BERLIN EMBASS

Berlin Embassy

William Russell

CARROLL & GRAF PUBLISHERS
NEW YORK

BERLIN EMBASSY

Carroll & Graf Publishers
An Imprint of Avalon Publishing Group Inc.
245 West 17th Street
11th Floor
New York, NY 10011

AVALON

Copyright © 1941 E. P. Dutton

First Carroll & Graf edition 2005
First published in the USA in 1941 by E. P. Dutton
Published in Great Britain in 2003 by Elliott & Thompson

Library of Congress Cataloging-in-Publication
Data is available.

ISBN-10: 0-7867-1694-0
ISBN-13: 978-0-78671-694-4

9 8 7 6 5 4 3 2 1

Printed in the United States of America
Distributed by Publishers Group West

Contents

CHAPTER ONE

AS I WALKED along the Hermann Goering Strasse toward our Embassy a siren shrieked with startling closeness. The unexpected blast of noise made me jump. I looked about to see where it came from.

Across the street, Adolf Hitler's new Chancellery stood long and quiet and pink in the early morning sun. Stiff sentries wearing steel helmets and massive black boots guarded the huge portals. I looked around back of me. There was Potsdamerplatz, its converging streets choked with army trucks, motorcycles, heavy motor-drawn cannon. Still the siren shrieked. I looked up at the roofs of the buildings and saw the long, slim barrels of anti-aircraft guns poked into the sky, but the siren itself was hidden. I walked on, looking curiously at the truckloads of soldiers rumbling past, at the silver airplanes which circled high above Berlin. The excitement of a city preparing for war pounded in my veins.

Before I left my apartment I had listened to tense news reports from Paris and London and Berlin radio stations. Today was Friday, the thirty-first of August, 1939. War was close at hand. It could not be true, of course, and yet it looked that way. All night long the crowded European ether had sputtered with angry words, with fearful words, with ominous words. A few days ago Germany had signed a ten-year peace pact with the U.S.S.R., and the lights were now green. My British and French friends were leaving Berlin on every train. Americans resident in Berlin had packed their most valuable and portable possessions and were poised for flight. Every moment brought a new telephone call, a new rumor, a new sensation. Poland had given in to German demands; Poland had not given in. Poland would fight, Poland would not fight. England and France had let Poland down, England and France were standing firm. The only truth was untruth and the only certainty was uncertainty.

The unseen sirens scattered over the German capital cut into the morning air and split it into a thousand fragments. They were being tested to acquaint the people with the 'alert', the 'take cover' and the 'all clear' signals to be used when enemy bombers appeared over Berlin. There were soldiers stationed on every roof in the center of Berlin; they peered aloft through their telescopes at the planes which circled overhead. Many more policemen than usual walked along the Hermann Goering Strasse; the side entrances to Hitler's private gardens were heavily guarded.

As I neared the Embassy I felt a touch on my arm. I turned around quickly and saw behind me a small man, seemingly bald, dressed in a wrinkled brown suit, a gray hat trembling in his hand. He looked back over his shoulder anxiously and then at me. 'I must talk to you,' he whispered.

'To me?'

'You work in the American Embassy, don't you? I've seen you in the Immigration section, haven't I?'

'Yes, I work there.'

'I tried to get in just now but there's such a crowd I couldn't get near the door.'

'We might as well walk along,' I said. 'You tell me as we walk.'

We started off. 'The police are after me,' he said, looking back over his shoulder again. 'The Gestapo ordered me out of Germany ten days ago. I've got to get out today, or never.'

'You're telling me the truth? A lot of applicants – '

'My God, look at my head if you don't believe me.' I saw that his head had recently been shaved. Underneath the newly grown hair were harsh red gashes. Then I saw that his left eye was half-closed and that the flesh around it had been broken.

He put his hat back on. 'War is going to start tonight. I have friends who know. If I don't get across the border, I'll lose my last chance to escape. God knows what they'll – '

'You want an American visa?'

He gesticulated impatiently. 'I've written and written to your Immigration section, and I never got an answer. I've been hiding out with friends in Berlin because I was afraid to appear on the streets. I waited a whole week for a letter from the Embassy but today I knew I couldn't wait any longer. I had to come down here, police or no police.'

'Come with me, then. I'll look up your dossier and see what we can do for you. You have affidavits from the United States?'

'Everything's in order. I was supposed to get my visa in July when my wife and son got theirs. Those gangsters had me locked up in Dachau and though I tried everything they didn't let me out until last week.'

'Are your wife and son in Berlin?'

'They're in Holland waiting for me. We have tickets on a Dutch boat that sails day after tomorrow. If I can't escape by tonight, they'll have to go without me.' He clenched his fists. 'But that just can't happen, not after everything else I've been through.'

The man looked at me excitedly. His eyes were bloodshot, his necktie wrinkled. He looked as though he had not shaved in days.

'How will you get to Holland?'

'I have a ticket on a plane leaving tonight at nine for Rotterdam.'

'Have you got a Dutch visa?'

'Not yet, not yet,' he said tensely. 'I have to get my American visa first and then try to get a Dutch visa.'

We reached the entrance to the Consular section of the American Embassy. A long line of refugees blocked the door; a thick crowd milled around the old porter who tried to keep them from pouring into our reception room. 'Come on,' I said to the harried man at my side. 'What's your name?'

'Hans Neuman,' he answered, pushing through the crowd to keep up with me.

'Let this man in,' I told the doorman, and we walked together into the waiting room. It, too, was full of Jewish refugees, many of them there to get their visas and the rest of them straining against the Information desk where Joe was trying to answer their frantic questions. 'Follow me,' I said to Neuman. I went down the corridor to my office. I motioned him to a chair in front of my desk. I went to the file room to get out his dossier.

There was a big red 'C' on the top of the dossier; that meant 'concentration camp case'. I checked his statements and found them correct.

The Embassy was a madhouse that morning. It overflowed with tearful refugees, clamoring American citizens, many fearful Germans. All of them wanted to escape from Germany before it was too late, before the war broke out and sealed the borders forever. There were not enough employees to take care of all these frantic people and they pushed each other around and tried to grab every consul, clerk or messenger who passed through the waiting rooms. I took the dossier back to my office and lifted my telephone. I dialed an inside number.

'Yes?'

'Nora?' I said. 'Look up the list of applicants for today and see if you can crowd in one more for a medical examination.'

'Can't do it,' Nora said promptly. 'We're issuing five times as many visas today as we usually do.'

'Squeeze him in,' I said. 'He's just one more. It may mean saving the man's life.'

'Consul Stratton said – ' Nora began firmly.

'Oh, all right,' I answered. 'Don't bother.'

Neuman was running his hand lightly over his scarred head. He wet his lips nervously.

'You have your birth certificate with you?' I asked. 'Four passport pictures, twenty-six marks to pay for your visa?'

'Everything, everything,' he assured me eagerly. 'Do you want to see them?'

I shook my head. 'Wait a minute,' I told him. 'I can't promise you anything, but wait until I've spoken to Consul Stratton.'

Taking the dossier, I went down the long corridor to Richard's office. He sat at his desk writing busily on a typewriter. Vice-Consul Paul Coates sat in a comfortable chair, leisurely reading through a thick dossier.

'Richard – ' I began.

'Can't it wait?' he asked, continuing to type. 'I'm writing a memorandum on a tip I just got from the Polish Legation – it's too hot to dictate.'

'I've got a pretty tough case here,' I said.

Richard was rereading what he had just typed. 'Sit down a moment,' he said absently. 'I'll be right with you.'

I looked at my watch. Ten-fifteen, the hands said. I sat down in a chair and stared out the window at the new Propaganda Ministry building next door.

It was a beautiful day; the sun shone brightly over the German capital, falling on the black asphalt streets and on the many trees which lined them and on the thousands of roofs which sheltered the four million inhabitants of Berlin. Every hour hundreds of men quit their apartments and places of business to report to the army. The people had been warned to stock up on black paper for use in the blackout and most of the shops were sold out already. Germans fought frantically to buy what pitiful surpluses of food and clothing they found still on display. Every railroad station in Berlin was crammed with fleeing foreigners, and German soldiers. Men in uniform, men in civilian, men in threadbare suits and women in expensive furs fought, crowded, shoved to get on the preciously few trains still allowed to run. Dutchmen, Belgians, Danes, Swedes, Poles, Frenchmen, Englishmen and Swiss jabbered in their respective languages as they fought for seats or standing room or any space whatsoever on the trains which were destined for some foreign border. Nobody knew whether the trains would reach the borders before being halted by German authorities.

Through the streets of Berlin, holding up traffic and proudly or fearfully beheld by many citizens, thundered tanks, heavy guns, truckloads of military supplies.

Telephone and telegraph lines from one end of Germany to the other were jammed and blocked with army messages. Frantic people, anxious to learn the whereabouts of loved ones, were told that it was no use to put in a long distance call or file a telegram.

The Berlin newspapers were black with angry headlines telling of LAST WARNINGS, and UNENDURABLE OUTRAGES and MURDEROUS POLES. The harried Berliners bought the newspapers and read them as they walked and sighed and folded their papers and continued on their uneasy ways.

The sky over Berlin was full of the roar of huge bombers headed east. The powerful throb of their motors rattled windowpanes and drowned out conversations. On and on they came until one thought there was not another bomber in the world, but still they came.

Germany on the verge of a new world war. Worried, anxious, trembling, terribly ignorant of what was actually going on.

I ran my fingers through my hair and looked at my watch again. Ten minutes had passed. Richard was still writing diligently. A fresh squadron of planes roared directly over the Embassy. All three of us looked up instinctively at the ceiling. Paul got up and went to the window to look out at the sky. 'Don't you want to see them?' he asked me.

'I've seen enough German bombers to last me a lifetime,' I said.

Consul Richard Stratton was not at all like Paul. He was also clever, but he was generous, kind and witty. His innocent-appearing face was surmounted by a crop of bushy brown hair which was never combed. He was a fascinating person whose telephone was constantly being rung by Berlin beauties. He was well liked by most of the foreign diplomats in Berlin and he stood in well with certain officials in the German Foreign Office and the Ministry for Propaganda and Public Enlightenment. The fact that Richard cheerfully hated their guts did not prevent him from making use of what information he gathered from these important sources. Richard played harder, attended more parties, had more hang-overs, lunched with more important people and got more work done than any consul in our Embassy.

He took the sheet of paper out of his typewriter and wrote his initials at the bottom.

'Richard,' I began again. 'This man just got out of Dachau a few days ago and the police are hounding him to leave Germany.'

'Are his affidavits in order?'

'Yes. But the important thing is that he must get his visa today.'

'Let's see the dossier,' Richard said, reaching for it. His telephone rang and he held the receiver in one hand and the thick dossier in the other while he talked. 'Yes,' he said. 'I've got it right here. Be right up with it.'

He hung up and rose from his chair. 'The Chief wants me in the Embassy section,' he said. 'This will have to wait until I get back.'

'But what can I tell Neuman?'

'He'll just have to stick around and see if we have a number free for him. There are a lot of people ahead of him, Bill. Maybe something will be free this afternoon.' He was gone.

'What do you let people work on your sympathies for?' Paul said. 'It's not fair to all the others.'

'I know it's not fair,' I said. 'Nothing's fair, if you want to be strictly truthful. It isn't fair of the German police to order this man to get out of his homeland when he has violated no law and when he certainly has no place to go to. It isn't fair to push a man around until he's half crazy. I'm not concerned about fairness.' Paul shrugged his shoulders. I returned to my office. Hans Neuman turned around in his chair as I entered. 'I don't know yet,' I told him. 'You'll have to wait and see if there is a quota number free.'

'I can't wait,' he answered nervously. 'It's noon already.'

'You have to wait,' I said. 'Sit down out there in the reception room and I will have you paged when I know something definite.'

There was a rough knock on the door frame. I looked up and saw a large, perspiring S.A. man, one of those middle-aged, pot-bellied, hard-faced Nazis who make up the ranks of the Brown Shirts.

'What do you want?' I asked.

The refugee looked around. When he saw the Brown Shirt standing in the doorway he sprang up from his chair in fear. The Brown Shirt looked at the refugee briefly. 'We've got a Jew out here,' he said loudly. 'He fainted on the sidewalk in front of your building.'

'Where is he?'

'My comrade and I carried him into your waiting room.'

'We'll take him to the doctor,' I said. The Brown Shirt stood aside to let me go out the door.

'You people ought not to make these Jews wait outside like that,' he grumbled, wiping his red forehead with a handkerchief. 'It gives people a bad impression of Germany.'

'We make them wait?' I asked, astonished. I walked across the waiting room to the bench where the old man lay. 'Help me carry him into the doctor's office,' I said to the pot-bellied Nazi. Together we carried the limp man into the doctor's office where the immigrants are given their physical examinations. We laid him on a cot and I called the nurse. She asked me anxiously what was wrong. 'Heat, I guess,' I told her. We left the man in charge of the nurse and returned to the reception room.

'I want to thank you,' I said to the two S.A. men. 'It was kind of you to bring the old man in here.'

'We always try to be of service,' the comrade of the pot-bellied one said. I had a quick mental picture of the Jewish shops which I had seen these Brown Shirts and the Black Shirts convert into shambles, of the burning of merchandise, of the bruised and broken people who came to us daily for protection.

'You know, it's too bad about these people,' the pot-bellied Nazi said expansively. 'If they only had sense enough to live like decent people, *der Fuehrer* wouldn't have to send them away from Germany.'

I looked at him and made no answer.

'Well, we have to be on our rounds,' Pot-Belly said. 'You haven't heard any news about Poland backing down, have you ?'

'No,' I said. 'Has she backed down?'

'I just asked. They will give in, of course,' he said confidently. 'A good war might teach those dirty Poles a lesson, though.'

'What lesson?'

He ignored my question. 'They've been persecuting Germans long enough. The Fuehrer has a great patience, but we ought to wipe those Poles off the face of the earth.'

I looked around the waiting room at the crowd of anxious refugees. Many sat on the benches waiting to be examined by our doctor and to appear before Paul to answer a few questions and swear that their statements on their applications were all true. The porter struggled with a crowd of would-be immigrants at the outside door. The line extended out to the curb, and curious Berliners stopped on the sidewalk to stare at the refugees.

'I have to work now,' I told the Brown Shirts. 'Thanks again for your help.'

Each of them gave me the flip-flop Nazi salute, boomed 'Heil Hitler,' and clicked his heavy heels together. I left them and returned to my office. Hans Neuman sat there, rubbing his head with his fingers.

'Give you a scare?' I asked.

He nodded grimly.

'They can't arrest you in the Embassy,' I said to reassure him. 'This is exterritorial ground.'

'I know,' he said. 'I just didn't think.' He got up. 'I'll wait outside, like you said. You won't forget that I'm out there?'

'The moment Consul Stratton comes back I'll ask him again,' I promised. 'You needn't worry.'

He left and I sat down at the desk and began to work on the dossiers. There were two tables in the room piled high with case after case. I worked on these dossiers when I wasn't interviewing the applicants. There were pleading letters and anxious telegrams from the refugees attached to the tops of the dossiers, and demanding cables from their relatives in the United States. I read the letter attached to the first dossier. The applicant wanted to know our answer to the all-important question: Were his affidavits from his friends and relatives in the United States sufficient to enable the Embassy to grant immigration visas to him and his family? My job was to appraise the attached evidence, the bank statements, the income tax returns, the plans for the support of their applicants, which were furnished us by interested parties in America.

The nurse telephoned me to report that the old man who had fainted was all right. 'Fine,' I said. 'Tell him to go to the Information desk and tell Joe his troubles. He'll take care of him.'

I interviewed several applicants and I finished as many cases as I could possibly work through, but at the back of my mind there was the persistent thought of war.

The telephone interrupted my work several times during the morning. Finally I realized that it was time for lunch. I walked to the window and looked out at the busy traffic. I lit a cigarette and drew on it thoughtfully.

RUMORS, RUMORS, RUMORS.

In the absence of any real information the wildest yarns circulated in the German capital as authentic truths. Hermann Goering, said the rumors, has told Hitler that Germany isn't prepared to make war and that he will resign from the government if the order is given to march into Poland. Adolf Hitler, said the rumors, is screaming wild because the Poles are proving so stubborn, and he rages at his adjutants when they come near.

Rumors. We listened avidly to every one of them.

The inhabitants of North Berlin (formerly a Communist stronghold), the rumors said, are booing Hitler's image in the movies and are shouting that they won't go to war for him. Adolf Hitler, said the rumors, is planning to appear at the last moment as an angel of peace, a real savior of mankind, and will propose disarmament to all nations of Europe.

These were nothing more than rumors but we repeated them eagerly.

I turned away from the window, ground my cigarette out in an ash tray and walked into the waiting room. I paused by the Information desk to listen to the applicants' questions. There were excited faces, tearful faces, faces scarred with the print of hard fists, faces flabby with soft living, faces of people who expected America to save them from death. There were the frightened faces of Jewish refugees, who were convinced that an outbreak of war would trap them within the borders of the German Reich.

Joe sat at the Information desk, listening patiently to the urgent reasons why the applicant speaking should be shoved forward on the waiting list so he could get his visa more quickly.

Other applicants whose turns had already been reached on the waiting list but whose evidence of support had been judged insufficient, were there to plead their cases.

'But I know my affidavits are all right,' an elderly refugee was arguing in German. 'I can get along in the United States fine. I can make a living for myself without any help from my relatives. I don't need anybody's support.'

'How will you get along?' Joe asked.

'Well, for one thing, I can sell insurance,' answered the old man.

'But,' Joe interrupted, 'you just told me that you can't speak English. How are you going to sell insurance?'

'I think I will get along,' replied the applicant quietly, with dignity. 'My relatives assure me that you can get along fine in the United States if you speak only Yiddish.'

Joe laughed. 'I don't know about that,' he said. 'You had better try to get your other relatives to send you affidavits. The evidence you have presented isn't strong enough.' I looked over Joe's shoulder at the applicant's dossier. That was what I had written a few days before – 'evidence insufficient'.

The old fellow moved away, dissatisfied.

I looked after him reflectively.

It was easy enough to write 'evidence insufficient' on a dossier when I worked alone in my office. It was not so easy to see the tragedy my simple, hastily scrawled words wrought on a human being. 'Hand me that dossier, Joe,' I said. 'I want to take another look at it this afternoon.'

A small woman, dressed in black and wearing thick spectacles, moved forward to the desk. 'My husband is in the concentration camp at Dachau,' she said simply, in a low voice. 'Tell me what I can do to help him get out.'

'What's his registration number?' Joe asked.

'Eight thousand four hundred and ten, Polish quota,' the woman said.

'I'm sorry,' Joe answered sympathetically. 'There are thousands of applicants registered before your husband. He has at least eight years to wait.'

The expression on the woman's face showed that she did not believe Joe's words. 'But you will just have to do something,' she insisted. 'He will die there. If war comes, they will never let him out of that place.'

Joe shook his head slowly.

The little woman began to cry as she gathered up the letters which she had spread out on the desk. She fumbled with the papers and when she had them all in her pocket-book she walked away.

It was like that all day, everyday, in our Embassy.

Some demanding. Some pleading. Some trying bribes. Some too wrought-up to speak. All wanting the same precious thing. A visa for the United States. An escape from an unnamed fear which rolled nearer and nearer with every passing minute.

The waiting room was a bedlam.

'Quiet,' Joe called at the crowd of refugees.

'Please get quiet.'

Outside the Embassy, I felt more at peace. The streets were full of Germans, many of them in smart uniforms, walking hurriedly to some personal destination. I crossed the Hermann Goering Strasse and walked through the Tiergarten, Berlin's Central Park. Frisky squirrels bopped over the grass, looking for food to store away. Three housemaids strolled past me, pushing baby carriages. A weather-beaten statue of a lion was bathed in peaceful sunlight.

I saw a familiar figure sitting on a bench, eating a sandwich from a paper sack. Hans Neuman looked up at me sheepishly. He pointed to the paper sack. 'They don't allow Jews in restaurants,' he explained, 'so I had to buy something and bring it out here.'

I paused in front of him. 'Do you want to eat lunch with me?' I asked. '1 think the maid can find something.'

He shook his head vigorously. 'Oh, no,' he said. 'This is fine.'

'See you later, then.' I walked on and left him sitting on the park bench, with the paper sack in his lap. I passed the lakes in the Park, the carefully tended flower beds, the white stone statues of departed German kings and queens and nobles, walked underneath the branches of great old trees: thoughts of the past shoved the terse present from my mind. How many German soldiers of how many generations had walked with their girls through this park before going off to battle? How many had come back to walk again?

These old wooden park benches had been sat on by important people, by lovers, by scholars, by soldiers, by thousands of peasants on a Sunday's excursion; most of them had long since left the scene. The Park conveyed the impression that mere people are the least important part of life – swords might dangle at military waists, trusting girls might look up at their lovers, old men might sun their ailing legs. Sooner or later they all moved on and were not missed at all.

At the front door of my apartment house, across the Tiergartenstrasse from the Park, I paused a moment to exchange a word with the *Portierfrau*. She was leaning against the building with her strong arms folded over her ample bosom. *'Na, wie geht's, wie geht's?'*

'Ich weiss nicht,' she said, shaking her head slowly. 'I'm afraid we're in for trouble.'

I twirled my keys on my finger and breathed deeply of the fresh air.

'Do you think there's going to be a war?' the *Portierfrau* asked anxiously. 'My husband has already been called up. He left before dawn this morning.'

'Perhaps some way out will be found,' I said unconvincingly. 'Don't worry.'

'Only think – to have to go through another dreadful war!' She fell silent.

A German lad, about four years old and dressed in a miniature Storm Trooper's uniform played with a toy cannon on the sidewalk in front of the house. He wore a wooden knife at his side and had a small tin helmet on his head. The use of such costumes is one method the Nazis employ to instill the military spirit into their young. Dress them that way, train them that way, and they will grow up knowing nothing but the boot on the foot, the weapon at the side, the steel on the head.

'Oh, yes,' the *Portierfrau* said. 'The postman told me today that you forgot to pay your radio tax last month.'

'Two marks, isn't it?' I asked.

The *Portierfrau* nodded. Every owner of a radio in Germany must pay a monthly tax of eighty cents to the Reich post office for the privilege of listening. As in most European countries, all radio stations are owned by the government. Since no advertisements are allowed, the cost of the programs must be borne directly by the people. 'Tell the postman that I don't listen to German stations,' I said.

'Tell him I consider London more accurate.' The *Portierfrau* laughed, somewhat uneasily.

Upstairs, I unlocked my door and entered the apartment. Hanna, my maid, smiled a tense smile at me and I saw that she had been crying. There was an envelope sticking out of her apron pocket.

'Did Fritz write?' I asked needlessly. Hanna nodded and went back to the kitchen. I strolled into the living room and walked over to the piano. With one finger I picked out a few notes of *St. Louis Blues*. I was too restless to play. I switched on the radio and waited for the tubes to heat up. The *Deutsche Allgemeine Zeitung* lay unopened on the living-room table. I glanced at the angry black type: NEW OUTRAGES OF POLISH CHAUVINISTS. I read no further. In these tense times, by the time a newspaper had rolled off the presses it was hours old.

Richard Wagner marched slowly into the room as the radio heated up. I smiled to myself. Whenever it was necessary to rouse the people into a fighting spirit, German radio stations trotted out their most stirring recordings of Wagner. Blustering old Wagner, as German as any German, with his violins shouting and his horns locking with each other. Was Hitler having this exciting music broadcast in order to give courage, or to get it?

Hanna came in, bringing a tall glass of rye and soda. 'Swell,' I said, and sat down tiredly. 'Everything all right with Fritz?'

'He's at the front,' Hanna said shortly.

'Which front?'

'Why, I can't tell you that,' Hanna said. 'That would be – '

'All right, all right.'

'Oh, Herr Russell what are they thinking of?' Hanna cried suddenly. 'Are they all crazy? What do we Germans want with another war, what will we do if war comes?' Her high voice echoed in the room and I took a drink. She recovered herself and straightened the shade on the floor lamp. 'I'm sorry,' she said.

'I don't blame you. If everybody felt as you do, maybe there wouldn't be any war.'

'Nobody knows what is going on. The newspapers don't print anything but Goebbels' lies.' Hanna pointed to the *Allgemeine*. 'You won't find anything there. They never tell us ahead of time what is going to happen. They just let us know after they have done it. Then it is too late.' ...'

I shrugged my shoulders.

'Is war actually coming?' Hanna asked.

'Yes.'

'When?'

'In a few days. Maybe tonight. Tomorrow. The next day.' Hanna sighed deeply and left the room. Wagner blared forth at me from the radio. Horns, oboes, basses. I sat there drinking my drink and waiting for Hanna to serve lunch. The sirens howled as they were tested all over the city of Berlin.

Not even the furniture in the room looked peaceful.

Our time? A century without sense.

Ommmmp. Ommmmp. Crash! Bang! Ommmmp. It was the band with the changing of the Guard, the daily parade which rounded our corner every day at noon. I looked out my window and saw the soldiers coming down the Tiergartenstrasse, accompanied by a large crowd of Germans which walked along beside the marching men. The leader of the band tossed his baton, the horns blared a stirring march. Wagner's music coming from the radio at my back became insignificant, a tinny whisper compared with the booming, shouting music of the military band.

Two policemen on horses strutted by to clear the street of traffic. All traffic stopped, and the line of stalled cars reached as far up the street as I could see. Following the band marched the soldiers, rows and rows of perfectly drilled men. There was nothing to be read in their faces. Their mouths were tightly closed, their eyes hard and set straight ahead, their guns carried over their shoulders making a line as regular as so many rails in a fence.

On the other side of the Tiergartenstrasse, under the shade of the trees, I saw an old man, probably a World War veteran, running along beside the soldiers on his feeble legs. As he tried desperately to keep up with the men, his face was aglow with the remembered glory of battle. The music had entered his blood, the sight of the marching men brought back the glorious old days. 'Paris by Christmas,' his blood was singing. 'My army, my wonderful German army!'

The last of the steel helmets bobbed past, the playing of the band was only a faint *ommmmp ommmmp* in the distance. The festive life which had surged beneath the trees at my corner had died into the routine of an intersection; the white-jacketed policeman stationed there was informal again, helping an old lady in black across the street. Wagner's music was broken off abruptly and a hard-voiced radio announcer began to read a summary of negotiations with Poland.

I ate a quiet meal, and left the apartment soon afterward.

Downstairs, the white-coated policeman – an old acquaintance – came over to me as I stood on the corner waiting for the cars to pass. 'Know anything new?' he asked me.

'Looks as though Germany will be at war soon,' I said, watching the planes overhead.

'Never,' asserted the pleasant old policeman. '*Der Fuehrer* will keep us out, like he did last time.' He watched the traffic casually as he spoke. 'I remember you said last September that war could not be avoided,' he reminded me. 'It will be the same story this time. They are afraid to fight Germany, Herr.'

'Don't you believe it,' I said. 'The fact that other nations want peace won't keep them from fighting if it is necessary.'

'They will be crazy if they fight with Germany,' the policeman said. Our conversation was drowned out by the roar of three large bombers overhead. Their motors screamed in our ears and deafened us. After the planes had disappeared into the distant blue sky, the policeman bummed an American cigarette off me and reminded me not to forget that he was saving foreign stamps for his nephew.

I think that every second German is saving stamps for his nephew.

I had a lot of work to finish in the short afternoon so I hurried through the Tiergarten back to the Embassy. The doorman cleared a path to the door; when I got inside I found the waiting room as crowded as ever. I pushed my way through the crowd. Hans Neuman stood near the Information desk. I nodded to him as I went through to my office.

For two years, everywhere we turned we had found applicants for immigration visas. The applicants wandered into our private offices, they explored the cellar in the hope of finding a stray consul, they waited on our stairways to grab one of the consuls on his way upstairs.

Our biggest thrill came when we unexpectedly found a nice old refugee lady sitting placidly in the small room marked 'Gentlemen'. She could read no English.

All of our consulates in Germany had the same problem. Refugees were to be found in every nook and cranny of their buildings, many of them begging to be allowed to spend the night under the safety of Uncle Sam's roof. When we opened the Consular section of the Embassy one morning in Berlin we found that a terrified Jew had spent the week end with us.

One reason we were so popular: There was no European country which would admit a German or a Polish Jewish refugee unless he could first show that he was registered with the American Consulate for an immigration visa.

We tried to handle the problem in the most humane way possible. There were times when the crowds got too much for us – especially the time they pushed through two heavy glass and brass doors. But we did not treat these Jewish refugees like cattle, as so many of the other consulates in Berlin did. We did what we could within the American quota laws. We probably issued visas to a multitude of undeserving and unworthy people and thus excluded excellent people who didn't understand how to push for their chance to emigrate to the United States.

I met Paul Coates in the corridor. 'Has Richard come back from lunch yet?' I asked.

'I haven't seen him. Are you still trying to get that man started to Holland?'

'Yes.'

'He'll never make it now.'

I walked away without answering. The room where the refuges' applications were taken by our machine-gun typists was noisy with the clatter of typewriters, the talking of the applicants, the howling of their babies. I went over to the desk of one of the typists. She was firing questions at a refugee, typing the answers as fast as he gave them to her. She glanced up at me briefly and went on typing. 'Herta,' I said hesitantly.

'No more,' she said promptly. 'Consul Stratton's personal orders. I couldn't possibly do another application today, and there are no more numbers anyway.'

'All right. Give me one of the application blanks, then.' Herta paused a moment and extracted a clean application blank from her desk. I took it, and went to the Information desk. I looked out over the crowd and beckoned to Herr Neuman. He came eagerly; we went into my office.

'Will I get the visa now?' he asked. 'I can just make it, if I get it right away.' I shook my head.

'I'm going to take your application. That will save time, if Consul Stratton says it is all right for you to get your visa today.' I uncovered my typewriter and filled the long application blank with Hans Neuman's answers to my questions. I pasted two of his passport pictures onto the forms, attached his birth certificates and affidavits with a paper clip, and told him to wait out in the waiting room.

'I'll never get my Dutch visa,' he said. 'The Consulate closes in an hour. It's no use.'

'If you can't get a Dutch visa, you may have to go without one.

'Without – How will I get over the border?'

'The plane doesn't stop between here and Rotterdam. If the Germans let you leave from here, the Dutch can't prevent you from landing.'

'They'll send me back,' he said with certainty. 'I know people who flew to London without landing permits. The English sent them back to Germany on the next plane.'

'Maybe there won't be a next plane,' I answered. 'If war breaks out tonight or tomorrow the Dutch will be too busy to bother about you.'

'The Dutch, maybe not. But I still have to go through the German customs – you don't know the Nazis.'

'Don't I?' I asked. 'Wait outside, and I'll do my best for you.'

The rest of the afternoon I interviewed applicants and kept on the lookout for Richard. All of the refugees looked at their watches continually, hoping against hope that their visas would be issued before our office closed for the day. Many of these refugees had already sent their baggage ahead – to Holland, to Belgium, to Denmark, to Italy. They had their railroad or their airplane tickets in their pockets. All they needed was the precious visa to the United States. Tomorrow might be too late. Tonight might be the last time the German borders would still be open for them, the disowned children of Germany. The applicants filed into my office and filed out again. They looked at their watches and they anxiously counted the minutes left to them.

Richard did not return to the Immigration section until five o'clock. When I saw him rush past my door I grabbed Neuman's dossier and followed him into his office.

'God, are they close to it!' he exclaimed, throwing his hat on a filing cabinet.

'Anything new?'

'Negotiations have been entirely broken off. The story now seems to be that Hitler is going to start a war with Poland whether the Poles give in or not.'

There wasn't much answer to that.

'The British and French are doing all they can to persuade Hitler not to try it.'

'What about Poland?'

'It seems that Poland is just about as willing to fight as Hitler is. That is, they might welcome a war to settle things once and for all.'

'I still can't believe it,' I said after a moment. 'I know it's coming, but I can't believe it.'

Richard motioned toward the dossier I held in my hand. 'Is that the case you wanted to talk to me about this morning?' he asked. 'What's the trouble?'

I told him the story.

'So the whole thing hinges on a German quota number?'

'Yes.'

He leaned back in his chair. 'Now, Bill,' he began, 'which clerk in this section is always saying that if we make an exception with one refugee we should do it in every case?'

'Several people are getting their visas this afternoon who aren't planning to leave Berlin for several days,' I explained. 'I suggest we give Hans Neuman one of the August quota numbers and let a not so urgent case wait until tomorrow.'

'Has Neuman's turn been reached on the waiting list?'

'Quite a while ago.'

'You think he's honestly in danger?'

'You ought to see his head,' I answered. Richard picked up his telephone and instructed one of the clerks to check up and see whether one German quota number could be assigned to Neuman without harming any other applicant.

'What time does his plane leave for Rotterdam?'

'Nine o'clock.'

'Why don't you take Neuman to the airport yourself, Bill? You can have my car.'

I was surprised. 'I hadn't thought of it. I guess my presence there would make it easier for him to pass the Gestapo agents, that's true.'

The telephone rang. Richard answered and listened a moment. 'Fine,' he said. 'Send him in to see the doctor right away.' He hung up and turned to me. 'Tell Paul to sign Neuman's visa in time for it to be issued today – if everything is in order, that is. And,' he added casually, 'you won't be at the airport in any official capacity, but if things start to go wrong just remember that firmness works miracles with German officials.'

I grinned. 'Thanks.' The messenger entered the room.

'An applicant to see you, Consul Stratton,' he said.

'Who is it?'

'Rabbi Jacobson.'

Richard groaned. I had to laugh at the miserable expression on his face. The Rabbi was one of our more persistent cases. He had been trying in vain for two years to get sufficient affidavits of support for himself, wife and five children to enter the United States.

The messenger lingered. 'The Rabbi said that he has something private to tell you.' He paused. 'He said that he won't go away until he has talked to you – and I believe him, sir.'

'Bring him in, then,' Richard said. I walked down the corridor with the messenger.

We had worked for two years day and night to help the immigrants. We worked Saturdays and we worked Sundays and we took work home with us to try to cope with the mounting piles of affidavits and correspondence. Our United States Senators and Representatives loaded down our mails with demands for assistance to this or that refugee. We did what we could to handle the flood of petitions and affidavits which poured in on us from all parts of the United States. We did what we could to help the worst cases; we gave visas by the thousands.

I think there is no decent American living who could have worked in our Berlin Immigration section without acquiring a deep hatred for the government which drove these people like cattle from unfriendly consulate to unfriendly consulate, from blocked border to blocked border. Nothing was too petty for the mighty German government so long as it could do some harm to a harried Jew.

The Germans practiced persecution not only by committing the major crimes at which they were past masters – murder, unjust imprisonment, arson, robbery. The Nazi government stooped to the smallest things, petty persecutions such as special yellow park benches for Jews to sit on; special restricted shopping hours for Jews, special laws for Jews, newspapers attacking Jews, which were pasted up on bulletin boards all over Germany. As terrible as were the beatings and the killings, I sometimes thought that it was the little things which hurt the average Jew most. One day he was a respected citizen of Germany; the next day he had to pack his belongings and move on somewhere.

Yet we had laughed about the Rabbi and his persistence. If we hadn't laughed occasionally we would have gone crazy listening to the miserable stories these refugees poured out to us.

Yes, we laughed occasionally.

'I feel rather sorry for Rabbi Jacobson,' the messenger said. 'If he has to get new affidavits from America he'll never get away from Germany.

'Don't you worry,' I said. 'The Rabbi and his family will get their visas soon.'

'Didn't you hear – '

'Doesn't matter,' I said.

I knew Richard too well.

He wouldn't say no today.

I saw Hans Neuman and arranged to meet him at the Embassy door for the drive to Tempelhof. It was, of course, too late for him to try to obtain a visa for Holland and he was nervous and worried. I left my office for the day and walked through our building to the Embassy section on Pariser Platz.

Our Berlin Embassy is housed in an old palace, originally a present from the German government to General Bluecher. Shortly after the United States purchased the rambling old structure it was gutted by fire and remained vacant for many years. In 1938 and 1939 our government spent a lot of money remodeling the Bluecher Palais. Our various offices which were scattered all over Berlin – the Embassy, the Consulate General, Commercial Attaché Treasury Attaché, Agricultural Attaché, Military Attaché, and the Naval Attaché were moved into the one building. It is an imposing structure but hardly a handsome one. Situated at one corner of Brandenburger Tor, the Consular section faces the Hermann Goering Strasse and the Embassy section faces the Pariser Platz, scene of numerous Nazi parades. We stood on the Embassy balcony many a time to watch Adolf Hitler drive down Unter den Linden on his way to speak in the Kroll Opera House or to review his troops when they paraded along the East-West Axis.[1] From this Embassy balcony we saw the German soldiers whom the Nazis insisted time and again were never sent to fight the Loyalists in Spain, returning from Spain. At that time, admiring Germans told each other: 'Here is indeed one of Adolf Hitler's greatest miracles. Thirty thousand soldiers who never went anywhere are coming back, and we are waving our little flags to greet them.'

When I reached the balcony the sun was just going down. In its fading gold and red rays I saw the silhouette of the massive Victory Column down the East-West Axis and the gold dome of the German Reichstag. Through the Brandenburger Tor poured a line of automobiles, bicycles, impatient taxis, military vehicles. German soldiers strolled by, saluting the motionless guard who stood at rigid attention before the Tor. Old Buergers walked along, content in their contemplation of a new and powerful Germany which would surely arise. What they had lost through their defeat in the World War, their sons would now recover – and more besides. The friendly traffic policemen in the center of the Hindenburg Platz, just on the west side of the Tor, waved their white arms, held up lines of cars, encouraged hesitant drivers to move on, move on.

---

[1] And on the Embassy balcony I once overheard a witty remark.

We were waiting for Hitler to drive past, and he was long overdue. At last, Richard leaned far over the balcony to look up Unter den Linden toward the Wilhelmstrasse. Drawing back, he observed in a bored voice: Get ready, people. Here comes *der Furor.*'

The sun disappeared abruptly. The street lights up and down Unter den Linden flashed on. The guard at the foot of the Tor was relieved and his pedestal was vacant. A large bomber passed directly overhead, its wings topped with red and green lights. Across the Pariser Platz the French Embassy was ablaze with light. People came and went in cars and taxicabs. In spite of the activity before me, the world seemed suspended, seemed filled with a ghoulish kind of waiting.

It was a little lonesome on the Embassy balcony. The light sinking. The day dying away.

I rubbed my tired eyes. What if war comes? I was thinking. What would happen to the things I liked, to the civilization of which I was an involuntary part? I wanted to see this Man pun-ished. I had witnessed three years of his terror, his pettiness, his cruelty, his negation of every human advance. He and his heavy-booted gang had lorded it over the rest of the people far too long.

Yes, yes, fix this man so he will no longer menace peace lov-ing people.

But what about the boys who will die fighting him and the boys who will die defending him? There were Heinz and George and Wowo[2] in his armies, friends of mine. Who could say how many would have to die – on both sides of the fight – before there could be an end to Adolf Hitler? I had no answer to this puzzle. It is something sitting down the street in the Reich Chancellery, lonesomely bent over a great desk, drawing lines on maps, dreaming big dreams of world conquest.

It is crowded around in a circle in Warsaw, racking its brains in an attempt to outguess Hitler.

---

[2] Unlike the other characters in this book, Wowo's name is his real one because he is now in a place where Nazi reprisals cannot reach. He was a tall, big-nosed blond who worked in the Associated Press when I was there. His father had been killed in World War I but Wowo was no Nazi and no believer in the Nazi's dream of recapturing an empire. Recently I received a letter from a reporter in the Associated Press Berlin Bureau. 'Wowo,' the reporter wrote me, 'died June 10, 1940, at Châlons-sur-Marne, of a shot in the lung. He was buried where he fell.'

It is gathered in a church in England, asking God for guidance at this fatal hour.

It is walking in the fields of France, where anxious eyes are trained on the secret hills across the Rhine.

It is in a thousand history books, in a million dispatches of ambassadors to their governments, in hundreds of capitals over the world, in the opinions of men talking excitedly on street corners, in the hearts of mothers and in the wild hopes of their sons.

It lies in the whims of the bosses, the whims of the dictators, the caprices of their women.

War is the biggest thing in the world. It is the massing of all that is the worst of mankind; it is the hatreds of people, their secret resentments, their greed, their firm convictions all rolled together and exploded to destroy the cities and the fields and the human beings who get in its unholy path.

That is war.

That night I drove up to the curb in front of the Embassy. Hans Neuman opened the door quickly and got in. The street was quiet; a single light burned on a high standard. A soft wind blew through the dark trees of the Tiergarten.

'Where's your baggage?' I asked.

'I had to leave it,' he said, seating himself stiffly. 'I have a few things in Holland, in our trunks.'

I started off and drove rapidly through the Berlin streets. We passed an occasional military truck and several police squad cars with their identifying blue spotlights. The night was warm and the Germans who strolled past the countless little shops were dressed in light clothes. We halted several times for stop lights; a long line of army trucks carrying soldiers and guns held us up for ten minutes at one intersection. It was a quarter to nine when we turned in at the huge Tempelhof Airport which lies in the south of Berlin. I locked the car and we went into the spacious lobby. Although the place was full of uniforms – army, air force, black-shirted Storm Troopers, Brown Shirts – there was a hush over everything. People scurried back and forth, but quietly, as though a little noise would bring the world down on their heads. Hans Neuman held back when he saw the line of passengers being examined by three Storm Troopers, obviously members of the Gestapo, and one customs official.

'Come on,' I whispered. 'Let's get it over with.'

We fell in line and waited uncomfortably while the other passengers were given a thorough investigation before being allowed to go through the exit to the waiting plane. We could hear the motors of the plane idling out on the field. We moved forward slowly until we were next. 'Passport,' one of the Storm Troopers, dressed in a cold black uniform, said to me. He was the youngest of the four officials; his face was hard.

'I'm not going,' I said. 'This man is.'

'Why are you here, then?'

'I'm from the American Embassy,' I answered. 'This man has a visa for the United States. I would like to see that he gets aboard this plane for Rotterdam.' There was a pause, while they looked at each other, and at me. 'His boat sails day after tomorrow.'

They drew away and whispered a moment. I knew that I was in no danger because I had done nothing wrong, yet I squirmed inwardly. That is the principal impression one carries away from Nazi Germany – the fear, the continual whisper, look over your shoulder before you speak, whisper, whisper, whisper. This nation-wide fear discourages any attempt to form a secret movement within the Reich. A man who fears that the Gestapo has information concerning his telephone calls, the contents of his letters, his private conversations with supposed friends – whether he is actually guilty of any wrongdoing or not – hesitates to work secretly against the Nazis. He is afraid that his first slip, however small, will result in his arrest and that the Nazis will use all of their accumulated Gestapo information to put him away permanently.

You want to know how a minority can keep itself in power against the wishes of the majority? This is one method: Make every citizen feel in his heart that at one time or another he said or did something against the government and let him think that the government knows about his indiscretion but is merely biding its time until he makes a bigger slip. Who speaks more patriotically to strangers than the man who fears immediate arrest by the Gestapo?

Who will say 'Heil Hitler' more loudly?

The officials came back to us. The youngest Storm Trooper took the brown German passport from Hans Neuman's trembling fingers. He looked through it carefully.

'There's no Dutch visa here,' he said.

'I didn't have time to get it,' Hans Neuman explained. 'I just got my American visa late this afternoon.'

'*Herr Neuman* has a visa to the United States,' the Storm Trooper said in a sarcastic voice to his colleagues. 'Well, isn't that nice?'

'Let him go,' one of the older men said. 'We'd have one Jew less. Let the Dutch worry about what to do with him.'

The customs official opened the passport slowly and laid it down on the railing. He checked the name with a type-written list he took from his pocket. He made a mark in the passport with his rubber stamp and handed it back to the refugee. 'See that you don't come back to Germany,' he warned. 'If you do, you'll be sent back to a certain place.'

In the crowded space between the railings and the German officials Hans Neuman turned and suddenly grasped my hand. He was too choked to speak. I shook his hand.

'You're holding up the line,' the customs official said to us. 'It's time for the plane departure right now.'

I stepped back and watched Neuman hurry through the terminal door to the blackness of the landing field. Now that he was safely through I felt curiously let down. Outside, I watched the large plane taxi down the field, turn around and take off. It roared close over the roofs of Berlin apartments and was soon lost in the dark sky. I drove back to the Embassy and parked Richard's car in our courtyard.

I was told that I was elected to spend the night in the Embassy. I was to sit in Alexander Kirk's office just in case anything broke in the early hours of the morning, while our Chargé d'Affaires tried to get a few hours of badly-needed sleep in the room adjoining. At three o'clock Kirk went to bed; at five o'clock I was trying desperately to keep awake. I walked back and forth in the lonely office, my feet sinking into the deep rug. I walked to the tall windows and pulled aside the heavy draperies. It was still dark outside. The street lights sputtered in the Pariser Platz, casting little yellow smudges into the darkness. Two drunks staggered past the Embassy, singing at the tops of their voices. The night air was soft and warm. The sky was a dark black, for the moment empty of airplanes. Trucks of every description rumbled under the Brandenburger Tor, carrying groceries, fruits, munitions – God knows what secret things were in those trucks. Across the street, light glinted from behind the draperies in the busy French Embassy.

I thought I heard a sound in the large room behind me.

I stepped back from the windows. Nothing.

The telephone was on the desk, silent, uncommunicative.

History will prove some day that it was in the hum of propellers, in the rattle of express trains, in the concert of claxons that some of the decisions were taken which changed the map of Europe. And every reopening of the horrors of war announced itself not by a gong or a clash of cymbals or a fanfare of trumpets, but by the ringing of a telephone. For Destiny – like all of us today – lives between these two companions of modern civilization: speed and noise.

I went back to the window. Day was beginning to break over the tops of the buildings. On the roof across the street I saw the long shadows of anti-aircraft guns. Stocky soldiers stood silhouetted against the sky, waiting, waiting. A faint soft redness appeared to the east, far up the Linden.

The street lights went out suddenly.

Deadly quiet.

A single car sped down the street, an official car with a Nazi pennant flying from its front fender.

The telephone behind me jumped into life with a horrible

scream of bells. I looked at my watch involuntarily – it was five-thirty.

I had hardly lifted the receiver from its hook when Alexander Kirk appeared in the doorway. 'I'll take it,' he said. He sat down at the large desk and held the black receiver against his ear. In his right hand he held a pencil.

There was a long moment while he listened.

Without one word of answer, he put the receiver slowly back on the hook. He drew a pad of white paper toward him.

'Russell, will you wake the code clerk?' he asked quietly.

'That was the British Embassy calling. The first German bombers left for Poland ten minutes ago.'

CHAPTER TWO

Since early this morning, we have been answering Polish terror with our cannon.

ADOLF HITLER in speech, September 1, 1939.

IT WAS 10:45 in the morning when Adolf Hitler rode past the American Embassy on his way to proclaim a state of war with Poland. There was a thin line of S.S. men standing along the route to the old Kroll Opera House, where the Reichstag members had been called into hasty session. The streets of Berlin were filled with sunshine and were empty of people. Loud speakers had been set up along the route and on many street corners over the city.

Across the street from the Embassy I saw a group of laborers moving some concrete blocks.

We looked at each other haggardly. None of us had had much sleep, if any. The loud speakers outside the windows blared forth recordings of soldiers' marching songs. Ringing, marching, inspiring songs. Artificial jubilation recorded on pieces of wax and scratched with a needle. Civilization.

Then came the Voice.

We had no radio in the Immigration section, so we leaned our collective and undignified heads out of the windows to hear what the Voice had to tell us.

The Voice was husky, tired. It told us of the horrors perpetrated against German nationals in Poland. It told us, for the thousandth time, of the injustices of Versailles which were going to be wiped out.

While we listened, we looked at the sunshine-splashed trees in the Tiergarten. Several silver airplanes roared overhead, one after the other. The workmen across the street were obviously unimpressed by the fact that their Fuehrer was speaking. They did not even stop their work to listen.

'Germany has answered Poland's aggression with action,' the Voice told us. 'Since early this morning German armed forces have been moving into Polish territory.'

The streets were absolutely empty, except for the Storm Troopers who lined the street to the Reichstag meeting. German citizens were at home or at work, listening to words which spelled tragedy for all of them. At my back a typewriter was clattering busily. Some clerk didn't care if there were war or not: she had to finish her work.

'I have put on the uniform of a soldier,' the Voice screamed at us. 'It will not be taken off until Germany is victorious. If I should fall on the battlefield, Hermann Goering is to be my successor. If Hermann Goering should fall, Rudolf Hess will be your leader.'

'Deutschland, sieg – ,'

'Heil!!' The four hundred-odd best-paid yes men in the world cried in one rough voice.

'Sieg – '

'Heil!!'

'Sieg – '

'Heil!!!' There was prolonged cheering by the honorable members of the Reichstag.

That is how a dictator country goes to war. Three 'heils' and the discussion was over.

The simple workers across the street had almost finished moving the concrete blocks. They were undisturbed by the declaration of war. After all, nobody had asked their opinion about it. They had their blocks to move. Let Adolf handle the war.

Deutschland, Deutschland, über Alles, the deputies were singing lustily. We scattered from our places in the windows. Now, that was a strange feeling we had then. The sun was shining, automobiles were moving along the street as usual. The immigrants were pressing eagerly against the barrier at the Information desk. It was hard to realize that anything had changed.

But a whole world had changed.

Germany was at war again. Only twenty years after the disastrous end of a great struggle, she was thumbing a ride on the same old merry-go-round.

One expected something terrific to happen immediately. Nothing did.

Now it is perfectly clear that Poland wants the catastrophe. –
From an editorial in the *12-Uhr Blatt*, September 1, 1939.

When Germany began her undeclared war against Poland, the United States was the only major power caught without an ambassador in Berlin to report on, and perhaps to have helped the world avoid, this new conflict.

Our Chargé d'Affaires in Berlin, Alexander Kirk,[1] was an excellent reporter, a hard and brilliant worker, a charming diplomat. But official doors which will open to an ambassador remain closed to a chargé d'affaires.

In these days of strictly censored news dispatches it is a good thing to have a man on the spot who can report directly to our government on true conditions in Germany. To deprive ourselves of such representation is something like having one's self locked up in jail because people in the street smell bad.

BOMBING OF POLISH CITIES BEGUN

Headline in all non-German newspapers on September 2, 1939.

The British and the French had not yet declared war on Germany, as they promised to do if Poland were attacked.

We wondered fearfully if they would break their word again.

This morning I bade farewell to a friend, a Canadian trade commissioner. 'Maybe it will all blow over,' I said as we stood on the train platform. 'Maybe you'll be back in a few days.'

'I wouldn't come back,' he answered. 'If we don't keep our word this time I would be ashamed to be seen here.'

---

[1] Kirk is at present [1941] in Cairo, serving as American Minister to Egypt.[1]

DER FUEHRER IS ON THE EASTERN FRONT WITH THE SOLDIERS WHO HAVE BROKEN THROUGH THE POLISH CORRIDOR

Deutsche Allgemeine Zeitung, September 5, 1939.

Two railroad coaches, chartered especially by our Embassy for the transportation of American women and children resident in Germany left Stettiner Bahnhof for Copenhagen, Denmark.

Train connections with other countries had been broken off in every direction, except to the north. There were a few persons in the special coaches who had simply put off their departures until the last possible moment, but the majority of the passengers were wives and children of our consuls stationed in Germany.

These families were being broken up, and none could say when or where or if they would be reunited.

The train was overflowing. Passengers sat on their suitcases, they doubled and tripled up on the seats, they hung out the windows, they packed the vestibules. As usual, the toilet doors had been opened to allow more room. Late arrivals stuffed their baggage in through the open windows, and had themselves pushed upward and in to follow their things.

I had come to see Betty off, but we had not talked much before the train pulled out. It was too much of a farce to try to talk about the future.

There was a long, long whistle from the front of the train. The engine, puffing heavily, pulled the string of coaches slowly out of the station.

Stettiner Bahnhof was full of small children wearing blue tags around their necks; they were being shipped away from the city to the safety of the country. Smart young officers, heavily braided, wearing dangling swords at their hips, crowded the platforms, carelessly pushing the humbler citizens aside.

Outside the Bahnhof we found that the sun was shining and people were walking slowly through the Berlin streets to enjoy an Indian summer Sunday. But there was no happiness. One felt as though a heavy weight had been placed on one's head.

My diary entry for that Sunday was:

September 3, 1939

Today is the third day of the war. It is now 11:15, and the English ultimatum to Germany expires at 12:00 noon. Forty-five minutes more of half-peace peace.

Now it is 4:10 p.m. In the meantime, England has declared war, France has declared war and somehow the sun is still shining.

We have gotten news that the special coaches in which the women and children left this morning have arrived safely in Denmark.

A postcard arrived from Hans Neuman; he has sailed by now.

The German radio stations are blaring marches, and the German memorandum to England is repeated every few hours in full.

The people I have met seem calm and sad and resigned. They stand around in little groups in front of our Embassy building, staring at us through the windows. I think this is nothing like the beginning of the World War in 1914. They marched through the streets carrying flags, then; they yelled with joy, they shouted their hatred of the enemy.

Today, I think they feel that they have been led into something which may turn out to be too big for them. The truth has been kept from them so consistently that surely not over two or three percent of all the Germans know what is going on.

The air is full of rumors, as usual. Some of them which I heard during the day are:

France will not take part in the war.

Russia has given an ultimatum to England.

The first Italian divisions are already pouring through the Brenner Pass into Germany.

Von Papen is in Paris to negotiate.

The German and French armies on either side of the Rhine River are fraternizing with each other and have refused to fight.

It is said that Saarbruecken has been shelled by the French and has been destroyed stone by stone.

Rumors, rumors. How they flew today!

Himmler made a speech today to his black-clothed S.S. ('If you want to be a member of the S.S., you must be out of the Church.') Himmler made a ringing appeal for obedience, which ended stirringly: 'Hitler expects every man to do *more* than his duty. God commands, and Heil Hitler!'

Consul Fulton wanted to go to church this evening. He walked down the street in Berlin-Dahlem to his regular Protestant Lutheran Church. He got there during the evening Sunday school classes, but the interior of the church was already packed with grown people who, by their great numbers, had pushed the children aside.

London, September 6, 1939. – The Prime Minister and Mrs. Neville Chamberlain took their usual morning walk today through St. James's Park with gas masks slung over their shoulders.
New York Herald Tribune.

POLES FLEE WARSAW AS GERMAN
ARTILLERY ATTACKS CITY
New York Herald Tribune, September 6, 1939.

I saw her in the vestibule of the Embassy, crying lonesomely.

'Is something wrong?' I asked. I held a stack of papers in my hand. And in the waiting room a crowd of refugees were waiting to be interviewed. But something was amiss here.

'Yes,' she sobbed. 'I don't know where to turn. They tell you to leave immediately but they won't help you get out.'

'Who does, who won't?' I asked.

'The Embassy.' She looked at me over her handkerchief. 'Oh, I'm sorry,' she said. 'Maybe I shouldn't have said that. You work here, don't you?'

I reassured her, and heard her story. She was an American who wanted to leave Germany, as the Embassy had advised her to do. She had made arrangements with the American Express to forward her trunks, but she needed a letter from the Embassy stating that she was an American citizen in order to get the trunks cleared through the customs.

Well, that is simple enough, I thought.

Simply write out a letter and give it to her.

But the consul in charge of American affairs refused to give her the letter, she said. Just flatly refused, and that was that.

I went into his office and inquired about the girl. 'No,' he drawled, leaning far back in his chair. 'We can't give out such letters. That is not our business.

'But we are here to give every American all the help we can,' I argued.

The plump consul – shook his head and turned around in his chair to look out of the window.

I went back to the girl, and we found another way to get what she wanted. She made out an affidavit, stating that she was an American citizen with passport number so and so, which the consul had to notarize. He couldn't get out of that.

The Embassy was swamped with American citizens who were stranded in Berlin. There were no ships available, since most of the places had been booked far in advance by the immigrants.

Many American citizens came in and asked in German how they could get back 'home.'

'Can't you speak English?' the consul or vice-consul would ask.

'Nein,' answered many of them, continuing to wave their red American passports in the air.

One man was born in Pennsylvania, reared in Rumania, attended college in Germany. He spoke Rumanian, German and French, but not one word of English. He was an American.

Not infrequently, people who had been living in Germany for many years, but who had retained their American citizenship, came dashing in to the security of the Embassy, gave us a cheery 'Heil Hitler,' and asked which boat we were sending them 'home' on.

We put all available energy and employees into answering the thousands of questions, and telephoning the steamship companies in an effort to wrangle berths for our citizens.

I suppose we were successful because finally they were all gone from Berlin. However, that was several months after the outbreak of war.

When are they going to send help to Poland? we all asked each other.

BRITISH RAID REICH AGAIN WITH LEAFLETS
New York Herald Tribune, September 6, 1939.

I looked up at the familiar window.

I had rushed down to the Associated Press to confirm a piece of information, and on my way back to the Embassy through the Markgrafenstrasse I had suddenly noticed my old window.

Memories rushed upon me and pushed the war from my mind. In the room behind that window I had lived for almost a year, during my student days in Berlin before I went to work in the Embassy. My room had cost twenty-five marks a month, which isn't much, and I had tea and a roll thrown in free, as breakfast.

At one time, for two straight weeks that tea and roll constituted my entire sustenance. Frau Hausen, my landlady, never had any idea how my stomach leaped up to greet that piece of dull bread each morning.

Well, those were the days.

We had no bathroom in the apartment. The toilet was halfway down the stairs and had no light in it. If we went there at night, we had to carry a flashlight with us.

Herr Hausen dreamed of the time when he would be prosperous enough to rent an apartment with a balcony and a bathroom. The balcony was the more important, he said.

Herr Hausen was a typesetter on Hitler's Berlin newspaper, the *Voelkischer Beobachter*, (which is a mouthful in anybody's language). He was a 150 percent Party member, although Hitler's coming to power had meant for him a permanent twenty percent cut in his wages.

Frau Hausen had formerly been a dancer. When her husband was at home, she was a thorough Nazi; when he was gone she beefed about everything Hitler ever did.

They had a son in the flyers' corps, of whom they were very proud. Sometimes when the son was home on leave, all four of us would go downstairs to the pub and sit there in the thick, steamy atmosphere until dawn, drinking beers and whiskys and vodkas and 'Eiercognac' and a peculiar form of dynamite called 'Himbiergeist.' That means, roughly, spirit of raspberries, and oh, my golly! We were sitting in that small pub the night the German army marched into Austria.

From my small room I had looked down on this Markgrafenstrasse thousands of times. Sometimes I had been lonesome, many times I had wondered just what I was doing in Germany.

Well, that was two years ago, and two years can be a long time.

I was standing there in the middle of the Markgrafenstrasse. My old window and my old street were the same. Only I had changed.

GERMAN TROOPS ENTER WARSAW
All German newspapers, September 8, 1939.

RATION CARDS FOR BICYCLE TIRES
12-Uhr Blatt, September 13, 1939.

Of course we knew that there would be rationing. But somehow we had been thinking of rationing of food and clothes and practically every necessity as a burden for the Germans alone.

We got our first rude shock, and taste of things to come, when Alexander Kirk told us of an experience he had in Braun's. Braun's is an ultra-swank store for men's clothes on Unter den Linden, the kind of place where the cheapest handkerchief costs one dollar.

Kirk had slept two weeks straight in the Embassy; he decided to buy himself a fresh pair of pajamas. Walking out for a breath of air, he wandered into Braun's, and asked a yawning clerk to show him several pairs of pajamas. The clerk refused, politely. 'We are not allowed to sell anything until the ration cards come out,' he said.

Our Chargé d'Affaires identified himself, and explained that he really needed the pajamas. The clerk was impressed, but he had his orders.

Resigning himself to the situation, Alexander Kirk started to leave. Near the door, he looked at a bunch of neck-ties on display. He fingered one tentatively.

'I am sorry,' the clerk recited. 'We can't sell any neckties either.'

He departed. The Chargé d'Affaires of the United States, many times over a millionaire, couldn't even buy a neck-tie.

That was only the beginning, we learned.

The German Foreign Office allotted us one spool of thread a month, exactly what the Germans were getting. Try as we could, they did not increase out quota one jot. When one is not allowed to buy new pairs of socks or new clothes of any kind, one spool of thread does not go far.

September 13:

The war is raging in Poland. What can England and France be thinking of? we ask each other. Why don't they attack Germany now, so she will have to fight on two fronts?

For the first few days of this war, the German citizens were thunderstruck. They were confident that England and France would fall upon Germany and destroy her completely.

But nothing has happened.

The Germans are regaining their confidence. The Propaganda Ministry is working on them day and night, by radio press, posters, speeches.

What are they doing on the other side of the Rhine?

Why don't they come on?

I talked to a high Party member today, who enthusiastically told me the following rumors as truths:

Poland will be finished in three days. France will remain neutral, after all. Our mighty airplanes will soar and smash London into bits. The Empire is quits.

RUINS MARK LINE OF NAZI ADVANCE
New York Times, September 15, 1939.

Refugees are still being allowed to leave, and we are still issuing visas as fast as possible.

Rabbi Jacobson went through this morning with his five children. They all have their visas already. In a way, we will miss seeing the Rabbi's face every day. We will miss his several urgent letters a week.

What will he find when he gets to the United States? We like to conjecture about that sometimes; about what kind of lives these people lead after they have passed Ellis Island in New York Harbor.

At least they are not living in blacked-out cities. Whatever other hardships they bear, they can at least see their way around.

Good luck, Rabbi. I wish I could see the smile on your face when you eat your first hamburger.

With onions.

RUSSIA THREATENS POLAND AS
HER DEFENSE CRUMBLES
New York Times, September 15, 1939.

I was having supper one night in my apartment alone, sitting tiredly at the table and eating the Canadian bacon which the Embassy imported from Denmark and the scrawny string beans which Hanna had found at some out of the way grocery shop, when the doorbell rang.

I hoped that I was not going to have company. After a hard day with the refugees all I wanted was to read awhile and go to bed.

The radio was going too loud for me to hear the caller's voice. I had tuned in London, to hear the eight o'clock news broadcast.

Since the war started, our supply of newspapers had been shut off. We didn't even get the hopelessly poor Paris edition of the *Herald Tribune* any longer. We depended on the London and Paris radio stations for our news of what was actually going on. The German newspapers and radio are so one-sided that from reading or listening to them one gets a distorted and confusing picture of the news.

Hanna came to my door. She looked frightened. 'Herr von

Uhlrich, from downstairs, wants to speak to you,' she said. 'About the radio.'

'Show him in,' I said, sighing.

He stepped from behind Hanna into the room. He was a little, red-faced Nazi who was feared by every German in our apartment house.

People ask me sometimes how one or two million Nazis can keep seventy million people under their control. Our apartment was a good example of how it is done. One Nazi was sufficient to spy on the other occupants. And of course, behind that one Nazi was the full and dreadful power of the secret police.

This morning at breakfast, Hanna had told me what occurred in our cellar last night during an air raid alarm. I had been working in the Embassy, and was not present.

When the sirens blow in Germany, every man, woman and child must go into the shelters. There are no exceptions.

Last night, the occupants of our house sat shivering in the crowded, dimly lit cellar. Captain S – an army officer who had been injured in the World War but who was now serving once more, sat there with his wife. His hands twitched nervously, and he seemed unable to breathe.

Suddenly, Hanna told me, he sprang to his feet.

'I've got to get out of here,' he said nervously. 'I can't stand this any longer.'

The other Germans sat still and looked at him. Herr von Uhlrich looked at him too. The air raid warden, who has complete police power during an alarm, tried to make him stay.

The Captain, who was really suffering, left anyway. There was a long, embarrassed silence. Nobody dared to speak. Finally, Herr von Uhlrich said in a cold voice: 'This officer has lived in New Germany for seven years, and to this day he hasn't learned how to say "Heil Hitler."

'This officer,' he continued bitterly, 'served in the World War but he doesn't know how to obey alarm regulations.

'This officer,' he said, 'would do well to watch his conduct more carefully, or he will learn what it means to be openly disloyal to our Fuehrer.'

The Captain's wife sat there in the dim cellar, holding her child on her lap. Nobody had dared to say anything.

Herr von Uhlrich was waiting.

'Well?' I said, getting up from the table.

'Will I be forced to have you taken to prison tonight?' he asked me through closed teeth.

'Wait a minute, Mister,' I said.

'You can hear that English announcer all over the building,' he said. 'Don't think that just because you are a foreigner you are exempt from our German laws.' He was almost too angry to talk.

'I didn't know that I am not allowed to listen to foreign stations,' I said truthfully. 'I read the law, and the preamble to it clearly states that it applies to "German citizens."'

'I don't care about the law,' Herr von Uhlrich said wrathfully. 'All I know is, you have dirtied this whole building with that English filth.'

'I'm not so sure about that,' I said.

'If you must listen to news broadcasts in English,' my visitor said, 'you can tune in on our station in Hamburg. It sends all the English you want.'

'Humph,' I commented.

'You will have to obey our laws,' he said. 'Just like everybody else. You're no different.'

'Well,' I said slowly, 'I read newspapers printed in Switzerland. Are you allowed to?'

'No,' he said shortly.

'I am,' I pointed out. 'Are you allowed to import butter?' This question hit him in a weak spot. He was already eying my large hunk of butter on the table, which was more than his whole family could buy in two weeks.

He did not answer.

'I can,' I said.

'I see there's no use talking to you,' he said, turning to go. 'Before denouncing you to the police, I shall ask the Propaganda Ministry about your status. I am a friend of Dr. Goebbels.'

I tried not to show that I considered friendship with Goebbels as something a little less than wonderful. After all, our government did not pay me to antagonize the citizens of the country in which I was living.

He left, slamming the door behind him.

Hanna came in to clear away the dishes. I had lost my appetite. I went over to the radio and turned it off.

'For God's sake, Hanna,' I said at last. 'Stop shaking before you drop every dish we have.'

What Goebbels had to say about my listening to London, I do not know.

I never heard from Herr von Uhlrich about that particular matter again.

POLAND ENTREATS ALLIES VAINLY TO RUSH MORE HELP; LONDON SAYS STRATEGY FORBIDS IT
New York Herald Tribune, September 16, 1939.

Today, from here and there, I noted two more items of 'hot' inside news:

There will be a government set up in Poland similar to that of Hacha in Slovakia, I heard.

One Nazi told me: We have made an offer of peace. If the others are impertinent enough to reject it, we will build three hundred submarines and starve England out.

I just found a clipping from the *12-Uhr Blatt*, September 9, 1939, in one corner of my desk drawer. The German propaganda machine has up to now consistently minimized the fact that England and France declared war on Germany on September 1. This propaganda theme runs through all the news stories: 'When we have taken care of foolish Poland, England and France will be glad enough to talk turkey.'

After nine whole days of war, the Nazis explained the parcel post situation to the German people as follows, according to my little clipping: 'Shipments to France and England will no longer be accepted by the German Railroad Company, owing to the *political situation.*'

A government which hesitates to tell its people the truth, even about smaller things, must be dreadfully afraid of something.

SOVIET TROOPS MARCHED
INTO POLAND AT 11 P.M.
New York Times, September 17, 1939.

With that, it was all over with Poland.

Only Warsaw still held out, despite headlines in German newspapers of September 8 which made a premature claim to the capture of the city.

Wowo came through Berlin from fighting in Poland, on his way to the West front. He had been allowed one day's leave.

We met at night, and sat in a smoke-filled pub. We talked earnestly, and occasionally kicked around with our feet the sawdust which covered the floor. He wore heavy black boots. I wore crepe-soled shoes.

Wowo is a tall, blond, clumsy lad, the same age as I am. We used to work for the Associated Press together,[2] before he was called to the army and I went to work in the Embassy.

We were having our last two beers before I could bring myself to mention a subject that had remained taboo. The lights were being turned off around the walls of the little pub. A drunk was leaning against the bar, muttering something about the blackout. The waiter came to collect for the beers we had drunk. He counted the pencil marks which he had made on each of our paper coasters under our glasses. Instead of writing it down on a pad every time you order another beer, German waiters simply make a mark on your coaster. They trust you not to swap coasters when they aren't looking; nobody swaps.

'Wowo,' I said finally. 'Did you kill anybody in Poland? Did you kill a man?'

---

[2] It will do no harm to tell Wowo's favorite story about the Associated Press.

At the Berlin office of the A.P., we frequently received cables from the foreign editors' desk in New York, requesting our reporters to follow up this story or that. During the summer of 1937 the Nazis were busy persecuting the

'Mostly I fought in woods,' he said. 'Thank God for that. If I killed anybody, I never knew it.' He thought for a moment. 'One time, the third day of the war, I winged a Pole in the arm. He fell over into a ditch, and when I came to the edge of the ditch and peeped over at him, he was lying at the bottom on his back, screaming with terror.

"Don't kill me!" he cried to me. "Please don't kill me!"

"I'm not going to kill you, you bastard," I said, climbing down the ditch bank to where he lay. "I'm just going to take you back to our field hospital."

'Another time,' Wowo said, 'I was one of a squad assigned to reconnaissance. We walked through a wood, following close behind a large group of advancing German soldiers. We came across a solitary Polish soldier lying there in the woods, dead. From a cigarette clenched between his lips, smoke still curled upward.'

After a while we left the pub, and parted in the blackout. On my way home, I tried to accustom myself to the idea that I too some day might have to become a killer. It was not a pleasant idea.

RUSSIANS DRIVE 40 MILES INTO POLAND
New York Times, September 18, 1939.

I awoke out of a sound sleep with a jerk. The telephone was ringing terrifyingly in the darkness.

How late was it? I turned on the light and looked at my watch. One-thirty.

I picked up the receiver. A long-distance call for me, the operator said. Copenhagen.

I was connected. 'Hello, Bill, is that you?' came the voice.

'Betty!' I exclaimed. 'How are you?'

Catholic Church in Germany, closing the Catholic schools and arresting the Catholic priests and nuns.

Wowo was alone in the A.P. office before dawn one morning. There was nothing going on, until the teletype began to clatter and Wowo was treated to an eyebrow-raising cable from a wide-awake editor in New York:

ASSOCIATED PRESS BERLIN PLEASE PURSUE NUNS AND MONKS

'All right, I guess. Except I'm so bewildered that I don't know what to do. Is there going to be a war, or not?'

'I think so,' I said.

'Because if it is going to stop when Poland surrenders, I think we should come back to Berlin.'

'I wish you would,' I said. 'But I don't think it will happen that way.'

'No, I guess not,' Betty said in a small voice. 'But when are the English and the French going to do something?'

'You probably hear more in Denmark than we do here,' I answered. 'What do the Danes think?'

'They have everything covered with sandbags, and are expecting the worst. They worry about the situation, but there is nothing much they can do to protect themselves at this late date. They think it will be either the English or the Germans who will invade them, and they devoutly hope the English get here first.'

'I do too.'

'But will they?'

'They haven't done anything so far,' I said. 'Maybe they will wake up soon.'

We were silent a moment. I thought of the terrible urgency for action by the Allies before it was too late. A low hum came over the wire.

'Are they still riding their funny bicycles?' I asked.

'Still riding,' Betty assured me.

Yes, the Allies and their friends were still riding, still blithely playing. There was nothing to be afraid of.

SOVIET AND REICH FORCES MEET,
MAP POLISH PARTITION
New York Times, September 19, 1939.

RUSSIANS RECEIVED ENTHUSIASTICALLY. SOVIET TROOPS GLEEFULLY GREETED BY THE POPULA-TION AS LIBERATORS FROM THE POLISH YOKE
B. Z. am Mittag, September 19, 1939.

He spoke again today, at Danzig. He told us what else he wanted to get. He did not mention anything that he was willing to give up in return.

He ranted.

Nowhere in his speech did he find time to thank those boys who had given up for him the only real thing they possessed, their lives. He had not a word of condolence for stricken parents, for new widows, for their children.

This is a new conception of the term 'Unknown Soldier.' He had words of thanks and gratitude only for the machines; the airplanes, the tanks, the steel and iron and copper machines. There was no casual word for the men who sat inside the machines and guided them, and died because of them.

He praised the machines. They will go on, filled with new men. Don't be impatient, boys. It will soon be your turn to ride.

As I sat by my radio listening to his tirade against every single thing America stands for, a vivid thought struck me:

Here is a man who has broken his every promise, and kept his every threat.

After hearing his bitter speech, Hanna told me: 'I can't help it. I like Goering's speeches better than I do Hitler's. They are a lot more fun.'

POLISH CAPITAL AIR-BOMBED THREE TIMES, SHELLED BY BIG GUNS

CHAMBERLAIN AGAIN VOWS TO CRUSH HITLER. ASSURES NATION THAT WAR IS GOING SATISFACTORILY

New York Herald Tribune, Paris edition, September 22, 1939.

What a strange, nostalgic feeling one gets from reading preserved copies of old newspapers.

There are the same headlines which seemed so full of truth at the time one first read them, while the ink was still wet from the presses.

Time has somehow turned them into lies.

If you want to feel superior, read the old copies. The smartest writers and the cleverest editors worked at top speed to give you the news and to anticipate events. When you read, you will discover that you know so much more than they knew.

Now, a few months later, their best work appears infantile when compared to the cold reality of events.

Go back and read again the old headlines which once made you secure in the belief that your side would win.

I was wrong. They will not make you feel superior.

They will make you very sad.

German soldiers entertain no hatred beyond the grave. It must also be stated at this hour that the German army along the Western frontier endeavors to preserve peace, in accordance with the wish of the Fuehrer. A grave cry goes across the frontier: What avail is useless bloodshed?
Funeral oration by a German officer at the grave of a French officer. New York Herald Tribune, September 22, 1939.

An Englishman, whom I shall call Blake, had just arrived in Berlin after a perilous trip across Poland from Warsaw. He had been secretary to Ambassador Biddle at the American Legation in Warsaw, and had remained at his post after the others had left.

Consul Fulton gave a lunch in Blake's honor. I was glad that he had thought of me because he served nine of us the most sumptuous meal I have ever put myself around. Most of the food had been flown from Copenhagen by plane. The caviar had come by plane from Riga, Latvia. Consul Fulton was a wealthy man; no consul's salary would allow such extravagances.

After lunch was over, the plates were removed and we sat around the large table, smoking and drinking champagne.

Champagne for lunch! Boy!

I thought fleetingly but guiltily of the roomful of applicants who were waiting for me at the Embassy. By this time, Joe had probably had to tell them several times that I was deep in my work and would see them in a few minutes.

I took a sip of the champagne and listened to Blake relate his experiences in Poland.

'On my trip across Poland,' he said, 'I spent one night in a middle-sized city. Blocks of the buildings had been destroyed by bombs and shells. It was an appalling sight, and in this city I heard a pathetic story. The occupants of one of the few buildings still standing came across an unexploded bomb in the cellar. They rushed to the German military authorities and asked them to remove the thing. The Germans nodded, and sent a group of soldiers back with the Poles to the building.

'With true Prussian efficiency the conquerors ordered everybody to leave the building. The Poles filed out one by one, children, old women, men – leaving their clothes and possessions behind in the rooms. The German soldiers came up out the basement, unrolling a long piece of wire. They moved back quite a distance, gave the wire a jerk, and the building collapsed with a terrific roar. The Poles found that everything they had owned was an indistinguishable part of the rubble.'

I lit a fresh cigarette and leaned back in my chair to listen to Blake's next story. The waiter entered the dining room softly and filled our glasses again.

Blake told us another story out of his experience In their mopping-up operations, the German soldiers came to a Polish count's mansion. He surrendered his weapons to them, and they proceeded to search the many-roomed mansion. When the Germans came to a locked door, the officer asked the Pole to whom the room belonged. 'It is my mother's,' the count replied quietly. 'She spends part of the year here and the rest of the year in Warsaw. She is in Warsaw now.'

The Germans broke into the room, Blake told us, and found in one drawer a small pistol. On the strength of this chance discovery, the count was accused of concealing a weapon. He was taken to the courtyard and executed in front of his own servants.

We nodded. We had heard many similar stories.

I looked at my watch secretly. It was three-thirty already, and time enough for me to be getting back to my applicants. I scratched my cheek nervously.

Blake had pulled a set of photographs out of his pocket, and he passed them around the table.

They had been taken with a small amateur candid camera, Blake said, by a Storm Trooper.

The guest on my right handed the first picture to me. It was a photograph of twenty Jews, who were digging something with shovels.

I was handed the second picture. It showed the Jews standing shoulder-deep in the long grave which they had dug out of the earth.

The third photograph showed the group posed for the camera, standing before the gash in the earth. The fourth print showed their backs, their hands above their heads. This picture was obviously taken from between the heads of two members of the firing squad.

When the man on my right handed me the last picture, I had to look at it closely to make out what it was. The print was dark because of underexposure. I finally made out at the bottom of the hole the sprawled bodies of the Jews who had dug their grave.

The men were pushing their chairs back from the table and getting up.

I got back to my refugees as fast as I could.

WARSAW MAYOR PLEADS ON (BRITISH) RADIO FOR ALLIES' HELP. TELLS OF MERCILESS ATTACK BY NAZIS, VOICE BREAKS

MAYOR: The brutal bombardment of towns, the destruction of hundreds of churches, hospitals and private dwellings, the murdering of thousands of women and children are continuing mercilessly.

ENGLISH RADIO: We, your Allies, intend to continue the struggle for the restoration of your liberties.

MAYOR: When will effective help of Britain and France come to relieve us from this terrible situation? We are waiting for it.
New York Herald Tribune, Paris edition, September 20, 1939.

I will write the grim story as the Commercial Attaché told it to us. He was in a small milk shop downstairs from his apartment. He heard a woman say:

'But you've got to give me some pure milk. You've got to!' The Commercial Attaché looked up from counting his change. He had already put his ration cards back in his wallet, after the shopkeeper had cut something from them to cover the bread and milk he had bought.

'I'm sorry,' the tired shopkeeper said to the woman in black. 'The government says we can sell pure milk to sick persons and expectant mothers only, and then only if they present a permit. Otherwise, I must sell you skimmed milk.'[3]

The woman had started to cry. 'You don't know how it is,' she said in a low voice. 'They brought my son home yesterday in an ambulance.' All the Germans in the tiny shop were listening to her.

'Well, I'm sorry,' the shopkeeper said wearily. He heard stories all day long. 'I can't help you.'

'They brought him home with both his hands gone. Blown right off, they told me.' The little *Hausfrau* took out her handkerchief. 'I can't stand it,' she said. 'He can't eat anything, and you sell me skimmed milk.'

'For the love of God,' our Commercial Attaché told the shopkeeper. 'Take my ration card and give this woman all the whole milk she wants.'

The shopkeeper was a man, too. 'Thanks,' he said, declining the card, 'I guess I can take the risk.'

After the little *Hausfrau* had departed with her precious

---

[3] It was just about this time that the Berlin newspapers were running stories to the effect that skimmed milk was actually more beneficial to a growing child than whole milk!

quart of whole milk, the customers in the shop – the Nazis, and the non-Nazis – stared at each other coldly, each group daring the other to say something.

The Allies cannot come yet, but I know surely they will come. We shall endure.
Warsaw radio announcer, September 20, 1939.

The applicant looked at me slyly.

He sat in front of my desk, rubbing his hands together. His eyes would not meet mine, and I do not like that in a man.

'Won't you just look over my dossier again?' he asked smoothly.

'Why?' I asked shortly.

'Your time would not be lost,' he said meaningly.

I deliberately misunderstood the man and told him it was no use for us to talk further.

For a long period, the Embassy employees were constantly being offered bribes of one sort or another. Large boxes of candy arrived by messenger, sometimes containing a hundred-mark bill on the inside. For a while, the clerks kept the candy and returned the money.

One day, however, a consul found seventeen boxes of expensive candy tucked away in a typist's desk and the delightful practice was stopped immediately.

At Christmas, embarrassingly large baskets of food, wine, champagne and delicacies of all sorts were delivered by shops in Berlin to our residences. Inside, we would find no card to identify the sender. About a week later, we would get a letter from some applicant asking a favor. Near the end of the letter would be an inquiry regarding the safe arrival of the Christmas present, followed by the name and address of the generous sender.

The refugees frequently offered our clerks large sums of money to help expedite their applications. Money was of no importance to most of them; they had to leave it with the government when they left Germany anyway.

These offers of bribes were made in secret, usually in veiled language. One desperate applicant, however, in front of a waiting room full of people offered to give one of our clerks one hundred marks – about forty dollars – if he would see that his visa was issued immediately.

The American Consulate General at Stuttgart, Germany, had a bad scandal, involving three clerks who had been employed there for years. The total amount of the bribes involved was several thousand marks; to our embarrassment, the German Gestapo was the first to uncover the whole affair.

One of the major tragedies of the last few weeks was that we should have had to watch the resistance of a gallant nation overborne, without ourselves being able to render such direct assistance as might have produced different results.
Lord Halifax in speech, September 21, 1939.

For a country whose every aim is to put away things religious and concentrate on gods of a more human form, nothing can be sacred.

The following item was broadcast on the official German radio. It was later mimeographed – perhaps because its author considered it such a masterpiece – and passed around to those who had failed to hear it. I have a copy, and I have translated it into English.

I will make no further comment; it speaks for itself and for the mentality of the rulers of Germany:

Our Father Chamberlain, Who Art in London,
Forgotten be Thy name.
Thy kingdom destroyed.
Thy will he done, neither on earth nor in heaven.
Stealeth not our bread from us anymore.
Pay Thine debts, which Thou never paid,
To Thine believers.
And leadeth us not into the abyss,
But delivereth us from Thee, the Worst Evil.

For Thine is no kingdom, nor Power, nor Glory.
For Thou art a scoundrel in Eternity.
Amen.

NAZIS ASSASSINATE PREMIER OF ROUMANIA
New York Herald Tribune, Paris edition, September 22, 1939.

WHO DID IT? – THE ENGLISH!
12-Uhr Blatt, September 22, 1939.

The war in Poland is practically over. Almost every day we expect the French and the English to attack. The German in the street expects the same thing. I think half of them expect to see foreign soldiers marching through Berlin in another month.

Goebbels is busy telling the people that no such thing is possible.

The continued inactivity has convinced a lot of them that Germany is invincible.

But there is still the half which fears otherwise.

One German told me today:

'I hope they hurry up and break through the Westwall. When our army is defeated, that will be the end of Hitler. If we lose we will not be free; but then, we are not free now.'

Today I made the following notes in my diary:

Here is the curious spectacle of two million men lined up against two million men. They are evenly matched. They remind me of two football teams which have the same line strength. The only way one side can win is through an aerial attack.

Almost a whole month of war, and each side has allowed the other to bring up reinforcements and supplies to the front without the slightest interference. I think that is unprecedented in the history of warfare. The Germans are dropping bombs in Poland and the English are dropping in Germany – leaflets!

HEAVY ARTILLERY BLASTS WARSAW, POLES UNSHAKEN
New York Herald Tribune, Paris edition, September 26, 1939.

Our corridors mill with Americans still trying to get home, and refugees trying to get to the United States for the first time.

I don't know how it was done, but the citizens poured out of Berlin. By the hundreds they came into the Embassy, and were found transportation of some description back to the United States. We never knew that there were so many American citizens tucked away in these tiny German villages, far up in the mountains. We got them all started on their long journey, somehow.

We, of course, remained behind.

The streets of Warsaw were reported to be strewn with thousands of bodies.
New York Herald Tribune, Paris edition, September 26, 1939.

'Is that you, Nora?'

'No! I am Dolly Koner.'

'Oh, beg pardon.' In the blackout, Vice-Consul Paul Coates didn't bother to tip his hat. No use to go to the trouble when nobody could see, anyhow.

I was waiting with him on the corner of Joachimsthaler Strasse and the Kurfuerstendamm for Nora Johnson. He had asked me to arrange a meeting for him, and the only way I could make Nora promise to come, was to come myself. Poor Paul.

If I tell you it was black on that street corner, you must believe me. There were no street lights. Cars drove past with heavy black paper pasted over the headlights, a tiny slit cut in the middle of the paper. The street cars were phantoms, which one could hear but not see. Germans shuffled along in the darkness, bumping into each other and growling unwilling apologies.

Nora was already fifteen minutes late.

Suddenly Paul grabbed an arm in the darkness. 'Nora!' he said with relief.

'What the hell?' the owner of the arm growled. 'Turn loose of me.'

Paul turned loose. He lighted a cigarette nervously, forgetting to offer me one. The flame of his match glowed brightly in the dark. Somebody muttered at Paul to keep his match covered.

That is a strange effect the blackout has on people. They all talk in whispers and low voices as they walk along the dark streets, almost as though they fear the enemy could overhear them and drop some bombs down on them.

In the process of becoming civilized, the poor human being has had to adjust himself to speed, to loud radios, to gasoline fumes, to bright lights and to many disagreeable things. He is having a little more trouble getting used to the idea that at any moment a few hundred pounds of high explosive are likely to fall on his head from the skies above.

A couple walked past us wearing tiny flashlight bulbs on the toes of their shoes which blinked on and off with every step to warn of their approach. Practically every German wore a phosphorous button on his coat; thousands of small buttons glowed and bobbed along the Kurfuerstendamm. Many people, the kind I call one hundred and fifty percent Party members, wore phosphorous buttons in the pattern of the Nazi swastika.

Shuffle, shuffle went the pedestrians. They talked little and concentrated mainly on avoiding the pillars and posts in their paths.

In the darkness, certain girls made easy pickups. It is still very much forbidden to ply the trade in Germany – two whole chapters of Mein Kampf are devoted to this subject – but it was hard to spot would-be offenders in the dark. Even the old girls, the wrinkled ones, stood on corners with their ugly features safely hidden in the darkness and shone their flashlights on their legs in invitation.

There was some excitement near where we stood. An old woman, carrying a big bundle, walked toward the subway steps. She missed her step and fell down the steep concrete stairs.

Somebody put in a call for a first aid ambulance, and it came and carried her away.

While we were watching the stretcher bearers work with their flashlights in their hands, somebody slapped Paul lightly on his shoulder. He looked around, but there was nobody near.

Like ghosts, people crept past. Feeling their way carefully over curbstones, avoiding the showcases which are built out in the middle of the sidewalk on the Kurfuerstendamm, muttering apologies for unavoidable collisions.

I learned one lesson in war-time Berlin: Cities were never built to be blacked-out. Cities were meant to be well lighted; they are unbearable otherwise.

Paul was grumbling because Nora was so late. Finally, she was there. 'You're late, Nora,' he muttered.

'I'm sorry,' Nora said. 'I got lost in the dark and missed this street. Where shall we go?'

'Let's go in Kranzler's,' I said. 'It's right here on the corner and we won't have to walk in this mess.'

I went ahead, and parted the heavy drapes which covered the door. When we came into the light of the restaurant, we blinked. The place was crowded, but a waitress found us a table in a corner.

We hung up our coats on a coat tree, and sat down. I had just picked up the list of drinks when I heard Nora gasp.

'Paul!' she said fearfully.

'What?' he asked, goggling at her.

'Look, there on the back of your coat.'

Paul and I turned to look at the coat hanging on the tree. Paul's mouth flopped open in astonishment. In the blackout, somebody had attached one of those red-lettered stickers to his coat. It read: DOWN WITH HITLER.

RIBBENTROP FLIES TODAY TO MOSCOW
FOR SECOND TIME
12-Uhr Blatt, September 27, 1939.

FRENCH CABINET PUTS FINAL BAN
ON COMMUNISM
New York Herald Tribune, Paris edition, September 27, 1939.

There is of course no need for me to tell which of our German employees in the Embassy it was. It would not help my story any, and it would only cause a visit to the employee from the German Gestapo after they get their hands on this book.

We will call her Fräulein Brandt.

Fräulein Brandt's mother and father had retired. The apartment was quiet; it was late at night. The maid had not yet returned from the movies, where she was sent to get her out of the way so Eva Brandt could listen to foreign news broadcasts.

Eva sat on the floor beside her radio and tuned in London very softly for the late news broadcast in the German language.

She had been listening for a few minutes before she noticed that the volume had increased. She turned the radio down even lower. The British announcer's voice grew louder.

She turned the volume knob down as far as it would go. The Britisher's voice filled the whole room with sound.

Eva was horrified; she was paralyzed with fear. If anybody overheard her tuning in on London, it would mean a long prison sentence for her. Had her radio gone completely crazy? she wondered.

She quickly turned the dial to the Berlin Station. That worked all right, and the broadcast was normal and quiet. Mystified, Eva twisted the dial back to London.

The British news came as loud as ever.

On a quick suspicion, and because she is a clever girl Eva turned her radio completely off. She could still hear the London station distinctly in her apartment, and she knew what was going on.

The man upstairs, either drunk or insane, was also listening to the London broadcast and hadn't bothered to turn the volume down.

These are the incidents that make a German's life so pleasant in Nazi Germany.

WARSAW AFLAME AND IN RUINS
New York Herald Tribune, Paris edition,
September 28, 1939.

We had a party at Richard's house.

At dinner there were candlelight and good wine, and Richard told us amusing stories about his experiences in Rome.

Consul Fulton was there; also an Italian Consul, and four dancers from the Berlin Scala – a music hall.

After dinner, we adjourned to the living room to listen to a news broadcast from London. Richard, being a Secretary of the Embassy, as well as Consul, has diplomatic immunity. He cannot be arrested, not even by Herr von Uhlrich.

Two of the girls were red-haired and the other two were brown-haired and they had beautiful dancers' bodies and they spoke a halting English which was quite sufficient.

One of the girls put twelve records on the phonograph and closed the lid.

Deep Purple, it played.

The evening swept on.

Two bottles of Scotch were carried in, executed, and carried out again.

Ice tinkled in the glasses. *St. Louis Blues, Star Dust, Melancholy Baby* were played over and over. They made America seem close, and the war far away.

It is strange how a few bars of some half-forgotten song can bring back home so vividly; how they tug at the inside of you until you want to put your head down on your arms and shut your eyes.

Two of the girls were looking through the large stack of records. Richard was dancing with one of the redheads, and I with the other.

Consul Fulton was talking earnestly with the Italian Consul; each was trying to get information from the other without giving any information in return.

This is an old diplomatic game, and one in which each side usually allows the other party a moderate victory just to keep things going. Many Americans have the mistaken belief that when one of our diplomats comes into close conjunction with a smooth foreign diplomat, America loses something every time.

Well, I don't think so.

American diplomats are probably as shrewd as those of any

other country and have the added advantage of being considered simpletons on the basis of their predecessors' mistakes.

The average United States consul has such a fresh look of innocence on his face – he probably hails from a small town in Kansas – that he is usually able to wangle more secrets out of foreign officials than a sleek Turk or a bearded Russian.

I drove the girls home in Richard's car, a hellish ride through the blacked-out streets. It was dawn before I got them all distributed to their various apartments and reached home. I left the car on the street.

The next morning I found a police ticket on the seat; I had left the automobile parked without hanging a tiny red lantern on the rear bumper.

I have already mentioned the unreliability of the German newspapers. One side of every question, and one side only, is presented. Nowhere in the press will one find anything even remotely detrimental to the German nation or the German race.

I have never seen in any Germany newspaper any criticism of the government, the bureaus, the army, the municipal governments, the state-owned railways (though they badly needed criticism), the weather bureau, the state agricultural program, the rearmament program and on and on.

On the other hand, practically everything foreign, with the exception of Italy, came in for constant vituperation. Following the Munich conference, during which Germany got everything she wanted at the time, the Propaganda Ministry unbent so far as to allow the newspapers to write the following single sentence in praise of Neville Chamberlain: 'It appears that Herr Chamberlain is a far-sighted statesman (!), but we prefer to wait and observe his attitude for a time before we say too much about him.'

A few days later, when Chamberlain told the British that they would have to rearm as never before, the German press leaped back on him with all its accustomed fury. We breathed sighs of relief; it just wasn't natural for the Nazis to say anything nice about anybody.

Sometimes real news is to be found on the back pages of the newspapers, among the death notices. In a controlled press, one learns to look for significant omissions rather than stories unlikely to appear.

If a notice announcing a soldier's death does not carry the words 'Died for Adolf Hitler,' one may well assume that here was no Nazi who fell.

Here are two black-bordered clippings which tell their own sad little story.

Remember that in Nazi Germany, the survivors of a dead soldier are supposed to show no grief and wear no mourning. They are supposed to be glad that their loved one could make the supreme sacrifice for Adolf Hitler.

Died for his Fatherland, 22 years old,

PETER MUELHENS,

Lieutenant of a Reconnaissance Detachment.
In indescribable sorrow over the death of their only child,

Dr. Anton Muelhens, Frau Emmy Muelhens, nee Drost, Berlin, September 13, 1939.

Today my beloved husband,

DR. ANTON MUELHENS,

Followed our only son Peter Muelhens who died on the battlefield. A heart attack released him from his misery and pain over our Peter. In unutterable sorrow and in the name of the survivors,

Emmy Muelhens, nee Drost, Berlin, October 7, 1939.

Both of the deceased will be buried on Tuesday, October 10, at 12 o'clock from the Chapel of the Luisen Cemetery in Berlin.

WE ARE WAITING FOR AID FROM OUR ALLIES
Warsaw radio, September 28, 1939.

I do not know why I save newspaper clippings. Perhaps it is because I once thought of being a newspaperman. At any rate, I like to take the clippings and shuffle them around and contrast them.

For instance.

On the twenty-eighth of September, I cut the following items out of a newspaper:

The French Army is using thousands of pigs to explode German mine fields in front of the Siegfried Line.

The French, it is reported, drive units of hundreds of pigs several kilometers into No Man's Land, where they explode the mines on contact, thus saving the lives of innumerable soldiers.

New York Herald Tribune, Paris edition.

Uncontrollable fires are sweeping Warsaw, having destroyed all food and other supplies. It is impossible to estimate the number of dead. With practically every hospital destroyed or under shell fire or airplane bombardment, the Poles are obliged to transport the wounded from place to place.

New York Herald Tribune, Paris edition.

'Heinie,' I said today, when the old newspaper vender laid my newspaper down on the desk, 'coming every day to the Embassy here, did you ever get the idea of going to America?'

'I used to want to go,' he said, taking off his thick glasses and polishing them on his sleeve. 'Have a brother in Detroit.'

'Why don't you want to go now?' I insisted.

'Well, I'll tell you,' he whispered confidentially, leaning over my desk. 'The landlord who runs the apartment house where I live is a big Nazi. When Germany loses this war, and the people start to revolt, I want to be here.' He put his glasses back on his nose. 'I want to be the first to kick that Nazi right in his fat ass.'

'Speak more softly,' said Paul, leaning across the table. 'There is a bunch of Storm Troopers at the table right behind us.'

It was the twenty-ninth of September, and we were sitting in the Kunstler Eck, a small Lokale far back in a courtyard which stays open all night. Its walls are covered with gloomy wood carvings, tiny models of cannon, death's-heads, coffins.

Richard was there, Consul Crom Fulton, Vice-Consul of the United States Paul Coates, my Swedish friend Niles, and I. Niles was an official in the Swedish Legation, a sophisticated, clever analyst of German internal politics for his government.

Our waiter was so old that he seemed to be part of the depressing furnishings. Against one wall there was a pump organ, on which a hunchback played endless symphonies, sonatas and lieder.

Niles was telling an interesting story about Dr. Brinkman, who had just been removed from his post as head of the powerful German Reichsbank.

'When Dr. Brinkman was made head of the Reichsbank,' Niles continued, 'he of course inherited a terrific burden from the brilliant Dr. Schacht, who had resigned as you know. Brinkman kept the office only two months, then resigned "for reasons of health". All Germany gossiped that Brinkman had lost his mind.'

'Who wouldn't?' asked Paul, drinking heavily from his wine glass.

The old hunchback played heavy chords on his organ, rattling every glass in the place.

'Right after he was appointed,' Niles continued, paying no attention to Paul, 'Brinkman began to behave in a strange manner. He ordered large signs reading KEEP TO THE RIGHT to be hung in the corridors of his office. These signs caused the Reichsbank employees to talk, but were nothing compared to his action of paying the Bank's official band to play in the building's courtyard, during working hours.

'A few days later, Brinkman called all the Bank's young messengers together in his office. He took them to the swank Adlon

Hotel bar in several taxis, and ordered cocktails for them all. Some of the messengers were only twelve years old. By this time, all Berlin was talking about the President of the Reichsbank. The day following the Adlon bar incident, Brinkman decided to call up Field Marshal Goering. Of course, as head of the Reichsbank, he was connected immediately. 'I have something important to discuss with you,' he said to fat Goering. 'Will you come over to see me?' In the presence of his adjutants, Goering irately slammed down the receiver and yelled, 'That guy must be crazy!'

Niles slowly exhaled his cigarette smoke. 'He was,' he added reflectively.

We laughed.

The Storm Troopers sitting near us were not talking.

They were obviously listening to what they could catch of our conversation. Their faces showed that they did not approve of our speaking English.

Richard looked up at Niles from under his thick eye-brows. 'Perhaps he wasn't crazy at all,' he said in his deep voice. 'Maybe he thought it was worth while to make a fool of himself in order to get out of that dangerous job.'

We talked, the organ played, the S.S. men sat silent, the old waiter leaned against the wall with his white napkin across his arm, we drank more wine, the air was filled with cigarette smoke, the world was in suspension.

The waiter came to life and brought us another bottle of wine. He poured our glasses full.

'I hear the Germans are cleaning everything out of Poland,' Richard said. 'They are even gathering up the spent bullets, so they can melt them and use them over again.'

'Somebody told me this today,' Paul said. 'The German soldiers are mainly interested in Czech girls and Polish geese.'

'That's not funny,' Niles said shortly.

Paul thought it was. He laughed anyway.

'Let's lower our voices a little,' I said, leaning forward. 'There is no use in our letting these three fellows start trouble.'

'You're right,' Niles agreed.

'I heard a very good story about the evacuation of the French town of Strasbourg,' Richard said, wrinkling his forehead to remember. 'The town was completely evacuated, so that nobody was left except the mayor and the priest. After a long and exhausting train ride to the south of France, it developed that many of the women who had left Strasbourg were pregnant. A French officer in charge of the evacuation asked a subordinate why all those women were allowed to get on the train in such a condition. The journey had taken so long that the subordinate felt justified in answering, "They didn't, sir."'

We laughed.

It was getting late. Several of the lights had been turned out and the Kunstler Eck appeared gloomier than ever.

The Storm Troopers drank their beers and looked at us. Only occasionally did they speak a word to each other, and then it was in a low, guttural German.

The hunchback was playing something that might have originally been written by Wagner. The waiter stood against the wall, waiting for us to leave.

'I think it about time we shoved off,' Niles said, rising to his feet. We agreed, and got up to get our coats from the rack.

The three Storm Troopers looked up at us. One of them saluted us with a ringing, 'Heil Hitler!'

Niles looked in the S.S. man's direction for a long time reflectively, before he turned away without answering.

We left the Kunstler Eck.

Outside, day was already breaking.

The morning newspapers were being delivered around the city. They said:

WARSAW CAPITULATES!!!
All papers, September 30, 1939.

WAS THERE A WAR AT ALL?
12-Uhr Blatt, September 30, 1939.

CHAPTER THREE

PEACE.
    Peace!
    Peace!!
    The word leaped at me, through the telephone receiver, shouted at me by people who rushed past my door.
    The English cabinet has fallen, they cried.
    Chamberlain is out!
    The English King has abdicated!
    Peace has come to Europe!
    Berlin began to rock with the news. It was October 10, 1939, a nice, sunshiny day, when the population first got wind of the news.
    The way out of the mess had been found, they said exultantly.
    On what terms?
    Doesn't matter. The main thing is that Europe shall once more be at peace. The whole war was just a bad dream, an especially bad Munich crisis which had simply gotten out of hand. Everything was all right now.
    I picked up the telephone and called my friend Willy at the Associated Press.
    'Hello, Willy,' I began.
    'No, I don't know anything new,' was his prompt reply.
    'Oh, you've heard the rumor already?'
    'Nothing else all morning,' he said.
    'Is it true, then?' I asked tensely.
    'I just heard it. That's all. Perhaps it is true,' he said.
    'Hope so.'
    I put the receiver down on the hook.
    The phone rang immediately, violently.
    It was Hanna. I could tell from her voice that she believed it already. She just wanted to make sure by asking me.

'I don't know anything,' I told her, truthfully, and hung up.

My telephone bell jangled noisily the whole morning. Nobody knew any details about the peace proposals, but everybody knew that peace had come. A German acquaintance – a Nazi – came by for a triumphant visit with me. He had taken a day's holiday to celebrate.

'All over but the signing,' he said joyfully. 'Hitler is still the smartest of them all. Let's go celebrate.'

I let him go his way alone. I didn't trust the whole thing, somehow.

Richard rushed by, on his way to the Foreign Office. He believed it.

Peace!

How the word took hold of the German capital that day. How wild with joy the people went. Every time the telephone rang, it brought more rumors and eager questions and flat assertions.

The average number of telephone calls in New York daily is eight million – more calls than are made daily in entire France. On October 10, Berlin far outdistanced the New York average.

I got more and more nervous. Rumors were well enough, but I wanted some confirmation.

The telephone rang. 'Call for you,' said the operator, her voice harried. I waited eagerly until the connection was completed.

'Yes?' I said.

'This is Max Lefkowicz,' the person said. 'I have number forty-three thousand and ten on the German waiting list. Can't you tell me when I will get my visa?'

God!

I looked up the number on our chart, and told him the discouraging news.

In Germany, where no adverse opinions are allowed to creep into the newspapers, the only way one can know what the people actually think about things is to talk to them in person and to watch how they behave in crowds. I felt I could not stay in my office any longer. I closed the door on the stacks of dossiers and walked out into the sunlight.

The Germans I met on the street were smiling broadly; the *Hausfrauen*, the soldiers home on leave, the younger stenographers, the workmen in dirty clothes.

I had not seen them smiling like that at the time of the *Anschluss* with Austria; they had not smiled on the street when Germany conquered Czechoslovakia bloodlessly; the fall of Warsaw had not caused such a general good humor.

For those who would understand what goes on in Nazi Germany, there is much food for thought here.

I walked past the Adlon Hotel, where most of the foreign diplomats meet for important talks. I turned the corner by the American Express and walked down the Wilhelmstrasse. I passed the old government buildings which line the street; they are only two or three stories high and their fronts are unimposing. I saw von Hindenburg's old palace, which was being ripped out inside to be remodeled for the use of Joachim von Ribbentrop. I strolled past the guards who stand at rigid attention before the entrances to the more important government buildings. Their heavy feet were spread apart on the sentry blocks and their hard eyes looked straight ahead.

Although the peace rumors were only a few hours old, a large crowd was standing in front of Hitler's Chancellery. Faces were lighted with radiant hope; the people knew that any minute their Fuehrer would appear on his low balcony and speak to them.

I waited a while with the crowd, and then moved on toward Potsdamer Platz. At this busiest intersection in Berlin I saw people who had gone crazy with joy.

Strangers grabbed strangers by the arms to tell them the wonderful news.

Peace, brother, peace!

Other people grabbed strangers and embraced them in a delirium of joy.

It looked like New Year's Eve in the daytime.

In front of the swank old Esplanade Hotel I saw Heinie, a newspaper vender familiar to foreigners living in Berlin. He was talking to everybody who came past his newsstand, acquaintance and stranger alike, completely forgetting to sell his newspapers.

'What do you think?' I asked him, when I finally got him to recognize me.

'It's all over,' he said, grinning. 'They've stopped fighting and Adolf Hitler speaks at three o'clock. He's going to announce peace.'

Everyone was repeating it.

'Hitler speaks at three.'

'Peace, peace, peace, wonderful peace!'

'Praise God and Heil Hitler!'

In Berlin-Wilmersdorf, an enthusiastic butcher, believing that the war was over and the necessity for ration cards gone, sold out his entire stock of meats and wieners to avid *Hausfrauen*.

One happy father, anxious to write his soldier son the good news, was told at a branch post office that he could not buy a postcard bearing the word '*Feldpost*,' since the war was now over and there would be no more free postal delivery to the army.

In a small grocery store on Wilmersdorfer Strasse an excited crowd of housewives were eagerly discussing the new peace. A man, entering the grocery just in time to hear one woman say, 'Chamberlain has fallen,' said to the woman matter-of-factly, 'Then Anthony Eden will take his place.'

The housewives were infuriated with his words, and cursed at him. One woman pelted him with potatoes snatched from a bin. When the man would not take back his assertion, the women – practically in unison – shouted, 'Eden can't be Prime Minister. He's a Jew!'

Of course Anthony Eden isn't a Jew, but he is so much attacked in the German press that he should be one. And there is no reason why a Jew could not head the English government; the British have had brilliant Jewish leaders in other times of crisis.

Most Germans left their businesses in order to celebrate. Every pub in Berlin overflowed; every radio was tuned in for Hitler's speech at three o'clock.

Peace?

I tried to analyze my feelings at that moment. Did I want the war to continue or not? A year ago, when the German troops marched into lovely Prague, I had inadvertently cried at the person who gave me the news, 'God, why doesn't somebody stop him?'

Peace? What kind of peace?

What would I say to my English and French and Canadian friends if they came riding back into Berlin? Would I shake their hands and say I was glad they had come back? Or wouldn't I despise them, and myself?

It was already three o'clock. I stopped in front of a radio shop, where a large crowd was collected on the sidewalk to listen to an outside loud speaker. Martial music blared from the radio. The Germans talked happily among themselves.

We waited for an hour, hearing the stirring music all the time. Finally, not at three o'clock but at four, came the Voice of Adolf Hitler.

The crowd on the sidewalk was deathly quiet.

Der Fuehrer spoke.

Our Fuehrer, may God bless him, will announce peace to the people of Germany, to the people of the whole world.

He never wanted war with England and France, anyway. He is a good, kind man.

The Voice began. It announced the opening of a new and more energetic campaign to collect money for the Winter Relief. Now, more than ever before, it said, we have to support our soldiers with every bit of strength and money. The Voice spoke for forty minutes.

It had finished, and the sound of rousing 'Sieg Heil, Sieg Heil, Sieg Heil!' came through the noisy loud speaker.

There was no mention of the new peace in any sentence.

The Germans on the sidewalk around me were puzzled. Could it be that everybody in Germany knew that peace had arrived, except Hitler?

Had nobody told him?

The crowd was bewildered, and disappointed.

That evening, after the sun had gone down, the evening papers appeared, and on their front pages there was printed a denial. The unscrupulous British Secret Service had played a dirty trick on the German people by starting false rumors of peace in Berlin, the papers announced.

Gloom settled with the night. The faces which had been alight with joy all day were secret and hurt. People who had augmented their natural elation with alcohol bought in every pub along their paths, by nightfall had their alcohol in them still; their elation had disappeared down the drain.

Well, that night Berlin was completely blacked out.

Just like every other night.

But in the hearts of the people it was much blacker.

Germany is ruled by a special kind of mob psychology, much as a symphony orchestra is directed by its conductor.

The rulers of Germany know how to bring forth from their people loud tones, and they know how to make them quiet.

The Nazis know exactly what the public reaction to any new law or any new turn in government policies will be.

They have built a mighty instrument on which they play to bring about the desired results; connected with the first manual is the battery of newspapers; regulated by the second manual is the official Reich radio; the third row of keys controls the speeches of Party members at mass gatherings; the pedals work the propaganda posters.

One man plays this mighty organ: Dr. Joseph Goebbels. The stops are at his command; whether he plays a soft chord or a harsh one, Germany reacts accordingly.

Where propaganda is the lifeblood of the government, there must always be something hot to dish up for the readers, the listeners and the attenders.

October was a month of no news, since there was absolutely nothing going on. Poland had been conquered. The border with France was best described as 'all quiet on the Western front.' England was far away, apparently slumbering.

What to tell the people?

What, what, what could Goebbels feed the editors?

The Germans were beginning to feel a dangerous letdown.

How to keep them keyed to a fighting pitch?

What would the headlines be tomorrow?

One of the officials in the Ministry of Propaganda (and Public Enlightenment!) had an idea. A super propaganda story designed to stir up hatred of the British in Germany. He put a reporter to work on the job. The resultant story, supposed to be the diary of a simple German girl who had been interned in England during September and part of October, was published in many German newspapers in installments.

I have condensed and translated the articles, not because I think they are remotely true, but because – true or false – they give an excellent picture of what eight years of Nazi propaganda have taught German youth to believe.

Perhaps there does exist a nineteen-year-old German girl named Lucie Krahmer. Perhaps she was interned in England for two months. Perhaps she did tell the story of her experiences to a reporter. If so, that would not be a reason for my repeating her diary here.

This is the reason: from the words of her diary, the American reader can form a better and more accurate picture of what the average German youth thinks – and how he thinks – than I could give in two hundred closely written pages of exposition.

'The English *gentleman*,' wrote Lucie Krahmer,[1] 'is known to the whole world. Therefore, I would like to produce for everybody's information the gentleman's behavior in this war, especially in regard to women. I was the first German to return to her homeland after having been confined in England.

'In the middle of August, I went to visit a German family in London – in order to study English. I soon left for Ireland, where I found that the Irish were exceedingly kind people. It even happened that the Irish people, in one little village greeted me with our "Heil Hitler".

---

[1] In the Berlin newspaper B. Z. *am Mittag*, and other German newspapers.

'When war broke out, I packed my belongings in order to go back to Germany. While crossing England in order to get to Holland, I was arrested. English policemen took me to a police station, where all my belongings were immediately seized.

'The *gentlemen* police searched me as follows: I had to stretch out my arms, after which they took off my wristwatch and searched my pockets all over with their hands, as they search convicts. I was acutely aware of possibilities which awaited a young German girl dependent on British mercy and decency.

'They carried me to the Woman's Prison, in Manchester.

'Only a short time ago, we girls talking together in our homeland had sworn to serve our Fatherland through all our lives. I felt that fate had approached me and that I had to stand the test as a German girl.

'I was given a gas mask.

'That made me laugh for the first time in days. I was in the Woman's Prison and evidently all English convicts had to have gas masks just like any other Englishman. They certainly seemed to be mighty afraid of the Germans. At last I knew it. That made me feel proud and the gas mask which I was given was like a pledge for the victory of our Fatherland... .

'The English gas masks, made out of rubber and celluloid, go just under the chin and up to the eyebrows of the wearer. They fit so badly that I could comfortably stick both my fists under mine. Later on, I found that the other prisoners could do the same. From that time on I was not allowed to take one step without carrying that gas mask with me. The nurses and all the other prisoners carried them too.

'A long time later, when I had been set free, my supposition was confirmed. After my release I met not one single Englishman without a gas mask hanging over his shoulder. I was allowed to part with mine only at the frontier. This showed me – in addition to the captive balloons over the towns, in addition to the shelters dug in English gardens which look like gigantic mole hills and in addition to many other things I saw – that the English live in a constant fear of German attacks.

'All five of us Germans were put into solitary confinement exactly like the English convicts. The only difference was that we were allowed to wear our own clothes.

'In the course of time, when we came together with the English female convicts to do prison work, they shoved us around and had the nerve to ask us for what crimes we were in prison. That is what a German woman had to endure in England.

'On Sunday when I was brought to the prison church for the first time, I was terrified. Even at church I had to sit behind a white lattice, a crisscross of wooden slats. I sat right among the English prisoners. The English criminals were sobbing and bowing their heads.

'Must I do the same?

'I, a German girl?

'Why should I bow down and sob? No, never. I was not conscious of any crime. I was not repenting any misdeed. I sat upright proudly and did not let one single tear drop from my eyes. Although the parson looked at me again and again, it did him no good; it did not change the fact that I had neither a feeling of penitence nor knowledge of any crime committed by me. All I felt in that hour was love for my country, for Germany.

'We had to go to church twice a week. And what did we have to listen to in church? Politics! Or rather, what an English clergyman considered to be politics. This clergyman was strongly anti-German. The divine service of the Church of England comforted us with the following words:

'"The Germans were people without any sense of honor, and there were no Christians among them.[2]

'"During this war, hospitals, children's homes and so forth had been bombed by the Germans."

'This was said by a clergyman of England!

'One day he brought forth a parable, the one which tells how the Pharisees tried to bring Jesus into temptation and how Jesus could not be induced. How could it have been otherwise?

[2] There are certainly not many in the ranks of the Nazi Party, where worship of Adolf Hitler comes before Jesus Christ.

'This crazy clergyman compared the Pharisees to Germany and Russia, and he compared Jesus to England, who in the end would be victorious.

'One day the parson admitted in his sermon that an English airplane carrier had been destroyed. My God! Didn't I listen attentively to his words! We knew nothing of what was going on at the front. Didn't I think gratefully of our youthful pilots! They would teach England a lesson! They had already showed her – and more convincingly than I had ever thought possible – what Germany's army was and how high her power was to be estimated.

'An English airplane carrier destroyed. The clergyman, in his stupidity, excused this event by saying that England was in possession of such ships and that Germany had none. This only made me laugh. My fellow prisoners behind the lattice were also smiling.

'It won't help the English newspapers any to revile my Germany either. I can see through them; I caught them in their lies.

'I certainly never thought that the English people had so little brains of their own, not to be able to see that everything in their papers was nonsense.

'The English are becoming narrow-minded; they don't feel at home in the rest of the world, as they did in former generations. They can't see the surrounding world, and that may be the reason why so many English people are taken in by the lies of their government and of their press.

'They are absolutely uninformed.

'Before my arrest, I had seen innumerable placards on the advertisement pillars around England: "OUR FREEDOM IS ENDANGERED!" they read. It is the freedom of fools that these English people are worried about.

'They surely must be aware of the fact that the Germans stand behind the Fuehrer like one large community, as imperturbable as a concrete wall.

'How often during my stay in prison did I think: The Fuehrer has given us the correct upbringing for a national community. That is where the English are going to bite their teeth off.

'The prayer of a German girl in an English Woman's Prison was that the strength of the Fatherland, of which I was sure and of which I was also a tiny part, might grow and increase.

'We were treated cruelly and driven hard. Did the English learn these methods by the way they treated the natives in their colonies?

'The attendant insulted me with the most rude and filthy expressions. I can still bear her crying: "We are not in Germany."

'I am just sorry that we are not, I thought.

'At lunch time we were allowed to write letters. I wrote, among other things: "We are being treated like convicts, are always hungry and freezing." Not one of these letters was ever received.

'Letters addressed to us were held back for a long time and delivered only when it suited the administration of the prison.[3]

'Once a week we had to stand in line with our lead combs in our hands. We called it the louse parade. We were examined one after the other, a nurse rooting up our hair with our combs.

'Don't you worry, readers. English filth will not stick to a German girl.

'It was a hard blow for me when after a month's time I was called to the office and "Madam" told me with a cold smile that I would be confined for the duration of the war. Now everything was finished, I felt. But I did not want "Madam" to have the satisfaction of seeing a German girl lose her self-control. When I got back into my cell, I let my tears fall. I now had to fight for my life. Nothing would hold me back.

'One of the English criminals had told me that if I wanted to exasperate the prison administration, I ought to sing in my cell – they could not stand it, she said.

'I cried until I could not stand it any more physically – then my tears dried up.

'I started singing the *Deutschland* song, the *Horst Wessel* song and other songs of my Fatherland. That gave me strength and

---

[3] In view of the fanatically strict censorship of mail which exists in Germany this should have made Lucie feel right at home.

courage. My fellow prisoners also joined me. I wonder what the English thought when they heard us.

'No. They could not manage the Fuehrer's Germany.

'Finally, I had a plan. I learned from an English newspaper that the Swiss Embassy in London had taken German citizens under its protection. I applied to that office. The Swiss worked on my case so successfully that one of my fellow prisoners and I were set free.

'I went home through Holland.

'On the German border I greeted every house, every tree, every single flower; had I trusted the English newspapers I would have expected to see a destroyed and neglected country. But I had known that Germany would hold her own.

'I was deeply aware of the tranquillity and the self-confidence which existed in Germany. I compared it to the nervousness and unsteadiness in England. In Germany there is security, positiveness and confidence in the future. After all I went through abroad, I certainly can say:

'The Germans at home have every reason for being happy!

'And how great and kind is Germany! She is strong and powerful, she looks into the future with the calm consciousness of her power that England has no conception of.

'I have to think again and again of my fellow prisoners and of all the rest of the Germans in England and in her colonies. They are comforting themselves in the knowledge of the greatness and the power of their Fatherland.

'*We must all think of the Germans beyond the border. We are bound to them and they, in return, rely on us. We will have to think of a good homecoming for them. They deserve it for their faith in Germany.*'

October 11:

We are marking time. We are waiting for hell to break loose. This is beautiful weather.

What are they waiting for?

On my way through the subway turnstile today, the ticket puncher asked me, 'Will there be peace?'

'No chance!' I answered him, and went on.

The Germans are not as frightened as they were at first but up to now I have seen practically no enthusiasm for the war. They will fight for Adolf Hitler, of course; but only if he pokes them in the behind with a bayonet.

Nobody asked the Germans if they wanted to go to war.

In 1935, when Germany quit the League of Nations, Dr. Goebbels screamed at the people: 'We will have an election every year, to ask the German people if it wants to keep on under National Socialism.'

The very next year the election was put off because of bad feeling existing among the people. No election has been held since, with the exception of the 'Ja' and 'Nein' farce which was held in 1938. 'Ja' meant, 'Do you like Hitler?' and 'Nein' meant, 'Oh, you don't, don't you?'

Guess who won.

Suddenly they found themselves at war. They had not voted on a single issue leading up to it.

How good would their morale be if the English and French armies attack now? Not very good, I think.

But in the meantime, propaganda, propaganda, propaganda. If the others don't hurry up, the Germans will have enough artificial morale injected into them to make them want to fight.

Please understand this, Allies.

Ask your envoys who have been living in Germany the last few years. Let them tell you how the propaganda works in Germany.

Attack now while the people are still uncertain of themselves.

Attack, attack, attack.

October 12:

Richard and I were riding on a street car at noon. We were on our way to Consul Fulton's house for lunch, and Richard's car was out of gas. He had run out of ration cards, and had to leave his car standing in his garage.

We were talking in low tones, as we always did when we were in public. Suddenly we heard a rough voice behind us say, 'That English stinks.'

We looked around. The speaker was a Storm Trooper, wearing a black uniform and a big swastika armband. 'Why can't you speak in German?' he asked, rudely.

Richard looked at him sharply for a long moment. Richard does not have too much love for the Germans at any time, and he has even less when they interfere with him.

'My good sir,' Richard said in his slow and halting German, 'in the first place, we are Americans. We don't speak English; we speak American. In the second place, I am a Consul at the American Embassy here. Third, and most important, I am here only *because I have to be.*'

That wasn't diplomatic speech, but it was effective speech and something any S.S. man could easily understand. The Germans in the street car immediately took sides, some of them criticizing the Storm Trooper for butting in, the rest of them agreeing that nobody should be allowed to speak the English language in Germany.

When we left the car at our stop, the trolley was in an inter-German uproar.

Richard said he didn't know what kept him from quitting the Foreign Service and joining the Canadian air force.

'Damned Heinies,' he muttered all the way to Consul Fulton's front door.

October 14:

Today, after work, I decided to go to one of the Finnish bath houses in Berlin. There is nothing quite like a good sweat to relax the muscles and the nerves. The place I went to was called 'Sauna,' and it was the first time that I had been there.

It was the men's day to take the baths, but there was a woman attendant in charge of the booths where one undressed.

I took off all my clothes and waited for her to go away so I could come out. Finally, she called to me, 'Aren't you coming out?'

'I'm coming,' I answered unwillingly. Wrapping a scanty towel around my middle, I came out to be weighed.

The female attendant was annoyed. 'You can't weigh with that towel wrapped around you,' she said. 'It must weigh at least two hundred grams.' I put the offending garment away reluctantly, and was weighed.

After taking an ice-cold shower, I entered a room which was heated to a high degree of temperature by a tin stove in one corner. The tiers of wooden benches were lined with sweating men, most of them overweight. I sat down on the wood planks, and promptly jumped with pain as I touched the hot wood. Sweat began to pour from my every gland. A man came into the room and threw some cold water into the stove. A wave of stifling hot air flowed over the benches. The man instructed us to breathe through our mouths. He brought me a bucket of cold water and a bundle of switches. I began to switch myself briskly, as the others were doing. Switching the body makes the blood circulate close to the skin. After about ten minutes, I emerged from the room and took another ice-cold shower. Then I went back to sweat for ten minutes more.

I was ready for my soap massage.

'Did you bring your own soap?' the masseur asked me.

'No ' I said. 'Was I supposed to?'

'Well, yes,' the man said wistfully. 'But if you don't have it, I suppose we will have to give you some of ours.'

I laid myself on the wooden table.

'So you're an American,' the guy said, smearing my back with soap paste. *Wham!* he slapped it on. 'When will the war be over, do you think?'

'Not for a long time, I'm afraid,' I said. *Wham!*

'And will America fight against Germany again this time?' He was pounding my legs and back. 'I wouldn't know,' I answered him. *Wham!*

The masseur turned me over on my back. He rotated my stomach violently.

'We will have peace by November,' he said, starting to pound again.

'You mean, you will have defeated England and France by then?' I asked incredulously.

'We will destroy England completely.'

'And France?' *Wham!*

'Oh, France will not fight against us after England is defeated. They want to be friends with us.' His strong fingers squeezed my neck muscles. 'Germany is united. Let the others come. We are ready.'

'But what if the others don't come?'

'Then we will go to them.'

'Well, I wonder,' I said reflectively.

Wham! Wham!

It was finished. I decided, as the masseur tucked me in the cot, that in the future I would not mix politics and massage.

The heat and the massage had relaxed me. That was the first time I had felt tranquil in months. I was asleep almost immediately.

October 15:

Although they are strictly forbidden to listen to foreign radio broadcasts, from my observations I would say that approximately sixty to seventy percent of all German adults do so regularly.

They do not dare to listen openly. They turn the volume down to a whisper, they send their maids out to the picture show in the evening, they sit on the floors with their ears directly in front of the loud speakers.

Old-fashioned headphones, which could be used for extra-private listening, were sold out in every German radio shop during the first week of the war.

In Berlin's military hospitals, soldiers who had been wounded in Poland lay ten men to a ward and every night, when the London broadcasting station started its news in the German language, one of the men left his bed to stand guard outside the door to the ward. Inside, the nine other soldiers crowded their heads close to a tiny radio in order to hear the truth about what was actually going on.

It was not difficult to tune in London or Paris, even on the cheapest of radio sets.

The Germans broadcast 'Wunsch Koncerts,' especially created to please their soldiers at the front. As soon as their officers left the bunkers in the Westwall, the soldiers tuned in Paris.

But not for news.

They wanted to hear the hot French dance music.

From my dentist I heard the following significant story:

He has a friend of long standing, who is foreman of a construction gang employed on a government project, and is a Party member of high standing.

This Nazi foreman was invited by his straw boss to a party in celebration of the straw boss's tenth year with the same construction company. Of course he accepted, since in Nazi Germany class lines are supposed to be nonexistent. At the party in the straw boss's home, the members of the crew and the big Nazi drank the usual German beers, schnapps, beers, schnapps and some more beers. As the afternoon wore on into evening, the Nazi rose to go.

'Oh, no,' objected his employee, slightly drunk by this time. 'Don't go yet, sir. The highest point of the evening comes at seven-fifteen.'

The Nazi had no choice but to stay.

And at exactly seven-fifteen, the straw boss staggered over to his radio and tuned in London. 'This is the one time in the day when we can hear the truth,' he said. 'All the rest is lies.'

The other Germans, simple fellows all, gathered around with their glasses of beer in their hands, and listened to the London announcer.

The Nazi, who wore his Party swastika proudly in his lapel could not forbid the men to listen to the British without making a fool of himself and deeply offending his faithful old straw boss into the bargain.

After he had listened in with them, he could not report them to the Gestapo without getting himself into trouble. He was just as guilty as they.

And if he had reported them, his best workers would have disappeared.

October 16:

Today I made the following notes in my diary:

STATISTICS: In 1933, Germany spent 748,000,000 reichs-marks for rearmament. In 1934, after Adolf Hitler had come to power and the last year in which such figures were published, Germany spent 1,452,000,000 reichsmarks.

ALSO: In 1900, there were 2,000,000 births in Germany, and 8,000 college graduates. In 1932, there were only 900,000 births and 41,000 college graduates.

FINALLY: In the World War, 4,578 war pilots fell on the German side. Among them were twenty-seven who had won the highest German honor or decoration, the *'Pour le Mérite.'*

Figures which remind one of von Papen's famous remark: 'Germans,' he said, 'do not like to die in bed.'

So often in connection with Nazi Germany one comes across the word 'total.' In the German language, this word is pro-nounced with the accent on the last syllable, instead of on the first as we pronounce it. Also, it has much more meaning. One hears about 'total' war, 'total' economy, 'total' rationing.

The Nazi government functions on a philosophy of 'totality.' Anything which it undertakes must be done 'totally', or not at all.

If any Jews are to be evicted from German soil, every Jew must be evicted. And this must be done immediately, else the 'total' way of doing things appears to be breaking down in the eyes of the people.

I do not know whether I make myself clear. 'Total' is a gov-ernmental system of no exceptions, of no deviations, of no crit-icism, of no waste.

In preparing for this war – and it was prepared for – the whole economy of Germany was put on a 'total' diet. Every bit of waste, every raw product, every possible saving of imports, every worker was utilized in a stupendous effort to save money, to build weapons, to train a huge army.

We who were stationed in Germany knew that the Germans were working day and night for two years before the war broke out to make guns, shells, bombs, planes. Of course the British and French envoys must have got the same information that we did.

With true German thoroughness, the Nazis set to work to build a war machine. They did it 'totally.' Those articles of which they were short – oil, certain metals, rubber – they acquired frantically from all over the world and stored them away.

Years ago, when I first crossed the Belgian-German border, I found that butter was strictly rationed. Other articles began to follow, and the closer the deadline for war approached, the tighter grew the supply of things.

It was a systematic, a 'total,' planning for war.

Everything for the State.

In Germany they sell little wooden plaques in novelty shops. They read:

'Thou art nothing. Thy State is everything.'

The 'total' theory applied most of all to imports from foreign countries. It must be understood that Germany was buying war materials in such quantities that her supply of foreign currency fell to nothing.

A government official sits down at his deck and figures the amount of foreign currency the Reich can save by stopping the import of butter. The figure is impressive; the butter stops coming in.

If the people can do without butter, another zealous Nazi reasons, they can also do without so many eggs. Forthwith, the Reich has to depend on its own meager supply of eggs. The scramble at the grocery stores for these few eggs is great.

Now look how much we have saved by cutting out imports of butter and eggs. Look how much foreign currency we have freed for purchases of steel and cotton. Let us look around and see what else the people can do without. Thus reason the Nazis. Discipline is what the people need. It will probably do them good to learn to do without some of the luxuries of modern life – especially those luxuries for which we must shell out foreign currency.

Tobacco, oranges and apples, bananas, cheese, foreign delicacies, medicines, cotton for bandages and clothes, wool for suits – WE CAN CUT THEM ALL OUT! The officials yell with joy.

That is 'totality.'

If you do anything, go the whole hog.

To save electricity in Berlin, for the past year many of the street lights have been eliminated. Why stop with street lights? one Nazi reasoned. Forthwith, all street-car headlights were unscrewed to save even more electricity. If a pedestrian were lucky enough to hear the street car coming at night or see the illuminated numeral above the conductor, he jumped. If he didn't, he didn't.

Hitler's ideas must be carried out quickly, and 'totally.' If a part of Czechoslovakia is in Germany's way, wipe the whole thing out. It is not important what the world thinks about it, but what it will do.

We cannot wait for problems to solve themselves. We will pass a law and the new law will go into effect the moment Adolf Hitler signs it – not two or three months later to give the people time to think about what it means. Slow evolution is not for our new nation. 'Total' change is what we are after, complete regimentation of thinking, of men, of their weapons, of the countries around us, of the world. As long as anybody thinks differently from the way we think, we must work to change them.

And if we cannot change them by persuasion and pacts, there is another way, the 'total' way. Invasion. When our soldiers and our Gestapo agents stand near these foreigners, they will soon learn to think as we do.

Yes, perhaps the 'total' way – the complete invasion of these upstart countries – would be best, after all.

So reasons a Nazi.

October 18:

If something doesn't happen, we will all go mad.

Today, for the first time since the war started, the German admiralty admitted the number of their submarines which have been sunk or lost.

Total to date, said the admiralty: Three!

Tonight a prominent doctor is coming to dinner at my apartment, but he is going to be disappointed in one respect.

He immensely likes good cigars. I sent Messenger out this afternoon to buy as many as he could, regardless of what they cost.

He came back without a single one. In every cigar store he had met with the same answer: 'There is a new law that you can buy only one cigar at a time, and you must clip and light it before you leave the shop.'

'*Mahlzeit.*'

Now there is a funny word in the German language. I usually had trouble explaining its meaning to American tourists who came through Berlin. It is translated something like 'mealtime,' and is used as a greeting – even when no mealtime is near.

I had lunch in a restaurant on Unter den Linden with a German friend recently. My friend was a regular patron of the restaurant. As I followed him out of the place, I heard him greeted in three ways.

The waiter bowed and said, 'Heil Hitler.'

The proprietor said, '*Auf Wiedersehen, Herr.*'

The pretty cashier at the door said, '*Mahlzeit.*'

In Germany, where 'Heil Hitler' is expected of everybody, greetings are significant and revealing. If a Nazi says 'Heil Hitler' to a non-Nazi, the latter may reply with the old Austrian '*Gruss Gott*' (literally, 'Greet God') and still be safe from arrest. He has also let you know where he stands politically.

I came up the subway steps last night near my home in the darkness. A man walked just in front of me and as he passed a young girl whom he evidently knew, he said 'Heil Hitler.' The girl said 'Heil Hitler' in return, and flopped her arm back in the Nazi salute.

A little farther on, the man met another acquaintance, an old lady.

'*Gute Nacht,*' he greeted.

'*Gute Nacht,*' she answered softly, and passed on by in the darkness.

Germans love their jokes.

They tell jokes about their leaders – which would land them in concentration camps if the wrong person were listening.

Although Adolf Hitler and other Nazis are notoriously lacking in a sense of humor, Field Marshal Hermann Goering pays five reichsmarks to any one bringing him a new joke about himself.

Unpopular Dr. Goebbels comes in for much ridicule, and is the object of many jokes. Example:

Two flies – a wise old fly, and an impetuous young fly – decided to have a race. They arranged to run from one side of Dr. Goebbels' notoriously wide mouth to the other. The young fly, confident of victory, set off across the Doctor's upper lip at great haste, but when he arrived on the other side of the Nazi's face, the wise old fly was already there, not at all out of breath.

'How did you do it, then?' asked the young fly in breathless amazement.

'Simple,' answered his elder. 'I just went around the back way.'

The Austrians, now part of the German Reich, are famous for their grumbling. They complained so much about their former governments that one might say they grumbled their way into the German Reich. Now, of course, their grumbling must be done in secret.

More plaintive than protesting was their comment on their forceful annexation by Germany:

'Before the *Anschluss*,' they said, 'times were good. Since the *Anschluss*, times are better.' Pause. 'We hope that times will be good again.'

As propaganda for the election which was held shortly after the annexation of Austria to determine the 'will of the people,' Nazi officials thought up a neat campaign slogan. Plastered everywhere, on walls, in trains, on banners suspended above the streets in Austria, were the words:

'One Country, One Folk, One Fuehrer.'

Since the *Anschluss* had caused the immediate death of their once-lucrative tourist trade, Viennese merchants privately repeated the slogan as, 'One Country, One Folk, One Customer.'

Our immigrants tell good stories on themselves and their woeful plight:

Two acquaintances of the Jewish race met each other on the sidewalks of New York, one immigrant told me.

'Whatcha looking so sad about?' asked the one of the other. 'Have you got relatives who are still in Germany?'

'No,' answered the other, dolefully. 'They have all immigrated to New York already.'

Another:

Just after the Austrian-German *Anschluss*, a Viennese Jew met a friend on the street.

'Well, Hermann, and how are things?' he asked sadly.

'Pretty good,' his friend answered in a cheerful voice.

'Are you crazy, Hermann?' the first Jew asked solicitously. 'We ain't speaking on the telephone.'

The following joke was popular, perhaps too popular, in Germany for many months just before the outbreak of the war:

Adolf Hitler and Dr. Goebbels were out riding, when they accidentally ran over a dog and killed him.

'Well,' said Goebbels, ' think I should find the owner of the dog, and apologize.'

'Go on, then,' Hitler growled 'but see that you come right back.'

One hour later, Dr. Goebbels appeared at the car, much the worse for alcohol. Seeing that Hitler was extremely angry, Goebbels hastened to explain his absence and his condition. 'It was like this,' he said. 'I found the house where the owner of the dog lived. I knocked at his door, and when he opened it, I simply said, 'Heil Hitler; the dog is dead.' 'Thank God,' the stranger said immediately, 'let's celebrate.''

A big Berlin banker – I shall omit his name – had an ardent Nazi

Party member as a partner in his bank. The two men quarreled frequently and bitterly. Finally, the banker succeeded in kicking the unpleasant Nazi out. A few months later, at a party, the banker was asked if he intended to reinstate his former partner.

'I?' he yelled. 'I ask you, did you ever hear of someone who wanted his appendix put back in?'

Even Hanna, who ordinarily kept quiet concerning political subjects and the Nazis, told me an innocent joke.

There was a newly rich Nazi, who had formerly been a poor worker and whose Party affiliations had boosted him to giddy heights. He strutted into a fine hotel one night, and engaged a room. The next morning when he appeared at the desk downstairs to pay his bill, the hotel clerk asked politely, 'I beg your pardon, sir. Did you take a bath?'

The simple Nazi looked astonished. 'Why?' he asked. 'Is there one missing?'

October 25:

The German propaganda being what it is, it is not surprising that the number of newspapers has fallen off considerably since 1933.

In format, most German newspapers are of tabloid size and have only twelve to sixteen pages. They don't contain funny papers, personal columns, editorial pages, society news or department store advertisements. They all have their continued stories, because statistics show that the average German *Hausfrau* reads five continued novels at one time.

Newspapers follow the Nazi Party line and ideology to the precise dot. Dancing is frowned upon; the having of babies, lots of babies, is encouraged, and so on.

The only newspaper likely to contain a bit of real news written between the lines of the propaganda is the *Frankfurter Zeitung*, and it is a paper hard to find at the newsstands.

The masses know nothing about what is going on, except what they learn over the radio from foreign stations.

I once told a German friend how curious I found it that in

the subway trains few, if any, Germans read newspapers as they rode. His comment was cryptic: 'They used to.'

I sat at my desk during the lunch hour today, cleaning out a stack of old newspapers. I came across the following clipping, and translated it because it is typical of the methods Nazi news-men use to inject propaganda into every story they write.

Gentlemen, the German press:

Washington, September 12. – *The sob story published in numerous American newspapers that the Philharmonic conductor Leopold Stokowski, who is very well known in America, was bombed in a refugee train near Paris by German airplanes has been denied by Stokowski himself.*

In reality, Stokowski is in Hollywood.

Stokowski, who is rumored to have close relations with Greta Garbo, was chosen by these inventors of horror stories in order to excite the tear glands of the Americans.

Wouldn't it have been wonderful to have been able to state the next day that Garbo had made her beautiful eyes red with crying after hearing the news? But it came to nothing.

How would it be if the American people would shed at least one tear for the thousands of unfortunate Germans who were victims of the vilest Polish terror in Bromberg?[4]

And if you want to enjoy a sarcastic laugh, read this clipping of a story which was printed today:

THEY HAVE TO SHUT UP!

Paris, October 25. *The announcement of a meeting of the French Chamber and Senate, which will convene about the middle of November, has been taken with satisfaction by the Paris press.*

People feel certain, however, that this extraordinary ses-sion will be of a short duration. It is considered to be self-

[4] *12-Uhr Blat*, Berlin, September 12, 1939.

evident that the French government will avoid engaging in any debates.

Debates would be apt to have a very unpleasant effect on public morale, especially should there be somebody in the Chamber or the Senate who would dare to express his real opinion.

The experiences of several French deputies in this respect destroy to a certain degree the impression one used to have of democratic countries where freedom, equality and brotherhood should be considered as the leading themes, and where hundreds of people are pining in prisons for having been so naïve as to believe it.[5]

We live isolated on our island in the middle of Berlin. The Nazis do not like us to get around too much so they ration our gasoline. They do not like us to spread any bad news around among the Germans, so they stop our French, Swiss and English newspapers at the borders. They do not want us to associate too much with Germans, so they tap all of our telephone calls, and discreetly let us know they are doing it.

But still, we get around.

This afternoon, for instance, I was visited by a German acquaintance who showed me an interesting manuscript written by a friend of his.

His friend had been von Hindenburg's butler.

The manuscript contained his memoirs, which he had unsuccessfully tried to get published. Since one of the Nazi propaganda policies is to glorify the late doddering old President of the Reich, publishers had been forbidden to bring the book out. The manuscript was not too flattering to von Hindenburg.

Glancing through it, an account of Hindenburg's first moviegoing caught my attention.

His butler had written:

Hindenburg never saw a movie. It was years before he let his family persuade him to sit through a few films.

[5] *Berliner Nachtausgabe*, October 25, 1939.

The first film chosen was directed by Luis Trenker and was a pleasant story of the woods, the hills and the lakes. Old von Hindenburg was pleased.

A few days later the second film was projected for his benefit. This film dealt with war, a subject dear to the old General's heart. However, the sight of a movie actor dressed as a Prussian officer amateurishly riding a horse caused von Hindenburg to snort loudly.

The third film was a lavish Lubitsch production depicting the capricious, giddy, romantic and amorous Madame du Barry. Hindenburg sat stonily and uncomprehendingly through nine reels of love and intrigue.

As he left the room, we servants heard him grumbling to his daughter. 'I didn't understand a bit of the love story,' he complained.

We heard his daughter exclaim in an exasperated voice: 'But fa-ther! I explained it all to you beforehand.'

October 28:

Vice-Consul of the United States Paul Coates gave a cocktail party this afternoon. His sandwiches were too thin, his apartment was too crowded and his cocktails were off color. But one can forgive him that because there were interesting people there.

I leaned against the sideboard talking to a disgruntled and disillusioned German film director He told me two first-rate stories, both of them true.

In a bored voice, he told me:

Dr. Sauerbruch, who is a world famous surgeon and an instructor in the University of Berlin lectured to his students one day on clubfooted men.

The most renowned clubfooted man in Germany is, of course, Dr. Paul Joseph Goebbels.[6]

'All clubfooted men are degenerate,' Dr. Sauerbruch told his

---

[6] 'Berlin quip: 'What does old Goebbels have in that box of a foot?'
'Batteries for his loud speakers.'

startled students. 'There is only one real exception in the history of the world. There was once a clubfooted man of compelling oratory, a revolutionist in word and deed, a man of great courage and unselfish devotion to his ideas. This man was also a talented poet.'

The students leaned forward in their seats, expecting to hear their hated Propaganda Minister named.

Dr. Sauerbruch concluded: 'Of course, I speak of Lord Byron.'

Paul Hoerbiger is one of the best-loved movie actors and music-hall singers in Germany. I have seen him perform many times, and each time I like him better.

The bored director told me a story about Paul Hoerbiger and Adolf Hitler.

Hoerbiger was commanded to sing before Hitler at a private party which the German Fuehrer gave. Hoerbiger sang, as his first number, the famous Viennese drinking song, *Wien, Wien, Nur Du Allein*. (Now forbidden in Vienna.)

This piece pleased Hitler so much that he had Hoerbiger sing it three times. At Hitler's fourth request, Hoerbiger demurred.

'I must tell you, *Mein Fuehrer*, that the author of this song was a Jew.'

'Doesn't matter,' answered Hitler expansively. 'He must have had a good moment.'

October 30:

Like hunters who gather at the close of a day's sport to swap tips about the best shooting places and the best places to fish, we sat around in Richard's office each day at noon to swap notes regarding the best and most generous meat markets, the stores where the clerks did not weigh too closely when it came to cutting squares from our ration cards.

Paul said that he had registered at the beginning of the war at his meat shop on the 'goose waiting list' and got a number up in the thousands. He waited two months and then went around to see how his registration was progressing. In the meat shop window was displayed a sign bearing the goose registration number already reached – number 310.

With rations so strict and food so difficult to buy, guests usually make allowances for shortages at the table and the host is consequently not embarrassed when the butter runs short or the precious few vegetables cook down to nothing.

Last night, however, I really got myself into a mess.

Hanna had called me up during the morning and told me that our number had finally been reached at the meat shop and that we would have goose and cranberries for dinner.

I promptly invited Richard and the two red-headed dancers from the Scala to dinner. We had swell wine ready to serve, a wonderful soup and even candles to light the table. But when Hanna saw the guests, she almost fainted. She had forgotten to tell me that my rationed share of the goose was – one leg.

October 31:

This is a crazy war.

Every three days, a new date for the beginning of the offensive is announced. Nothing happens.

I heard from one of Hitler's personal adjutants yesterday information which everybody is eager to know. What Adolf Hitler is doing. The adjutant told me that for hours at a stretch he looks at enlarged pictures of airplanes. He just sits and looks and studies. In the meantime, we wait for the war to start.

Rumors are rife and are hard to separate from truths.

Here are some of the things the German masses now firmly believe:

In death rays which will destroy whole regiments.

In a new system which will put the Maginot Line under water and drown the French soldiers inside like rats.

In 85,000 airplanes in the German air force.

In a gas, which carries itself forward under its own power.

In disease germs, which will find their way alone to England.

At the beginning of this month, a remark often heard from the Germans was: 'On October 12, the English-French friendship pact will expire. Then France will find her way to Germany's side.'

Of course when one mentions this false prediction now, no Nazi has ever heard of it.

October was gone. Forever lost, if that was of any importance.

CHAPTER FOUR

I LOOKED OUT my office window onto the Hermann Goering Strasse.

Gusts of cold wind blew leaves across the street and beneath the automobile wheels. Six Polish prisoners of war trudged by, pulling and pushing a two-wheeled cart loaded with slabs of heavy stone. The trees in the Tiergarten were bare; between the gray trunks I could see the bleak benches, empty of people. A few cold drops of rain spattered against the glass of my window. I shivered involuntarily because I knew that winter was finally here.

The long-awaited destruction of England had not yet happened; it would now probably have to wait until spring.

The policeman on duty outside the Embassy paced slowly by, swinging his chilled arms. A large wagon full of beer kegs rattled down the street, drawn by two white dray horses. The squirrels had disappeared from the Tiergarten to their hiding places, which were sheltered from the world, and warm.

The rain drops had become thicker and heavier and they fell from a sky which turned darker and gloomier every moment.

Outside my door, typewriters clattered busily, people talked in low incessant tones, the immigrants clinked money down on the counter to pay for their visas, telephones rang and rang. I looked at my telephone for a moment. It had rung so constantly during the past three months that I now expected it to burst into life every time I looked at it. There was no sign from the telephone, and in reality I knew of no message that it could bring me. The winter months stretched drearily ahead, the poor food, the lack of heat, the blackout, the impasse on the Western front. No, I expected no message.

I turned to the streaming window again. Three sets of clumping heavy boots ran by, three gray-clad soldiers chased by the rain. My window quivered with the water, making the scene outside look like a reflection of a landscape in a rippling stream. A dirty yellow street car stopped reluctantly in front of our Embassy door to take on the three soldiers, then whirred on happily again.

An Embassy messenger stood on the sidewalk, vainly trying to hail a taxi. He tucked the large envelope which was addressed to the Foreign Office under the protection of his arm, and whistled again and again at the taxis speeding past. A Storm Trooper in a long, ominous black overcoat walked by my window, shielding his face from the rain with his brief case. An official car pulled up before the new government building next door to the Embassy building. A group of uniformed men got out and rushed to the door of the Propaganda Ministry with their coats held over their heads. I saw the diminutive Dr. Goebbels hobbling along behind them.

The rain fell faster now, splashing violently as it struck the pavements and the streets. I thought of the soldiers at the front – on both sides of the Rhine River – who were splashing around in the mud, practicing maneuvers, flopping down on their bellies in the cold mud, getting up again.

The rain had turned into a torrent. Water poured down the sides of buildings into the streets; gutters filled up with the dirty cold water; street drains became clogged with floating leaves and brown pools began to form at the inter-sections. The little Spree River, which flows through the middle of Berlin, received the accumulation of the city drains and passed the rain water on to the next river. Other cities gathered their waters and passed them on, from one winding river to the next, until the mass of dirty water emptied itself into the Rhine River. On either bank of the Rhine millions of men were lined up dejectedly, staring across at each other, the cold water dripping off their steel helmets and flowing down into the river in between.

November

The third month of a new world war – a useless and insane one. Nobody wanted this war; everybody had it. It seemed that Europe was doing its best to strangle itself. Politicians and militarists held the whip hand everywhere; simple people cringed, and marched. Food was daily growing scarcer; factory hours were increased.

For the average German, every bit of social progress was being wiped out. After all, what a man of any nationality wants is a bit of leisure time and enough money to buy his clothes and food and beer. The simple worker doesn't care about *Lebensraum*. Realistic Germans have seen all to clearly that with every acquisition – Austria, Czechoslovakia, Poland – their plight has become worse. *Lebsensraum* sounds good on a speaker's platform, but it doesn't fill a stomach.

Balzac once said: 'The politician's most difficult feat is to furnish the people cheap bread and to pay the farmers a high price for wheat.'

Of course, Balzac was speaking for politicians in a free country, where they stand for election.

In Germany, no election is held and the masses are given no time or chance to discuss the advisability of bringing in new leaders.

In November, when the first real pinch of shortages began to be felt, the Nazis concentrated on keeping the people quiet. Nazi philosophy is that if you can keep the masses from rebelling against the small and unimportant things, it will not occur to them to revolt against the big things.

Soldiers who are caught dancing swing are given three days in solitary confinement;[1] but the big Nazi bosses sit in Berlin's Scala Theater and tap their comfortable feet to the good jazz of Otto Stenzel's orchestra.

Peace or war, keep the people in line. Don't let them forget that they are part of the great new Germany, the Germany

---

[1] A good friend of mine, a captain in the German army and an enlightened man, had one of the soldiers under his command reported to him for dancing swing in a Berlin night club. Under army regulations, the captain was bound to sentence the soldier to the guardhouse. First, however, he summoned the noncom who had seen and reported the soldier for swinging it.

'Are you sure this soldier was dancing swing?' the captain asked the noncom.

'Yes, Captain,' the noncom answered promptly.

which will not be downed by the conspiracies of others. Germans, we must all think alike, whether we be in the great Reich or in some foreign country! Discipline. Obedience. And we will rule the world some day.

If the United States goes into this war, there is one thing I do not want to forget. There are millions of people in Germany who do not agree with the policies of their leaders. And there are other millions, simple people, who believe exactly what their leaders tell them – especially when they tell them the same thing day after day. I do not want to go blind with hatred and forget that. You cannot punish a whole nation, as you might punish a single criminal. You can't get a whole nation to stand in the corner and cry. That was tried once, and it failed miserably. When it is over, try to help them recover from what they have suffered. Try to remove the causes for the rise of such people as Adolf Hitler. There should be enough intelligence kicking around in the world to accomplish that.

A small paper boat, which some kid had folded and placed on the surface of the water, floated down the gutter past my window. It was already waterlogged, and riding deep in the swirling water. The trees in the Tiergarten waved and shook themselves angrily to throw off the heavy water which streamed along their branches.

I had never imagined that war would be so dreary and boring. But it was.

I heard a slight noise behind me. The messenger stood there, looking over my shoulder to see what I was watching outside. 'Well?' I asked, shortly.

He jumped. 'Oh, I just wanted – I mean, there's a couple out here in the waiting room who say they want to go back to the

'And what is your definition of swing, sir?' the captain asked coldly. 'Why, why – I can't describe it exactly, sir,' the confused noncom stammered.

'Obviously, then, you have reported a soldier for dancing swing when you don't even know what it is,' the captain said sternly. 'A serious thing, sir.'

The noncom withdrew his accusation. The soldier never knew that someone had been watching him as he enjoyed himself in the night club.

United States. I don't know what kind of information to give them.'

'Well, bring them in,' I said, sitting down at my desk. A moment later the messenger reappeared with two nicely dressed people. 'Sit down,' I said, wondering if I should speak English or German with them.

'Thanks,' the man answered, in a Chicago twang. I asked them the usual questions for our records, and wrote down their answers on a memorandum sheet.

'How long did you live in America?'

'Seventeen years.'

'And when did you come back to Germany?'

'In January, 1939, to see my parents.'

I waited a moment for the rest of it.

' – They were sick.'

Yes, they always were sick in these re-entry cases.

'Before you left the States, did you get a re-entry permit?' I asked.

The man looked at me nervously. 'No, sir, I didn't. They told me that I could come back any time I wanted to.'

'Who told you?' I asked him drily.

'My friends,' he said evasively.

'Not a very reliable source of information in such an important matter,' I commented.

'I know that, now,' he said.

'Of course the German Consulate in Chicago didn't give you that false information, did they?'

The man hesitated. 'Why, no,', he said.

His wife broke in. 'Can't you do something for us, sir?' she pleaded. 'We only left America because we didn't have a job. A man came to us and told us that everything was wonderful in Germany and that we would be able to get good jobs with no trouble. He fixed everything up for us.'

'I thought you said you came back to see your husband's sick parents,' I said.

'That was another reason,' the woman said with agitation. 'We didn't think it was a crime to come over here to look for a job. The man in Chicago told us that we wouldn't have to join the Nazi Party or do anything here but work. After we got over here, the war broke out and then my husband went to work for a while. But it's not like they pictured it to us. I hate Germany like it is now.'

'There have been a lot of cases like yours,' I said slowly. 'If you came back to Germany to look for work you apparently came back to stay and according to the immigration law you may not be issued non-quota visas as returning aliens.' I paused, and tapped the desk with my pencil. 'Why didn't you take out citizenship papers during all the years you lived in America?' I asked curiously.

The man pulled a ragged piece of paper out of his pocket and placed it before me. 'I took out the first papers,' he said. 'I really don't know why I didn't keep up my application until I got to be a citizen. When it came time to apply for the second citizenship papers, I was sick. Somehow the time just slipped by, and I never did anything else about it.'

I looked at the piece of paper and returned it to him.

'Did you leave any possessions in the United States?' I asked. 'Any furniture, or an automobile or a bank account to show that you intended to return and live there once more?'[2]

He shook his head.

'Well, the law provides for re-entry permits to be issued to persons who are not citizens of the United States and who want to go aboard for a short time. One has to get re-entry permits before leaving,' I said.

I felt sorry for them. They were just as much Americans as so many naturalized people I know. They were simple people,

[2] The most spectacular example I know of a person getting a non-quota visa to return to the United States after she had sailed without procuring a re-entry permit and had evidently come to Germany to live, was that of a widow who had sold everything she owned before getting on the boat bound for Bremen. After she had lived in Germany a while, she changed her mind and wanted to go back to the United States. She finally got a non-quota visa because she could show the consul proof of a bank account in the United States in the amount of one cent!

not aware of the twists and turns of our immigration laws. Somebody had given them the wrong advice – probably intentionally – and here they were before me, unable to get back home.

'Well, couldn't we immigrate all over again on regular visas?' the man asked, breaking out in a sweat. 'I have a sister in the United States and she will give me an affidavit. You don't know what it is to be locked up in Germany, with no way of getting back to America.'

'I'm sorry,' I said. 'A few years ago, you could have produced your affidavits and you probably would have gotten your visas without any trouble. But now, the waiting list for the German quota is full for years ahead. We have sixty thousand refugees registered in Berlin alone, and all of them must have a chance to apply before your turn would be reached.'

'Won't you let us go back?' his wife pleaded. 'We have learned our lesson. If we ever get back, we will be the best Americans you ever saw. We will take out our first papers all over again, right away. Don't make us ruin our lives because of this one mistake.'

This is what one has to listen to in the Immigration section. It was too big for me, too important, too much a matter of life and death.

'I'm not keeping you here,' I said. 'It's the law. If I could, I would give you visas this afternoon. But there are thousands registered before you.' I picked up the dossier. 'But, wait a minute,' I said, and left my office. I walked down the corridor to Consul Richard Stratton's office, and found him in.

'Richard –' I began. I told him about the case, all the details. He leaned back in his chair and put his fingertips together.

'I suppose you have worked here long enough to know the answer,' he said.

'Yes,' I answered.

'Well, that's the answer,' he said, bending to his work again.

'I spoke to Consul Stratton,' I said.

'And – ?'

'The best thing you can do is to register yourself on the waiting list,' I said.

'And how long will that take?' the man asked anxiously.

'Like I told you before, several years.'

I found myself biting my lower lip. God, how I hated these scenes. If the immigration law gave the consul any discretion about whom to admit to the United States, we could avoid causing these heartaches, I thought.

'Well, I guess there isn't anything else to say,' the man said in a low voice.

'I'm afraid not,' I agreed.

They left, pulling the door carefully shut behind them. I nervously completed writing on the memorandum sheet, and signed my name to it. I could hear the cold rain falling and splashing on the window sill behind me.

On the ninth of November, 1939, a terrific blast was set off in a simple Munich Bier Keller which was heard around the world with profound regret. The regret was caused by the fact that the blast came twenty minutes too late to accomplish its purpose.

Adolf Hitler, leader and self-appointed savior of eighty million people, feared and hated by at least one hundred million more, escaped meeting his angry Maker by exactly twenty minutes.

He had spoken before a gathering of old Party faithfuls in the Nazi holy of holies – the Munich Bürgerbraü Keller – the very place where the Nazi Party was founded only a few years after the end of the World War. Hitler usually speaks for three hours or more. That night he spoke only a few minutes and picked up his coat and left, accompanied by his adjutants.

Nobody had known that he was to speak there. It was a surprise visit. But obviously, one person had not been surprised at Hitler's appearance at the Bürgerbraü. This person was only surprised at Hitler's unusual shortwindedness.

After the explosion, caused by a time bomb carefully installed in a column near the speaker's stand, the Keller was in a frightful mess. Huge timbers pinned Party members to the floor; several were killed. The Munich police ordered the city's lights to be turned on in order to apprehend the culprits, and the

Bavarian capital was immediately illuminated with dazzling white lights.

Germans walking along the dark streets rubbed their eyes in amazement.

Their first thought, at seeing the street lights turned on for the first time since the beginning of September, was that the war was over. People began to come out from their homes and apartments to gather on the streets. They slapped each other on the backs in happiness at the finish of the war, and tried to adjourn to pubs and beer halls to celebrate. They found that every place of amusement had already been closed on order of the police.

If what happened in the Bürgerbräu that night was an explosion, what happened when the rest of Germany heard about it the next day was a major earthquake. The Germans had never dreamed it possible that an attempt on Hitler's life could come so close to succeeding.

Nobody dared to say what he thought about the explosion, or ask any questions about it.

The official radio began broadcasting a message from the Gestapo to the effect that any person who had overheard any of his neighbors say, 'Curious that Hitler left just before the explosion went off,' should report this fact to the nearest police station immediately.

Many Germans put on a false appearance of joy at their Fuehrer's narrow escape, to cover their glum thoughts as they remembered how close they had come to getting rid of That Man forever.

This morning, a new milkman whom we had never seen before, commented to Hanna that 'Germany was cursed with the worst luck of any nation on earth.' Hanna did not trust him, and she took the milk bottle without answering.

We did not think the English planted that bomb, as the Nazis loudly asserted. Neither did we think that it was all a trick by Hitler himself, just to make him a hero in the eyes of Germany. It was a little too well-timed just to have been a fake.

Who in Germany so ardently wished the death of Adolf Hitler that he was willing to risk his neck by planting a bomb in the very place the Nazis would consider themselves safest? The stupid German who was arrested and accused (but never tried) of making and installing the time bomb did not quite fill the bill.

Who put that bomb there?

Don't you think that that is a question that Adolf Hitler would like to have answered?

A day of Embassy life consisted of work, rumors, jokes and talk. I always made it a point to jot down notes and key words to help me remember interesting things which I had heard or read.

On November 27, for instance, Nevile Henderson, the British Ambassador to Germany at the time war broke out, was the object of an attack in a Berlin newspaper. Among other things, the newspaper saw fit to claim that Mr. Henderson has cancer of the tongue.

In the *12-Uhr Blatt*, a saucy Berlin tabloid, the editor in chief referred to the world-famous concert pianist Paderewski as a 'violinist'.

Rumor of November 10:
> Public opinion in Belgium will force King Leopold to call Adolf Hitler the 'Savior of the Belgians'. If the King does not yield to public opinion and do this, Belgium will split into two parts, the French-speaking Walloons and the German-speaking Vlames.

Rumor of November 21:
> The S.S. *Bremen* has been swapped in Murmansk for one hundred Russian submarines.

Herr von Ribbentrop recently received the 'Annunziaten-orden' from King Victor Emmanuel, of Italy, which entitles the former champagne salesman to call the King his 'cousin.' The last two persons to receive this honor were King Zog, of Albania, and Haile Selassie, of Abyssinia.

* * *

On a large sign advertising the Berlin Sportpalast (scene of Hitler's speeches) one may see flags of many nations. Still there, after three months of war, are the English flag and the French flag.

Today, a prominent German doctor said to me during our conversation:

'Life is so boring. I would like most of all to be a shepherd, or to emigrate, or to read, read, only read. The big shots make life insufferable.'

A rhyme contest conducted in Berlin grammar schools was won by the following ditty, submitted by a little girl of eight:

Don't cause yourself and Germany trouble;
Don't dodge the air-raid protection.

A friend of mine thought up the following:

Three dictators utter profundities typical of their natures:

The dictator of Russia, STALIN – 'The Russians are the world's greatest people, and Russia is the greatest land.'

MUSSOLINI – 'Rome is glorious, given by the gods to enrich the world and be a cradle for Fascism.'

HITLER – 'When did I say that?'

And the current jokes which the Germans are telling:

Hermann Goering and Paul Joseph Goebbels died and went to heaven.

'Well, you may come in,' said St. Peter to the unwholesome pair, 'but for each lie you told on earth, you have to make one trip around heaven'

Goering peeled off his be-medaled coat and in spite of his great bulk soon completed seven or eight laps. St. Peter stopped him, and said, 'You may pass, but where did that little friend of yours go?'

'Oh, him,' said Goering. 'He's gone back to earth to get a motorcycle.'

Dr. Goebbels, Minister of Propaganda and People's En-lightenment, falls far short of filling the Nazi ideal of tall, blond

Aryanism. In fact, he is little, dark and repulsive to look at. Hitler, Goebbels and Goering, goes the story, were out riding in an automobile which got stuck fast in the mud.

Goering got out of the car, and waddled across a field to ask a farmer plowing there if he would lend his horses to pull the car out of the mud. The farmer said 'No,' explaining that he was so busy trying to keep up with Goering's Four-Year Plan for increasing production that he had not a minute to spare. 'But I am Hermann Goering,' the Field Marshal said.

'Yes?' said the farmer sarcastically.

'And that man in the front seat is your Fuehrer, Adolf Hitler,' Goering continued.

The farmer eyed the occupants of the mired car carefully. 'And now,' he said, pointing toward the back seat, 'you'll try to tell me that that little Jew is Paul Joseph Goebbels!' And this joke I heard only in foreign circles. It has a little too much barb in it even for joke-loving Germans.

A Spanish newspaperman in Madrid took what he thought was a bang-up story to his editor. The editor thought the story was good, too, but he said cautiously, 'We'd better ask the big boss before we dare to print it.'

Thereupon, he put in a long distance call from Madrid to Rome. After a while, a voice in Rome answered the telephone in a guttural German, '*Was gibts?*'

Richard Stratton and I left our dripping raincoats with the pert hat-check girl near the entrance, and walked into the large lobby of the Haus Vaterland in Berlin.

Most Americans who have ever visited Berlin have drunk and danced at the Haus Vaterland, because it is more or less a tourist 'must'.

The entire building, which is situated directly on Potsdamerplatz, is given over to bars, cabarets, ball rooms and game rooms, all under the same management.

The different bars on the four floors of the Haus Vaterland are decorated to represent some foreign country. America is represented by a cowboy bar.

Richard and I headed for the Bavarian beer hall on the second floor, and as we swung open the doors to the large room a blast of singing and music and smoke and beer fumes hit us in our faces. Oh, how often in my life would I like to be hit by such a pleasant blow!

There were at least five hundred Germans in the beer hall, all drinking from big stone mugs of beer and singing folk songs and locking arms and rocking around the tables to the lusty tunes of a Bavarian band. We found a table, at which two husky, generously-proportioned girls were sitting. They appeared to be housemaids, out for a spree on their night off. They looked at us and smiled broadly, one of them displaying gold in her teeth.

Of course they wore no lipstick or powder or paint, but when we asked them to have a beer with us, they giggled, blushed and accepted and were obviously pleased to be drinking a beer with two foreigners.

The sweating waiter brought us four large mugs of foaming beer, which we clinked together in salute. Richard and I secretly admired the girls' prominent muscles; I think they could have lifted our table with us sitting on it as easily as they lifted those mugs.

The Germans around us were as happy as only Germans can be when they are together and smoking and drinking beer and singing at the tops of their voices and not talking politics. The band on the platform overlooking one end of the room was composed of fat, fat Bavarians, wearing the typical Bavarian short leather pants, having small green hats with brushes perched on their shaven heads. On their music racks, instead of conventional sheets of music, the Bavarians had set large foaming steins of beer which ran over and spilled down the music-rack supports.

One beer followed another to our table. Richard was like a high-school boy. He sang, nay roared, with the maids. He turned around and made friends with the soldiers, the *Hausfrauen*, the chauffeurs and the *Bürgers* who sat at neighboring tables. He gave them American cigarettes, which were greeted with shouts of joy. The soldiers became serious, and stood up to toast

Richard's health. I wondered what they would do with those steins if they knew what we thought about their government.

'Trink, Trink, Schwesterlein, Trink,' the Germans sang, locking arms and swaying, first to the left, then to the right. Strangers locked arms with strangers; the band blew and sweated; the hall was filled with the sound of lusty singing.

'Trink –

'Trink –

'Schwesterlein, Trink.'

We all unlocked arms, and laughed together.

'Don't you like our Germany?' one of the girls asked Richard.

'Yes,' he said, taking out another pack of cigarettes.

'And don't you think our Fuehrer is wonderful?'

There was a moment's pause.

The girls waited with their steins held in mid-air.

Richard dropped his pack of cigarettes and had some trouble finding it under the table. The band struck up another tune, and the girls forget their question and drank their beers.

At the other end of the hall was a stage, on which had been built a theatrical set which depicted a scene in the Alps. Every fifteen minutes during the evening, the Bavarians laid down their instruments, the lights in the hall were turned down, and the miniature stage came to life. First, there was rain accompanied by loud crashes of thunder and bright streaks of lightening. The rain fell harder and harder, then turned into snow. The lights were blue as the snow fell softly. At last, the dark clouds rolled away and a sunshine-filled sky took their place. The mountains and the closer meadows of the Alps were gay and peaceful in the bright sunlight. The little scene was over, and the lights went up in the hall again.

The two maids, beaming happily from ear to ear, insisted on buying us a round of beers. Not to hurt their feelings, we accepted. The Bavarian band started up again, and the Germans at the tables sang lustily and locked arms and swayed as they sang. I looked at their clean, happy faces

'This is the Germany I like,' I thought. 'This is the Germany the whole world likes.'

* * *

I finished up my work early, and cleaned off my desk It was three-thirty in the afternoon, and a messenger had already come around to lower the wooden shutters outside my window. The Germans had sent us instructions regarding the time of the day our shutters were to be closed for every week during the winter. I had noticed that in January we would have to black-out at two o'clock every afternoon. That is an example of what people mean when they speak of 'German thoroughness.' Black-out at two.

I left the building, and walked in the direction of Alexander Platz, which is in a poorer section of Berlin than the one in which we lived and worked. I have a good miniature camera, and I wanted to buy a telescope lens for it before they were unavailable. Having no other safe thing in which to invest their money, and not wanting to keep the unstable currency in a bank account, many Germans were investing in good cameras and lenses. They figured that these objects could be easily hidden and would still be valuable after the war was over, no matter which side won. I had been unable to find a telescope lens anywhere, but I had the address of a small camera shop and a note from a friend of mine addressed to the owner of the shop.

The old Berlin Schloss at the end of Unter den Linden looked stern and colossal under the clouded sky, a grim reminder of what can happen to the great, the seemingly invincible. As I passed the great gate to the Schloss, I looked through and saw the huge courtyard from which had once rolled the carriages of kings. As recently as 1918, this great mass of architecture had been occupied by royalty. Before his downfall, the last German Kaiser had realized the dream of seeing most of continental Europe – even part of Russia – under German domination. Yet how quickly it all fell to pieces, once it started to fall.

How many European palaces are museums today! How many are now the tramping grounds of tourists.

The cellar windows of the old Palace were stacked with sandbags for protection against bombs; most of the great windows in the upper floors were covered with black paper.

I walked through the small streets which begin at the end of

Unter den Linden. Every candy store which was open had a line of Germans in front of it, waiting to get a small ration of one or two pieces of pralines. Of chocolate, there had long since been none. Other candy stores had signs on their doors, reading 'PRALINES SOLD OUT FOR TODAY.' Or, 'ALL OUR STOCK GONE FOR THIS WEEK'. In their show windows were displayed beautiful boxes of chocolates, and down at the right-band side of the displays were small signs reading: 'DISPLAYS ARE MADE UP OF EMPTY BOXES.'

Berlin at war.

From the exterior, Berlin looked the same. The shop windows were full of tempting wares: shoes, foods, everything and everything. But once the would-be customer entered the stores, he was met with the same dreary and disappointing answer: 'Sorry, that's all sold out already.'

In many of the shop windows in which the most tempting and unavailable objects were on display, there was a small sign glued to the glass: 'GOODS DISPLAYED IN THE WINDOWS ARE NOT FOR SALE.'

It is typical Nazi psychology that every show window must be full of goods for the looks of things, even though no such goods may be bought anywhere.

Many people were busily accumulating what they could in the way of bric-a-brac for their Christmas presents.

Soldiers walked along the streets, wearing the gray-green uniforms of the artillery, or the blue of the air force and the anti-aircraft. Many of the uniforms I saw had recently been the black uniforms of the Storm Troopers; they had simply been dyed a new color. Young, newly inducted infantrymen passed me, dressed in the light-brown uniforms of the compulsory Labor Service; a yellow band on their sleeves identified them as members of the German army. Other soldiers were dressed in uniforms stolen from the old Czechoslovakian army.

Hausfrauen prowled along the streets, peering hopefully into the grocery stores in the vain hope that some fresh vegetables might be on display. Vegetables were rare, however, and the women generally had to be satisfied with a few potatoes. On their arms they carried their large shopping nets which contained only one or two withered apples and the inevitable potatoes.

German officers passed, stern-faced, their long swords dangling grimly at their sides. Every passing soldier was compelled to salute the officers, and simple soldiers as well had to salute each other. After watching one German soldier give three stiff Prussian salutes in four yards, it occurred to me that a soldier's leave in Berlin might not be very pleasant.

The little camera shop was full. I had to wait twenty minutes before the one overworked clerk got to me. I told him what I wanted to buy.

'Telo-lens?' he asked incredulously. 'I'm sorry.'

I whispered the message I had been instructed to give him. The clerk looked around behind him, then said, 'Wait a minute.'

I interested myself in some cheap cameras lying on the counter. After a few minutes, the clerk came back with a small already-wrapped package in his hand. 'Here is your film,' he said loudly. I understood. He gave me the sales slip, which was for an amount more than the list price. The owner of the shop risked a prison sentence for selling the lens, bootlegging we call it, at a higher price than that set by the government. That sort of bootlegging, of articles, of food, of clothing, was going on all over Germany; I had heard of many eases where Germans paid fifteen to twenty dollars for a pound of cheap coffee. I paid the clerk and left. The shop was still full of people who were trying to find something they could put their money in.

Outside, the sky had become darker and a few rain drops began to fall. People ran for cover, and I ducked into the subway. The air in the train was bad, and the car was crowded.

The Germans sat or stood looking at each other; they were not reading, or speaking or thinking. This is National Socialism, I thought grimly. In order to rule people more easily, the Nazis just reduce them all to the same level and dare them to have any ideas of their own. Where do they expect to get the leaders to head future German governments? From the machine-similar products of their moronic propaganda-education?

Do foreigners realize what a prison Germany has become for those Germans who do not agree with the principles of Nazism? They are the hope of the world, these people who have swallowed nothing, who live in the hope of a day which will spell the end of Hitler and his whole horrible nightmare.

I counted the Germans in the car with me. There were eighty-five there. Seventeen of them wore army uniforms; six more wore the swastika Party buttons on their lapels. There were also three Red Cross nurses, and eleven similar-looking Berlin workmen wearing gray overcoats and smoking cheap cigars. When the subway train came to a halt in a station, those few Germans who had been talking closed their mouths immediately.

What could they say that could be said aloud and still be worth saying?

I left the subway and had supper in a good restaurant. I mean, the restaurant was good, not the food. The prices were the same as they had been in peace time, but the portions were smaller and inferior. It took me an hour to get my indifferent meal; it cost over a dollar. There were only three waiters to wait on one hundred people; Berliners came to the restaurants because they could not get enough to eat on their ration cards. Of course, at the restaurants the meat and bread and butter were as severely rationed as they were in the groceries, but there were potatoes and a few vegetables and sometimes fish to be had in public eating places. Before I was brought my meal, I had to give up the exact amount of ration cards required on the menu. The waiter took a few grams of my butter-ration card because, as he explained, the meat I had ordered was cooked in grease. Of course there was no butter served with the bread.

Afterward, over a glass of weak tea, I read the *Nachtausgabe*, and smoked a German cigarette.

'Who really sank the *Athenia?*' was the newspaper's leading news story. I quickly looked at the masthead of the paper to be sure I had not picked up an old copy, from September. No, it was today's paper.

'America sees through the *Athenia*-English lies,' the story asserted. 'It was obviously a trick of the English to bomb the *Athenia* and try to make it appear as though the Germans had done it. It was all done to get American public opinion aligned on the side of England.' After I had read and yawned and glanced at the sports and the death notices, I paid my bill and walked out of the restaurant into the blackout. By a miracle, I found a taxi, and instructed the driver to take me to the American Church at Norllendorf Platz.

'Is this an official trip?' the taxi driver asked suspiciously.[3] Taxi drivers in Berlin are generally unpleasant fellows and I have an intense dislike for them all.

'Yes, you so and so,' I said in English. He did not understand my words, but he assumed that if I were a foreigner and still living in Berlin I must be an official of some sort.

When I got out at the Church, I went straight upstairs. In the big recreation room there I found thirty Americans, all gathered around in a semicircle listening to the pastor of the Church talk. These thirty were all that were left of our once large American colony in Berlin.

The pastor heads the Church, and works during the week as a translator in the Embassy. I suppose otherwise he would starve.

This was Thursday evening, and a big fire was roaring in the fireplace. We could hear the rain beating down outside, but in the meeting room it was warm and *gemütlich*. I looked around at the people gathered there. Most of them were Americans, but there were a few pathetic Germans who found these Thursday evenings their only outlet for the accumulated tension of living in Nazi Germany.

There sat Jim, who was an art student from Pittsburgh. He

[3] It is forbidden to use one of the hundred-odd taxis still allowed in Berlin for pleasure trips. They are to be used only by government officials, persons going to a hospital, and so on. Germans think up many artful dodges to get around these strict rules. One day I saw a beautiful blond step out of a taxi, on crutches. She paid the driver off, and hobbled painfully around the corner. Curious, I followed her to see where she was going. The moment she was out of sight of the taxi driver, the blond tucked the crutches under her arm and jauntily continued on her way.

had been studying architecture in Berlin and was now waiting for a berth on some ship headed back to the United States.

And Mabel. I have an especial fondness for Mabel, perhaps because she had a heart as big as her body. And her body was conspicuously big. She was from South Africa and had been studying singing in Germany. Although she was one of our American Church faithfuls, her loyalty failed her when we sang *America* at the beginning of the Church service on Sundays. At the last line of *America*, the music of which is also that of the British national anthem, Mabel always roared 'God save the King' while we feebly competed with 'Great God Our King'.

The pastor had finished his informal talk. We all gathered around the piano and sang American songs. Mabel told me that she had succeeded in getting permission to leave Germany in three days.

'I can do just two things,' she told me. 'Sing and cook. I rather think they need my cooking more right now.' She had volunteered to cook in an English camp.

These Thursday nights were a little bit of America, surrounded by stiff unfriendliness. We came together and cracked American jokes and wished for American films and described American food to each other. Every week some of the familiar faces would be missing, having left for home.

Tea was served, and slices of a cake which a good soul had donated. I stood in front of the fireplace and sipped the hot tea. The windows were rattled by the wind and rain outside. *Old Black Joe*, we sang. *Swanee River*, and *John Brown's Body*. Then Margaret played some popular songs on the piano, most of them at least one year old – we were always that far behind in Berlin.

In peace time, we had always met new students and tourists at our American Church after the Sunday services were over. The faces were different at every service. A pretty American girl one had admired one Sunday was gone the next – to Rome or Paris or back to America.

In war time it was different. The little crowd grew smaller every Sunday.

After the meeting broke up, about half of us walked around

the corner to a genteel pub. We ordered our beers, lighted cigarettes, talked about the war, how it would end, when it would begin and all of that. The door to the pub opened, and we looked around.

The pastor entered, and we gladly moved aside to make room for him. He had stayed behind to lock up the Church. He was our pastor, but he was a good fellow and liked his *Malzbier* as well as the next.

We lifted our mugs together, '*Prosit!*' we shouted in unison. '*Prosit! Prosit!*'

CHAPTER FIVE

IT IS CURIOUS how one's ways of thinking change, and change so quietly that one does not realize it himself. In looking back over the first pages of my diary, I saw that I constantly referred to an attack by the English and French, and that I expected that such an attack would undoubtedly succeed.

Today, near the end of December, I realized that all of us constantly asked each other the question, 'When will he attack?' and, of course, we meant Adolf Hitler. It was strange how the passage of a few short months could have made us think that the entire initiative belongs to the German army, and not to the Allies. Is this the effect of steady propaganda on us, or worse still is it the effect of steady propaganda on the Allies? Has Hitler bluffed the rest of the world into thinking that he, and he alone, can give the command? Has he somehow maneuvered England and France into a position of uncertainty regarding their own strength, so that they would rather wait to see what Hitler will do before they try anything of their own? There was no doubt in our minds that the Allied armies could beat Hitler, but we wondered why they gave him time to consolidate his positions, to turn out armaments night and day, to strengthen the German people's morale through the constant pounding of his propaganda machine.

And so, through December, we wondered about these things. And we worked hard. We saw most of the Americans go at last, and we were alone on our Embassy island. One of our two American dentists in Berlin closed his office and came to work in the Embassy as night watchman. We fought with the German Foreign Office for food-ration cards, for clothing-ration cards, for coal to heat our houses and apartments. We issued immigration visas as fast as ever, and at nights we gave each other parties to provide some relief from the monotony of war. Four beautiful, blonde, American roller skaters played for a while at one Berlin variety house, and we had parties for them because the girls from the Scala were becoming afraid to be seen too much with foreigners. The roller skaters left us, to perform in Amsterdam, and later they came back through Berlin on their way to Copenhagen. When I want to think of something brave, I think of the pretty American roller skaters, shuttling back and forth in darkened Europe – because they did not have the price of passage back to the United States and would not ask the Embassy to buy their tickets.

I lifted my head from the stack of dossiers one day long enough to ask Richard Stratton if I could have two days extra for Christmas, in order to go skiing. I had an invitation from the friend of a friend, who lived in the Harz Mountains, and a few days away from Berlin seemed worth any amount of trouble.

Richard put his head down and looked up from under his brushy eyebrows and said no and then he laughed and said he meant yes, of course, and please would I have a good time and get rested up.

The train ride down to the Harz was gruesome: the cars cold and unlighted after sundown, the passengers gloomy and depressed. The train was two hours late, which wasn't much in war time, but still too much for any time.

I left the train, cold, cramped and blue.

Large flakes of snow were softly falling as I stepped from the tiny railroad station. Many small lights burned along the one street, the first outdoor illumination I had seen since the first of September. A row of horses breathing steam was attached to a row of sleighs, lined up before the station exit. Beside them stood their stolid drivers, waiting stoically for any traveler who might approach them and ask to be driven to some destination.

As I looked at the little shops which crowded together on either side of the street, at the blinking street lights, at the dim sharp rooftops of the residences, the weight of the war seemed to fall away from me. Could such quiet and beauty exist in a world of steel helmets and heavy boots and screaming propaganda?

It was cold there in front of the station, and large flakes of snow drifted down. The snug little village was buried in snow to the eaves of the roofs.

It was another world from the unpleasant one I had known for the past four months. It was peaceful here, and there was no need to exert one's self. I walked over to one of the sleighs and spoke to the driver. One word, the address of my host, and he was tucking me into the sleigh, big, warm blankets all around me. The stars had come out, and even they seemed friendly. After all, they shone over the United States, too.

Hitler had not yet occupied the stars.

With every breath I took, the deep cold air made ice particles in my nose. I put my hands into my overcoat pocket for more warmth; my fingers touched the numerous keys which every inhabitant of Berlin must carry. I will not think about keys and Berlin, I decided – and pushed them into a corner of my pocket. The sleigh runners crunched on the hard snow, making a whine as they bit into the well-packed whiteness. Tall, dark fir trees walked silently past us, creaking with their heavy burden of snow. The old driver said something soft to his horses, cracked his reins against their flanks, and they strained themselves in an effort to go a little faster.

'*Unglaublich schoen,*' I said.

'*Ja, ja,*' came back to me, neatly wrapped up in a cloud of human steam.

We left the lighted street of the little village, and rode past small houses sitting in the middle of fields of snow, heavily shuttered, every light hidden.

The sleigh climbed the low mountain, creaked upward past houses which were set more lonesomely apart from their neighbors. We rode over a small bridge, under which the muffled tinkle of water could be heard; then we made a sharp turn to the left and kept on climbing. The horses strained, and the runners bit into the snow. The driver clucked at the horses and talked to them in guttural German as patiently as though they could understand what he said.

Suddenly the sleigh stopped before a house, and to my left I saw a stream of unaccustomed, white light shining over the snow. My eyes followed the light to its source, and I saw a door which was wide open. Out of the door into the snow, three people and two frisking dogs flowed to meet me.

I asked the old driver what I owed him. I paid him, really only half of what I had expected to pay, and twice what he had expected to get.

The friends of my friend pulled me into the house, laughing, greeting, taking off my overcoat, my scarf, my gloves. The two beautiful dogs jumped up against me continually, wanting to make friends at once, vigorously sniffing my pockets even before we had been introduced.

In the living room, with dark wooden walls and old picturesque German furniture, I went immediately to the great porcelain stove which one finds in every German home. I sat down on the wooden bench built around the tiles, and put my back against the stove and listened to the soft grumble of the coals inside it. I took off my cold shoes and the maid, Elsbeth, brought me some warm slippers.

Then the questions:

' – Berlin?'

' – the coal shortage?'

' – still dark and disagreeable as ever?'

' – how in the world do you stand living in the city?'

All spoken in German.

Nobody could speak English except the dogs.

They had a small but sufficient vocabulary. They had already discovered that I was the only man in the valley with a bar of chocolate in his pocket.

We talked about the war, about the snow in the Harz, about the prospects for skiing.

I was most interested in the opinions of German farmers on the war. What they said about it, what they didn't say about it.

I drank some hot soup as we talked and decided immediately that I liked Herr Maass, my host. He was a tall and sturdily built man. His face was covered with the good wrinkles a man gets from farming, and his skin was tanned a healthy color. His wife was on the plump side, and she sat knitting and listening, rarely interrupting. Elsbeth, the maid, was darning socks and once or twice I thought I saw her chewing gum, though that is impossible since gum-chewing is practically unknown in Germany and considered a good example of American degeneracy. Still, I thought I saw Elsbeth chewing gum.

Herr Maass had played an important part in local politics before the coming of the Nazis in 1932. After he had watched his work fall to pieces with one sickening thud, he had retired to his farm, to work and read and think.

'Will America enter the war against Germany?' he asked suddenly, puffing furiously on his pipe.

'That is a question I cannot answer,' I said. 'We are so shut off here from the United States that it is difficult to know what people there are thinking.'

'Well, what do you think yourself?' he asked.

'I think not,' I said at last. 'The Americans are still disgusted at the Munich agreement; they are disgusted not only at Germany, but also at England and France for giving Czechoslovakia to Germany.'

'You don't think they had any other choice, do you?' Herr Maass interrupted.

'I really don't know,' I answered. 'I only feel that right now the United States is mainly interested in letting Europe have her fling alone, and then helping to clean up the devastation. I don't think my country has any intention of getting in.'

Herr Maass thought a long while. 'And when Germany starts dropping bombs on English towns and killing civilians?'

I had to admit it. 'Then our sympathy may be aroused, and we might be pulled in.'

'Yes,' he said. 'I thought as much. During the World War, I never believed it possible that America would come three thousand miles to intervene in Europe's fight. But having done it once, I believe the United States may very well do it again.'

I sat against the warm stove, silent. What was in store for many of us? I wondered. When would hell break loose in all our lives?

Herr Maass took the pipe out of his mouth. 'It is a hard thing to say,' he said deliberately, 'but in my innermost heart I would rather have it that Germany should lose this war than go on under the Nazi regime of Adolf Hitler.'

The words were spoken so quietly that I did not at first grasp the hatred behind them. I saw Frau Maass glance up quickly at Elsbeth, and give her husband a warning look.

I had heard that same sentence before. I was to hear it twice more before I left Germany. Let Dr. Goebbels know whereof he speaks when he screams of one hundred percent unity behind Adolf Hitler.

I never saw any evidence of an underground movement in Germany against the Nazis. On the other hand, I never saw any evidence of even seventy percent support of Hitler.

There are, perhaps, two million members of the Nazi Party. That is not many in a nation of seventy million people.

One Sunday morning Richard and I were walking with a brilliant man who is high in the German government, a man whose opinion I respect highly. Richard asked him the simple question: 'What percentage of the German people do you think are behind Hitler?'

The official, a member of one of German's oldest aristocratic families, walked along beside us for a minute before he gave his well-considered reply. 'Well,' he said, 'I think it is about like this. Four percent of the people are for Adolf Hitler, six percent of the people are against him, and the other ninety percent don't care one way or the other.' This was said before the outbreak of war. I have often thought about this man's words; I have often tried to discover what meaning they could have for the rest of the world.

I try not to indulge in wishful thinking. I know what I would like to see happen, but that does not make it happen. I dislike newspaper stories and magazine articles which paint a rosy picture of revolt in Germany, of dissatisfaction among the ranks of the Nazis, of inferior materials used by the Nazi armament makers, of the imminent shortage of oil in Germany. On the other hand, if one pays attention to what is going on all about him, he sees weaknesses in the whole German regime – weaknesses which are not going to develop into a general breakdown without intelligent intervention from the Allies.

In this diary, I have set down stories, incidents and, yes, even jokes, which I think show the temper of the German people. Leaders of other countries may read these lines and draw their own conclusions. They will know what use to make of them.

One might ask, didn't these foreign powers have ambassadors in Germany to furnish them with a picture of what was going on? The answer to this question is 'Yes,' but the resultant policies lead one to suspect that the ambassadors were drinking too much tea, attending too many official Nazi parties, reading too much in their history books. They should have been drinking beer in pubs, attending church in a small village, buying bread and eggs at markets, listening to the women talk among themselves and walking out in the fields to hear what the farmers had to say.

The world might have been spared those false stories of Germany's impending bankruptcy; of Germany's weakness in guns, planes, military equipment; of revolt against the government and fighting in the streets. The world might have been spared a war, by acting when there was still time to act.

For what exists in Germany today, I have two simple illustrations:

The first is: Imagine that Herbert Hoover were still President of the United States, and as unpopular as he was at the time he was defeated for the Presidency. Imagine that the United States had been forced into a war under his leadership. He would be supported by every man, woman and child in the Union. Each person would do what he asked of them, in order to insure victory for our country. But, in spite of their support of the President, many people would be firmly resolved that as soon as peace had been won, they would vote at the next election to kick the President out.

Many people feel that way in Germany today. They will support Adolf Hitler until the war is won; as soon as it is over, they have the firm intention of getting rid of him.

Others do not support Hitler even now.

For them, I have another illustration:

One may take a rubber ball in his hand and with his thumb push deep into the rubber. That is what Hitler has done to the conservative element in Germany. As long as one keeps a pressure on the rubber, it will remain compressed. But the power to spring back is always there in the ball – and muscles eventually grow tired of maintaining the pressure. This illustration does not apply to the Nazi-trained youth but I think it is very true of the majority of intelligent citizens of Germany.

The dogs came up to me and laid their heads in my lap. I fondled their long ears and rubbed my palm over their cold noses. Frau Maass rocked back and forth in her chair, counting stitches. Her hair was braided and coiled on the top of her head. Elsbeth sewed placidly.

Yes, I could not deny it. There was a curious suspense in the room. I felt as though it had something to do with my presence. I looked at each of the three. I could read nothing in their faces. They looked peaceful enough. Still, there was something.

I saw Herr Maass glance casually over toward the radio in the corner. Then, I realized what had caused the tension.

'Do you ever tune in on London?' I asked, innocently.

'Well, yes,' my host laughed, somewhat abashed. 'It is just about time for the news in German now, and I hesitated – well anyway, you have no objections?'

'I think you should know me better than that already,' I said.

Most Germans listen to foreign news broadcasts, but not in front of people whom they do not know well, or whom they do not trust.

Herr Maass went over to the radio, and carefully turned the dial. We listened to the news from London, but there was nothing new that night. Nothing had started to break the deadlock; no attacks, no troop movements, no sign of activity from either side.

'Well, at least,' Herr Maass said, shutting the radio off at the end of the broadcast, 'we know that there still is a world outside our borders. We are so shut in that one tends to forget that, sometimes.'

A little later Frau Maass rolled up her knitting and stuck it under the table. We all went upstairs to go to bed, separating in the upper hall to go to our respective rooms. I had a small, attractive room, one corner of which sloped away under the roof. I threw off my clothes and hurried into woolen pajamas. After the light was extinguished, I opened the window and looked out at the snow falling in a faint moonlight.

The world out there was still.

Somewhere, from far down the valley, a church bell tolled the hour.

Bong!

Bong!

Ten bongs, ten deep silver bongs.

I crawled into the bed, sleepily trying to balance the huge 'zeppelin' filled with feathers balanced on my stomach. Tomorrow will be Christmas Eve, I thought.

My first war Christmas.

With terrified eyes I saw the soldier come nearer and nearer. In his dirty hands was a steel-cold pistol; his left arm hung limply in a white sling. My back was flat against the wall; there was no escape for me. I looked deep into his grim eyes. They were gray, slanted, oriental. The pistol came nearer to my face. The steel ring of the muzzle was pushed firmly against my quivering left cheek. It was cold, like ice.

I woke up.

'Bo, my God!' I grumbled at the beautiful brown dog, whose cold nose was exploring my face. He wagged his tail violently, glad to see me awake. The oriental soldier was gone; his place had been taken by a small, neat room whose only window framed a scene of falling snowflakes.

'Come on,' Bo said impatiently. 'Get up. Let's play in the snow.' And then, looking up from underneath his shaggy eyebrows, 'Say, you haven't got any more of that chocolate, have you?'

Bo munched a piece of candy while I tugged at the ski pants, found a bright blue jacket to wear, washed my face in water so cold that it burned my face. Bo and I went down the steep wooden stairs to the living room, where the fire had already been lighted. Nobody was up but Elsbeth, and she put a cup of hot milk in front of me, and two rolls and jelly.

'Snowing outside,' she said, perhaps fearing that I couldn't understand anything more complicated. I ate my breakfast slowly, looking all the time out of the window at the peaceful world which was quiet and softened as though it had been covered with a thick soft blanket. I heard a kettle rattling in the kitchen, and the old clock ticking slowly in the hall. Bo lay on the floor and looked up at me wistfully, watching every bite I put in my mouth.

After a while I got up, and walked through the kitchen to the little lean-to where the skis were stored. I borrowed a pair which looked as though they could support me and I could support them. I took them out into the back yard and put them on my feet. Bo and Hermann, which is a much too formal name for such a handsome dog, leaped about in the snow and jumped against me while I was still trying to get the hang of standing upright on two slippery planks.

I had walked around the yard twice when Herr Maass came out the back door, wiping breakfast crumbs off his mouth. 'Well, what's about a trip down to the village?' he asked.

'Have they got a good doctor there?' I asked, trying hard to keep my balance.

'Why, yes. You mean for broken bones, I suppose?' I nodded and he laughed. 'We can ski down to the Dorf, drink a Devil's Beard at the tavern and ski back up again before lunch,' he said. 'That's not too much for your first morning on skis this year.'

I agreed, and he put on his skis. We started off down the road. The snow had ceased to fall, and the light was steadily growing brighter. The snow was two feet thick on the road, hard-packed by automobiles and sleighs and horses. It was swell to be on skis again, because skiing is one of the few forms of locomotion where Mother Earth helps man instead of holding him back.

The sun came out definitely, and shone brilliantly on the white crystals. Up on top of the mountain, the wind stirred up great clouds of snow but here in the valley the air was still. Each tree and bush along the side of the winding road was topped with a crown of soft snow. Each fence post wore a thick, white baker's cap.

We skied to the single street of the village, avoiding the sleighs and automobiles which passed us. Townspeople and tourists walked along, looking into the tiny shop windows along the street. Everybody was dressed in reds and blues and purples; their eyes were bright and their cheeks were red from the cold. We stopped in front of an old inn, and took off our skis and leaned them against the wall beside the heavy oak door. When we entered, we had to bend our heads to keep from bumping ourselves against the rafters of the low ceiling.

'Heil Hitler,' said the enormously fat bartender. The little pub was only large enough to hold the owner, two shelves of bottles, a bar and a maximum of six thin customers. There was one table in the small room, mainly used to hold the customers' gloves and packages.

'Heil Hitler,' Herr Maass answered. 'Give us two Devil's Beards, *bitte schoen*. And how is the Christmas season with you?'

The fat bartender sighed as he tipped the bottle of white liquor, known locally as the Devil's Beard, over the two small glasses. He looked over his shoulder before answering. 'All right, I suppose. But I don't know how much longer I will be able to buy liquor and beer. They are tightening up already.' He wiped a large, dirty rag over the tiny bar, and in its wake we miraculously found two small glasses of Devil's Beard.

'*Prosit*,' said Herr Maass heartily, lifting his glass.

'*Prosit*,' I answered. The Devil's Beards went down in one hot blaze, and we ordered two more.

The fat bartender leaned over close to us.

'You know, everybody around here listens to London,' he wheezed. 'Of course they are afraid to admit it right out loud, but they do listen anyway.' He looked over his shoulder again, expecting to see God knows what. 'Yesterday, old Frau Prause, who's got a son on a submarine, was at home and old Herr Illman came and told her that he had dreamed the night before that her son had been captured by the British – and was safe in a prison camp in England. Frau Prause just thought he was crazy, until four more neighbors came in during the day to tell her that they had dreamed the same thing the night before. She finally believed that it was true. Everybody around here heard her son's name read on the London news broadcast in a list of prisoners they had taken, but they won't admit that they had listened to a foreign station.[1]

'They just have "dreams". Last night, Frau Prause sent over here for a good bottle of brandy, and she and her neighbors had a quiet celebration. She knows now that her son is safe until the end of the war.'

'Everybody "dreams" things now,' Herr Maass told me. 'When somebody hears something from London or Paris which he simply can't keep to himself, he tells it around as though it came to him in his slumbers.' He paused, and picked up his Devil's Beard. 'That shows what cowards you can make out of a nation if you try hard enough,' he said bitterly.

'Ssssh,' the bartender said and without changing the expression on his jolly face shouted 'Heil Hitler!' as three Germans came into the bar. There were two men and a woman, and they too ordered Devil's Beards. 'Heil Hitler,' they answered in return.

We paid for our drinks, and left.

The tiny village looked peaceful in the sunlight. People going about their simple business. Soldiers speeding past on skis, looking more like vacationing youngsters than grown-up men of war. Children riding down the street on sleds, their feet dragging in the snow.

War.

War.

---

[1] Anyone caught listening to a foreign station in Germany was liable to several years in a federal prison; anyone caught repeating news that he had heard from abroad was executed. Recently, the death sentence has been extended to foreign-station listeners.

Modern war is a thing of cities.

Modern war starts in cities, it is fought with the strategy of cities and it is decided in cities. Modern war is not concerned with mere territory, with so and so many square miles of hills and woods. That was in the old days, before society had grown so complex, so dependent on the cities with their radio stations, their big newspapers, their telephone systems, their distribution of vital supplies, their power stations.

Modern war is fought with the psychology of city people. It has as its chief aim the destruction of city integrity and morale. This little village in the Harz Mountains interested the politicians and the generals only in the number of recruits it had to offer the armies and the amount of raw material it could feed to the war machine. This compact village opened its gates long enough to release its youngest and strongest men to the army. Later on, it opened its gates again to take in the remnants, the left-over trash of its men with their shot-out eyes, their missing legs, their vague minds. Many of its men never came back, not even in halves.

War is not fought here. It is not felt in the daily life of the villagers. War is fought in the large cities, where men build barricades in the streets against the enemy. Where their defeat means living under a new flag and a set of foreign rulers, where politicians disappear and newspapers change their policies in a flash. One captured government building is worth a thousand square miles of captured territory today. A radio station is worth more than the destruction of a regiment.

War is a city affair, because when it comes men and women fight against each other to form long lines before the exhausted groceries, and whole families sit together in one room to keep warm because the trains do not bring coal to the city.

The orders of war originate in a city office, where a fat official sits and writes instructions on a little piece of paper. When these instructions are made known by radio and telephone and newspaper and post, every person feels their effect, but none so much as the beleaguered city inhabitants.

A man in a village can go into the woods and pick up twigs

if he gets cold, and he can plant vegetables in his yard if he gets hungry and he can squeeze his chickens to make them lay eggs faster. It is difficult for a country man to starve in wartime. But the city man, cold and hungry, looks out his window at the bare walls of other buildings and the hard surface of the streets and knows that he is at the mercy of his government or his conquerors.

Villages which sell to each other and co-operate to provide for their safety against an enemy do not make war against each other. They have seen too well the benefits of peace.

But cities demand a hasty solution of problems, and the word war springs too easily to the lips of city people. City people are in a hurry; they cannot wait for negotiations.

No man alive today could sit in a village pub with his genial neighbors and send out the order for war.

A man in a city office could.

Herr Maass and I skied back up the hill toward his house. I was silent, enjoying the feeling of being out in the open after so many dark, confining months in Berlin. It is a glorious thing to know that one has legs, that one may stride through snow and forget the pressure of artificial diplomatic life.

We met an old weather-beaten farmer, who stopped his horses to exchange a word with Herr Maass.

'Heil Hitler,' the farmer said to me, giving me a sharp look.

'Herr Russell, Herr Smetana,' my host introduced us, adding, 'Herr Russell ist ein Amerikaner.'

'Oh,' the old farmer said, smiling, 'I'm sorry. Good day, sir.'

'Good day to you, sir,' I said, liking him for his spontaneous show of friendliness for an American.

'Afraid a lot of our game is being starved out by this snow,' he said to Herr Maass. 'They can't find anything to eat. I found a young buck this morning wandering around in the snow. Took him over to the forest ranger, but he died a while later.'

'Do you think we'll have a late spring,' Herr Maass asked the farmer, 'like it was last year?'

'Ja, I think so,' he said.

The farmer flipped the reins softly against the horses' flanks as he talked. With every sentence a cloud of steam came from his mouth. He spoke a local dialect which was hard for me to understand.

The two men talked a few minutes about farming prospects for next year, and then we parted.

'*Auf Wiedersehen,*' we said, pushing off on our skis.

'*Auf Wiedersehen,*' the farmer said, waving his gloved hand.

'He didn't seem to be much interested in the war,' I commented as we skied.

'These peasants are all the same,' my host said. 'They are all well off, and they do not interest themselves in national politics.'

'I wouldn't call war "national politics",' I said.

'You know, that is a curious thing. Most of the people here in the mountains – those who are not Nazis – more or less consider this war to be a private venture of Adolf's. It is curious how they separate themselves from the whole fact of war.'

'Are many of them Nazis?' I asked.

'Few. Farmers, German farmers at least, do not identify themselves particularly with any party. They are mainly concerned with getting good prices for their products and paying low prices for the things they buy. Whether the government is a monarchy, a republic or a dictatorship, it's more or less the same to these peasants.'

'You said they were prosperous,' I said. 'They don't look progressive or prosperous to me.'

'You'd be surprised,' Herr Maass told me. 'They don't like new methods of farming or breeding because they make all the money they can use with their present methods. And they know how to hold on to what they make. I suppose German farmers are the people least affected and least interested in National Socialism.'

'But it must affect their lives,' I objected.

'Nothing affects a farmer's life so much as pests and the weather,' Herr Maass said.

'Will they ever revolt against the Nazis?' I asked.

'No,' he answered firmly. 'No more than they will go out of

their way to support the National Socialists.' We moved out of the road to let a sleigh go past. 'During the inflation which followed the last war, the German farmers suffered least of all. They exchanged their money for goods, and when the comedy was over, they had something to show for their labor.'

'How do they feel about the currency now?'

'Cautious. They are buying things already. I heard about Herr Hummel, who lives in the next valley. He went into a store in the city, and looked at electric ice boxes. To the store owner's delight, he bought the most expensive ice box he had, and paid cash for it. He arranged for the electric machine to be delivered to his farm, and two days later it arrived accompanied by an electrician to connect it. The electrician looked around and discovered that Hummel isn't connected to a power line. When he started to ask questions, old Hummel growled at him, 'Never mind. Just put her over there in the corner. She'll keep until the war is over, and then I'll have at least one thing I can realize money from.'

As we skied along home, I turned over in my mind all that I had heard that morning in the village and on the way back.

After I had taken off my heavy skis, I found that I was dead tired. I clumped through the kitchen into the living room. I lay down on the couch and dropped off to sleep almost immediately. When I awoke, it was night and Elsbeth was closing the shutters to hide our lights from any chance airplanes. My legs ached. The long trek, had tired me out since I was used to nothing more exhausting than subways steps. It seemed that only a moment ago it had been morning; the day had literally sped by on skis. Full of peace, I looked at the two dogs lying under the freshly decorated Christmas tree, at Elsbeth slowly arranging the plates on the dining table, at the old German prints which lined the walls.

After I had gone upstairs and dressed, the smell of good food came floating through the upper hall. When I came down I saw that the food had already been placed on the table. Frau Maass had produced a goose from somewhere; I doubted if the matter of the goose could have stood extensive official investigation. But there it was, and smelling right handsome.

There was no pepper on the table – British blockade.

After dinner we sat around the big porcelain stove and drank coffee (which I had brought along as a present). Frau Maass beamed all over as she drank her first cup of real coffee in three months.

Herr Maass settled himself in his easy chair, and took out his glasses. While he read the newspaper, I helped his wife and Elsbeth take out the dishes. Elsbeth did a lot of giggling about men helping in the kitchen, but I noticed that it was she who broke the plate. The giggling stopped. We sat down in the living room, Elsbeth with us, and talked. Frau Maass told me about her son, who was in a flyer's corps, somewhere on the front.

'I had a letter from him only yesterday,' she said. 'He wrote that they will have a celebration in the bunkers tonight, with lots of food and drink. But, of course, he would rather be at home on *Heilige Abend*.'

Elsbeth pulled a picture out of her apron pocket. 'Here's a picture of him,' she said. 'Looks just like him, too.'

'Elsbeth!' Frau Maass said, staring at the maid. 'Where did you get that picture, may I ask?'

'Oh, let her have it, Mother,' Herr Maass said, looking up over his newspaper. 'Let her keep it.'

I took the photograph. He was posed by the side of a bomber. I guessed that he was about twenty-two. He had a handsome face, a friendly and open face. His flyer's uniform made him look tall.

I handed the picture back to Elsbeth. Over what country will he be shot down? was all I could think of.

'Is he a – ? Does he believe in National Socialism?' I asked.

Herr Maass shrugged his shoulders and spread his hands in a gesture of resignation. 'What else do they know?' he asked in return. 'What else have they ever heard?'

We sat silent and the clock ticked slowly in the hall. I sat with my back against the stove and looked at the brown dogs. Frau Maass sat, rocking quietly. Over what country will they get him? was all that ran through my mind. Do these people know it will end like that?

Yes, I supposed they did know.

The clock ticked and the dogs thumped their tails on the wooden floor.

'Well!' my host exclaimed sharply, holding the newspaper closer to his eyes. 'Please listen to this.' He was reading the morning edition of a Berlin newspaper. 'They've got a letter here on the front page from Rudolf Hess[2] to a girl whose betrothed died on a battlefield and who is expecting a baby. Hess says[3] that the fact that the German nation will be benefited by the birth of a child is far more important than the girl's personal feeling or any moral scruples. The main thing is, he writes, a pure-blooded soldier who has fallen for his country has left behind him a child to help carry on the German race.'

'Father,' Frau Maass interrupted, nodding her head in the direction of Elsbeth.

That young lady was all ears, of course.

'Well,' Herr Maass said slowly, 'Rudolf Hess is one of her leaders. What he thinks is fit to be printed ought to be fit for her to hear.'

'If you think it best,' his wife said, sighing.

'Hess says that the National Socialists will make this child as legitimate as one springing from a legal marriage. Instead of the father's name appearing on the child's birth certificate, the words "war father" will be inserted.'

Frau Maass reached under the table and took out her knitting. I found a pack of cigarettes in my coat, and took one out. My host read directly from the article.

"As all National Socialists know," Hess writes, "the highest law in war, as in peace, is as follows: preservation of the Race.

---

[2] Rudolf Hess was one of the three or four Nazi leaders who ruled Germany before his abrupt flight to Scotland. Adolf Hitler, Hermann Goering, Rudolf Hess and the army generals were the most powerful, in the order named.

[3] 'Rudolf Hess Addresses an Unmarried Mother' – *Berliner Morgenpost*, December 24, 1939.)

Every custom, law and opinion has to give way to and adapt itself to this highest law. Such an unmarried mother may have a hard path. But she knows that we are at war; it is better to have a child under the most difficult conditions than not to have one at all. It is taken for granted today that a woman and mother who is widowed or divorced may marry again. It must also be taken for granted that a woman who has a "war child" may enter into marriage with a man who is not the father of that child and who sees in the woman's motherhood the foundation of a marriage companionship. The family is the basis of the country; but a race, especially during a war, can not afford to neglect to keep and to continue its national heritage."' Herr Maass paused to read a little ahead. Then, 'Listen to this: "The highest service which a woman may perform for the community as a contribution to the continuation of the nation is to bear racially healthy children. Be happy, good woman, that you have been permitted to perform this highest duty for Germany. Be happy that the man whom you love lives in your child. Heil Hitler!"'

Herr Maass put down the newspaper. 'Maybe I'm a little too old-fashioned,' he said slowly.

"Well, I told you not to read that aloud,' his wife said.

'I don't know why not,' her husband said, ruffled. 'If Germany is going to dispense with morals, Elsbeth might as well know it and make plans accordingly.'

Frau Mass made a little gesture of dismissing the subject and went to the cupboard and took out a bottle of Moselle wine. Before she took down the glasses, she handed me a long taper which she lighted at one end. 'Please light the candles,' she said graciously. 'You may do it in place of our son, if you will.'

I carefully lighted every candle. Germans prefer candles on their Christmas trees to electric lights. They make a most beautiful picture: the branches bending and turning as they swing over the candle flames, crackling briskly; the soft drop of wax on the white paper underneath the trees; the reflection of the lights in the people's eyes as they sit around and watch the flames blowing to and fro – these are things surely never found in a string of eight colored lights on an electric cord.

The flames sparkled against the silver tinsel and the colored balls. Elsbeth had turned off the center light, and we lifted our wine glasses in the light of the candles.

'To peace,' said Herr Maass quietly. 'May it soon come to the world.'

We drained our glasses, each of us having a different reason for wanting peace. I dared not look at Frau Maass in that moment.

The old clock ticked in the hall, as it had been ticking when Napoleon had all Europe under his power, as it had been ticking when Woodrow Wilson came to Europe with fourteen sane points, as it would probably be ticking when the last disillusioned soldier had been disarmed after the end of this struggle.

I wound up the gramophone, and danced with Elsbeth. She was a fair dancer, but wine, Christmas and a foreigner in the house had excited her.

Later in the evening I was given several small white packages. In Germany, presents are distributed on Christmas Eve. There were presents for me from each of them and I treasured them beyond their actual worth since I knew only too well the difficulty Germans had buying anything.

Before I had left Berlin, I had found it almost impossible to buy Christmas presents. To my closest friends I had given coffee ordered from the free harbor in Hamburg. A pound of coffee was a princely gift. For my friends in the Embassy I had had to search harder. Everywhere in Berlin I met with the same answer – 'all sold out.' The show windows were stacked full of things, but in the right hand lower corner was the now-familiar sign: 'GOODS DISPLAYED IN THE WINDOWS ARE ABSOLUTELY NOT FOR SALE.'

Berlin, and all of Germany, had gone on a buying spree. It was frequently rumored that the government intended placing a fifty percent tax on all purchases of articles not regulated by ration cards. That rumor only made the people buy more furiously.

In Kadewe, one of Germany's largest department stores, I bought a teddy bear for the daughter of a friend. Two days later

I returned to Kadewe, to buy another teddy bear for a child I had forgotten. The teddy bears were all gone, as were all the Christmas toys. The only toys one could buy were tiny wooden carvings selling at five and ten cents and – Easter toys! Easter rabbits were for sale because the store already had them in the warehouse, and there were no other Christmas toys left in stock.

Inside all of the more expensive shops of Berlin, one found only empty shelves. Many salesgirls on hand, many customers but – empty shelves and storerooms.

The telephone rang, and Frau Maass got up to answer. 'It's for you,' she said to me. 'Long distance, I believe.'

I went to the telephone in the hall.

It was Jean, of our Embassy. She had called up to wish me Merry Christmas.

'I wish I were there,' she said wistfully.

'Well, I do too,' I told her. And I did.

I think Jean was homesick, and so we talked awhile and I said light things, and she was in a better humor and we hung up.

We drank two bottles of Moselle in the living room and talked in the unconstrained manner that comes with candlelight and good wine and friendly people. One by one the candles sputtered out until only one stubborn candle burned on. The room was full of pipe and cigarette smoke; the discarded Christmas wrappings were scattered around the floor (they would be gathered up shortly and saved to wrap-up next year's Christmas presents); even the dogs looked as though they could never stir again.

At midnight, we went out on the front porch and stood in the snow which had blown up there. Distant, tiny lights twinkled far down in the valley. The houses were blacked out but a few street lights were allowed to burn The air was quiet and the cold was everywhere. Quietly, the church clock struck the first of twelve strokes. I felt my skin tingle at the sound. I looked at Frau Maass. Her face was sad and her eyes were watching something in the distance. She was thinking about her boy, of course, and he was far away, dressed in a blue uniform, cold steel helmet on her blond-head. There were two tears on her cheeks; I looked away. The last silver bong rolled up the valley to where we stood and was followed by pure silence.

The day of Christ's birthday had come.

It was as simple and beautiful as that.

The next morning, Christmas morning, we went early to church. We skied down to the Dorf and placed our skis with the others against the side of the little stone chapel. A crowd of villagers stood outside the door, talking in the brilliant sunshine. In Berlin, Sunday finds no such crowds of people around the church doors. The Party trains the children to look down on the church and on religion. Every Sunday the Nazis carefully plan a program of morning activity for the Hitler Youths and the Hitler Girls and those infants too young to belong to either organization. They set the children to the task of collecting money from house to house, or collecting bones and tinfoil, or marching, marching to the accompaniment of their own military music, or planting gardens or attending Party pep meetings.

Deep tones from the organ inside the chapel signaled the beginning of the service. We went inside and sat down. Long white candles burned on the altar at the front of the church. The windows were small, and made of stained glass. The small church had the feeling of peace within its aged walls, and this peace seeped into our bodies and our hearts.

During the sermon, I looked about me. I saw several women in mourning, though mourning is forbidden to be worn for a soldier. 'Germans should rejoice that their loved ones might be able to give up their lives for the Fatherland,' the official announcement had stated at the beginning of the war with Poland.

The pastor avoided politics in his sermon, and the theme of his talk was that the present war is the punishment of God for our falling away from Christ. The pastor said, 'Falling away from Christ,' instead of 'Falling away from the church,' since the latter interpretation might be construed as a criticism of Nazi policies toward religion.

I have heard from friends that the church services are only slightly better attended since the beginning of the war than in peace. This fact contrasts strongly with 1914, when German churches overflowed with worshipers. War-prayer hours have been gradually introduced, but young people pass them by. I suppose of the approximately one hundred people in this little village chapel, less than ten were of my age or younger – I was twenty-four.

When the sermon was over, we drifted out into the warm sunshine. We took our skis from against the wall, and clamped them on. We skied back up the mountainside leisurely, Elsbeth and I throwing snow balls at each other on the way. Elsbeth was proud at having been to church with a foreigner. She had no clear idea as to where I was from, but anyway it must have been very far away because I spoke so funny.

The next day, Herr Maass suggested that we go down to the local police station and register me. When one has lived three days in one place, German law requires that he register at the nearest police station. If the newcomer does not do this, his landlord or host – and this law applies to house guests as well as tourists and business men – is subject to a heavy fine. We skied down the snow-covered road to the Dorf, and walked into the small police office. There were two old policemen sitting at their desks – they did not look young enough to be Nazis. We arrived a few minutes before noon, closing time for the station, and stood waiting until one of the policemen should finish writing.

The outside door behind us flew open with a bang, and a young man dressed in the black uniform of the S.S. strode into the room.

'Heil Hitler!' he barked officiously, flinging his right arm out in salute. To his surprise, the two old policemen kept on writing. The S.S. man glared at the officials, and repeated defiantly, 'Heil Hitler!'

A full quiet minute ticked by before one of the elderly policemen closed his register, looked up at the clock which showed the time to be two minutes after twelve, and then said coldly, 'It is noon, young man. And what did you want?'

That afternoon, Herr Maass and I undertook to ski up to the top of the mountain which overlooked the valley: It was a hard climb for me, since I was unused to such activity, but we went slowly. At the top, we had a wonderful view of a snow-blanketed valley. Miniature house tops nestled together; from their chimneys came light blue smoke. We drank a not very good hot coffee at a restaurant on the top of the mountain. We rented a bobsled to ride down a chute to the bottom of the mountain, and the ride was thrilling and freezing.

We got off the bobsled and walked along the road toward home. Many young people were on the road, skiing. They looked good: blond heads, tall figures, athletic girls, dressed in blues and reds and yellows. There were many soldiers, clad in the gray of the infantry. I took out a pack of cigarettes and one soldier saw that they were American. He skied over to me, and asked if he could have one.

'Certainly,' I said, offering him the pack.

'Up on vacation?' asked Herr Maass.

'Yes, sir,' the soldier answered promptly. 'Have a few days, so I came on up here. I have skied in the Harz Mountains every year since I was a boy.'

After we had gone on I thought: They all look alike, people in uniform; they must all obey the same orders and live the same lives and think the same thoughts. But somewhere behind them lies a family, a girl friend, a life very different from that led by the soldier who sleeps in the very next bunk.

I thought:

Two thousand soldiers get on a train, homeward bound on a week's leave. Because they are all individuals, they somehow know where they are headed – so that Hans doesn't go to Werner's mother, and vice versa. After their leaves are over, they come back to the front again and when the train stops, they are just two thousand soldiers again, each similar to the other.

I had two more days' vacation in the Harz Mountains before I had to return to the Embassy. While skiing I broke no bones, I suffered no painful sunburn, nothing happened to keep me from going back to the city.

By New Year's Day I was back in Berlin, pushing my way along in the blackout, struggling with the dossiers, fighting four million other people for my daily food, listening to the endless rumors. Over everything still hung the endless question:

When will it happen?

And what will it be?

CHAPTER SIX

IT WAS BITTER COLD in Berlin in January; deep snow had covered the sandbags which were stacked against the Embassy cellar windows; snow was piled in great mounds between the sidewalks and the streets because there had not been enough gasoline or enough labor available to carry it off; snow was on the roofs of Berlin and in the parks. We had industriously flooded the tennis court in the Embassy back yard in order to make an ice-skating rink.

The intense cold forced us to buy ear muffs and heavier clothes (from Denmark). We scurried around to dig up old electric heaters to help our apartments' faltering radiators. People said that the new friends of Germany, the Russians, threw this cold in, gratis, along with the friendship pact. At any rate, it was the coldest winter Berlin has seen for twenty-five years. Coal was hard to get, and food harder.

In bunkers in the Westwall and the Maginot Line, soldiers sat shivering around their stoves. When they had to go out on watch or reconnaissance detail the cold metal of their helmets burned their flesh, and their guns were icy to the touch.

We had no idea of how the war would end, or whether there would be a war at all.

The English dropped leaflets on Germany in the vain hope that people reading them would be incited to revolt. They might as well have saved their gasoline. The people who hated Hitler already could never hate him any more intensely; the people who worshiped him were still intoxicated. The only way an impression could be made on the Hitler-lovers was to drop steel on their heads, not paper.

The British thought in terms of 1918. They did not realize that today was not to be compared to 1918 – but to 1914. The Germans did not lay down their arms in 1918 because they were hungry; they did not force their Kaiser to flee just because they had no more clothes to wear and no fuel for their stoves.

They quit in 1918 because their leadership was gone.

The headquarters of the government in Berlin was a maze of indecision, of non-leadership. The entire German fleet turned Communist, hauled up the red flag of Communism over its ships in German harbors. At first the Berlin government ordered the Communist riots stopped by force, then later rescinded its orders. Germans, accustomed to being led with a strong hand, felt this hesitation in Berlin, this indecision, this lack of leadership. They began to revolt, the workers, the women and the soldiers.

Whatever weaknesses the Nazis have, lack of leadership is not one of them. They will rule with an iron hand as long as they can force the German nation to obey their orders. When they cease to lead, they will be torn to pieces.

Too many of us are thinking in terms of 1918.

When I first came to Germany three years ago, I was amazed. Where did the Germans get enough coal to run their trains? I wondered. Since 1933, I had been reading that Germany was a bankrupt country, due to collapse at any moment.

Well, here it was before my eyes. Huffing and puffing and looking quite hale and hearty. Like most Europeans, Germans live in well-constructed houses, behind which are pleasant gardens. German cities are clean and the streets are not filled with dirty urchins. Not in all of Germany, even in what they called their slums, did I see anything approximating the shacks which people in my native Mississippi call houses.

This well-being of the Germans had nothing to do with the Nazis; it had been built up over hundreds of years.

The thought that the Nazi-controlled Germany would go under in six months had been a pleasant one. I had liked to read this, and the foreign correspondents had written dispatches from Europe which confirmed the idea.

In every magazine, in every edition of our newspapers, in radio news broadcasts, we heard about the imminent downfall of the Nazis, the starvation in Germany, the riots in the streets. Dorothy Thompson even told us so.

But here Germany was, right before my eyes, working and living and going strong.

Our consuls have told me the curious sensation they get on their first trip back to America from some foreign country; everybody there tries to inform them of what is actually going on in the country which they have just quitted.

Miss Stevens, a clerk in our Embassy in Berlin, talked to her mother in New York by long-distance telephone one night. Almost immediately, Mrs. Stevens asked her daughter, 'What about the revolution over there, daughter?'

'But, Mother,' said the alarmed Miss Stevens, 'there isn't any revolution. Everything is quiet here.' Her mother shouted over the wires from New York, 'Oh, no it's not, darling. I know there is fighting in the streets there, but you just can't tell me over the telephone.'

Not all Germans like Adolf Hitler.

Many – I do not know how many – do not like him. But most of them will support him until the war is finished. Many – I do not know how many – German soldiers are fighting simply because their country is at war. They were not asked to decide whether or not their country should go to war; they do not even ask themselves whether their cause is just or unjust. The simple fact is there: their country is at war, and they have been called to fight.

When I hear foreign news reports to the effect that the German people will soon revolt, there are two things I try to remember:

They have nothing to revolt with.

And nothing to revolt for.

The Nazis had planned for some time on this war; they had calculated to the pound how much food, to the inch how much clothing, to the degree how much heat the people would have to have.

But they did not include this fierce cold weather in their calculations. People sat in their apartments and shivered in their overcoats. Germans owning stoves instead of having central heating had one advantage: they could scurry around and get enough coal and wood to keep one stove burning. On the other hand, the janitors regulated the furnaces, and I mean regulated.

This afternoon I went to visit a friend, who has four children and whose husband is at the front. She answered the front door herself and brought me into the kitchen, where she and the children had been trying to keep warm by the kitchen stove. She had been cooking supper in her fur coat and – gloves!

She asked me to supper, and I stayed. It would give me a chance to send over some groceries the next day, without offending her pride. I called up Hanna and told her not to fix anything for me.

For supper, my friend had macaroni and a piece of soup meat. 'I couldn't buy one potato in this neighborhood,' she apologized. 'They are all frozen, the merchants tell me. Green vegetables won't be available until summer and of course fruits are out of the question. Even salt is hard to get.' She laughed bitterly. 'Salt! Not even that.'

I knew she told the truth. Hanna constantly reported the same things.

'Yesterday, I waited at the market for two hours and finally got a head of cauliflower,' she continued. 'Many women waited that long and got nothing. I was more successful because I told the clerks that I have four children and had to have something to feed them. Lots of women send their maids to market every Thursday morning to stand in line the first two hours and the housewife comes down to the market to relieve the maid for the final hour or so of waiting. Most women let their maids eat at the same table with the family. There isn't enough food available to fix one meal for the family and one for the servant.'

She rose from the table, and began to take the dishes over to the sink. 'The greatest problem is variety,' she said. 'We are all getting fatter and fatter simply because we eat nothing but starches, bread and macaroni and meal soups. Johann has already started to complain of stomach aches.' She paused. 'I'll fix you some coffee, since you have been kind enough to bring us some.'

'It wasn't for me,' I objected. She fixed it anyway, and we sat around the kitchen stove, dressed as though for a park bench, drinking the steaming coffee from the tiny Meissen cups.

'Beautiful cups,' I admired.

'Beautiful coffee,' my friend said simply. After a while, I asked her, 'How are people in this neighborhood taking the war?'

She shook her head at me, shaking it slowly and pointing meaningly at the telephone in the hall.

I raised my eyebrows in silent question.

'Yes,' she answered, just as silently.

Her telephone was being tapped. That, too, I thought grimly.

January 12:

I took my first diplomatic bath today. Two large, tin bathtubs have been installed upstairs in the Embassy, one for women and one for men.

We don't get hot water in our apartments any longer, except for two days each week if there happens to be enough coal in the basement to heat the water and the building too. There usually isn't.

Berlin bath houses have been overflowing with Germans anxious to sponge themselves off. I telephoned the Finnish bath house, but they said that they were fully reserved for the next two weeks.

To prevent people from heating their bath water over gas ranges in the kitchen or from using electric water heaters, apartment owners have been forbidden to use more gas or electricity than they used in peace time.

Women employees of the Embassy must telephone one of the stenographers a day ahead if they want an appointment for the bathtub. They have twenty minutes to take their bath, and get out.

We men have not been put on bath schedules, it being practically impossible to tell a man what newspaper he shall read or what hour he shall take his bath.

I came close to washing the Embassy from its foundations. The tub was hastily installed and was not firmly moored to the floor. When I reached over the side of the tub to recover a piece of soap it was only by the most frantic maneuvering that I kept the whole thing from tipping over and spilling its burden of water and Embassy clerk onto the floor.

Deliveries of coal to apartment houses were practically stopped because of the shortage of trucks, gasoline and man power. There was a certain amount of coal piled up in the coal yards near the railroads. The city government invited those who wanted coal to come to the coal yards and get it themselves.

Baby carriages, children's wagons, old suitcases and gunny sacks were utilized to bring the lumps of coal from the railroad yards to basement furnace rooms. In those cases where an entire apartment house had absolutely no coal, the people who lived in the building had to take time off from their jobs and household duties to trek to the nearest coal yard. Not much coal can be carried in suitcases and gunny sacks, so these people had to make a trip at least once a day. The very old and the very young, who had the most free time, had to make several trips to the coal yards each day. It got to be a common sight to see an old man of seventy-five or eighty years trudging along the streets with a heavy coal sack slung over his shoulder. Beside him usually walked a youngster pulling a toy wagon full of lumps of coal.

Things got so bad that we had to open a commissary in our Embassy building for the use of the American members of the Embassy staff.

In a room just off the grand lobby of the former Bluecher Palace, we eagerly bought soap, flashlights, chocolate, sardines, coffee, dried fruits, milk, matches and anything else the Embassy was able to import from Denmark and the United States.

Most of us had a standing order with the Danish dairies for a weekly shipment of Canadian bacon, cheese, eggs and butter. Without these four important items, which, of course, were not available to Germans, we Americans would have had even slimmer meals than we had.

It is difficult for me to write down all the things one could not buy in German shops. Just think of anything you would like to buy, anything at all. It was a cinch that it wouldn't be in the store when you asked for it. Or if it was, it wouldn't be for sale.

An automobile? You cannot get permission to drive it.

Shoe strings. None.

Toilet paper. None.[1]

Suspenders. None.

All canned goods. *Verboten.*

Rubber bands and paper clips. Sold out.

Other things which one could not buy in German stores: shaving soap, electric wire, candles, any metal object, phonograph records (in order to buy a new record, the customer had to give up an old one), typewriters, electric razors, electric water heaters, clothing of all kinds (except on ration cards), furniture, thread (one spool a month), many kinds of paper and stationery, color film, vanilla, spices of all kinds, pepper, gelatin, leather goods such as suitcases and pocket books, buttons, cigars (one to a person each day as long as they lasted).

Soap was extremely scarce. Germans were permitted to buy one cake of 'unity' soap a month, of inferior quality. This cake was supposed to suffice for face washing, dish washing, bathing and all laundrying.[2]

An acquaintance of mine who was shortly to be married went to Berlin's leading furniture store to pick out a dining-room set. She found just the thing she wanted on display, and bought it then and there. The clerk entered her order on his sales book.

---

[1] Later on, the government brought out a toilet paper called 'unity paper'. This paper had the appearance and texture of American brown wrapping paper, and would surely have removed the paint from any woodwork over which it might have been rubbed.

[2] We Americans in the Embassy fared a little better than the Germans as regards soap. On December 20, we received a ration card entitling us to buy one pound of toilet soap and three pounds of powdered soap – every three months. We noted on the backs of these ration cards that they were the special cards issued for children, the sick and professional nurses active in the care of the sick. Everybody else got one cake a month.

'I will give you the address where you may send the furniture,' my acquaintance said.

'Oh, we don't need it yet,' the clerk answered. 'We won't be able to deliver the furniture to you sooner than twelve to eighteen months – if then.'

I was told the story of the German *Hausfrau* who went to Goldpfeil's, an exclusive department store on Leipziger Strasse in Berlin, to buy some common oilcloth.

'We don't have any more oilcloth,' the tired clerk told the shopper. 'But we have a new kind of oilcloth; it isn't wax and it isn't leather.'

The *Hausfrau* looked closely at the substitute. She opened her mouth to ask concerning the wearing qualities but the clerk interrupted her wearily.

'Just examine it well now,' the clerk said, 'because you won't be allowed to return it and complaints will be useless. It is a new *ersatz* product which hasn't yet been tested.'

The *Hausfrau* wasn't so dumb. She bought as much as she could of the stuff.

After all, even the *ersatz* might shortly be unavailable.

January 15:

Richard told me that yesterday he was standing in the snow reading advertisements of movies in Berlin on one of the many advertising columns which are a typical feature of Berlin street corners.

In addition to the advertisements, a Goebbels' propaganda poster was plastered on the column. An old Berlin worker with black ear muffs and a red nose walked up behind Richard and began to spell out the words on the poster to a companion.

'NOBODY SHALL HUNGER OR FREEZE' the poster stated.

'Hell,' the old Berliner grumbled, 'even *that* is *verboten* now!' And as the food shortage got more serious, a barbed joke went the rounds:

'What is the difference between India and Germany?'

'Well, in India one man starves for everybody.'

'In Germany, everybody starves for one man.'

January 17:

A line of women waiting patiently in front of a grocery store in our neighborhood was broken up today by a bunch of Storm Troopers. The women, who had been waiting in the cold for an hour in the hope of being able to buy some little something to eat for their husbands and children, were told by the S.S. men:

'If you don't have any other use for your time than to idle around in front of stores, Germany can think of plenty of things for you to be doing.'

The S.S. men thereupon loaded fifteen of the women in a truck, and took them to Party headquarters where they were consigned to work in the potato fields of South Germany.

One reason for such harsh action lies in the fact that the Nazis lay so much emphasis on appearance. They don't want foreigners in Berlin to see the pathetic lines of hungry people waiting in front of shops which are such a common sight in Russia.

January 19:

Where is all the coal, anyway? we all asked each other.

Except for the few piles of coal in the railroad yards, there was none. I had tried since the war began to buy some coal bricks for use in our laundry stove.

Hanna did all of our washing, the clothes, sheets and towels, because the express laundry service took from four to six weeks and the ordinary service took two months.

When you sent your clothes to a laundry, you honestly felt like giving them a farewell party. It was that long before you saw them again.

Every coal dealer gave the same answer: 'We don't take on new customers; anyway, we don't have coal enough for our old customers.' I had a ration card for coal bricks, which had taken six weeks to wrangle from the German Foreign Office, but I found that possession of a ration card was no guarantee that I would get what I needed.

From the middle of December until today, one of our vice-consuls has had little or no heat in his apartment. He called up the city administration every day to complain – his apartment house had been taken over by the city with the intention of tearing it down to make way for a projected area of new government buildings. Days passed and no coal arrived. Finally, our Embassy got in touch with the German Foreign Office which got in touch with Berlin officials who promised to remedy the situation. At last, a coal truck rolled up before our vice-consul's apartment building door. People who lived in the building had to go downstairs and help the janitor unload the coal from the truck and store it in the basement. There was plenty of coal – enough for four days' heating.

To honor the first bit of heat which had shown itself around his apartment most of the winter, the vice-consul invited several of us to lunch. 'I request the honorable presence,' his memorandum-invitation read, 'of Bill Russell at a *Modest* table and a *Gentle* heating, at 1:15.'

The table was all right, but the heating was so *gentle* that we sat around the board shivering in our overcoats.

The German Foreign Office apparently had a firm idea that we should be forced to battle for our daily necessities along with the Germans. We ordered what we could from Denmark, but one couldn't very well pay to have sacks of coal shipped by express, or pay postage on everything from thread to noodles.

Every month the Germans tightened up on our ration cards – which were jokes anyway. We started out with four pounds of meat a week and later got two. We started out with four pounds of rice a month, which was cut to one pound – and not a store in Berlin had any rice to sell. We had ration cards for oil, eggs, peas and beans. None of these articles was to be found, ration card or no ration card.

I asked the Germans for permission to buy a set of six napkins. Four weeks later, the permission came through – for three napkins!

One month Hanna took into a shop my ration card which entitled me to buy a spool of thread.

'It's a disgrace,' she said indignantly to the storekeeper, 'to allow foreign diplomats only one spool of thread a month! Can't you see the headlines in America sir? "ONE DIPLOMAT – ONE SPOOL OF THREAD."'

The store owner took my ration card from Hanna.

'I want at least three spools,' Hanna said with determination, remembering the many pairs of undarned socks lying around my apartment. 'Germany can't let foreigners think it is so hard up and stingy.'

To my astonishment, Hanna came home with three spools of thread. The extra two spools were permanently subtracted from the storekeeper's stock since he had no ration card to present for two new ones.

We heard so often this comment made to us by hungry Germans: 'Oh, *you* foreigners have all the food you want, don't you?' And they said it in a tone which implied, 'While we don't have anything at all.'

There was no answer to that but a rude answer, or perhaps a dangerous one. We usually did not answer. Once, however, the chilled vice-consul I mentioned above was asked at a party given by some Germans: 'Is it true that all you diplomats actually get six pounds of butter a week for each member of your family?' The questioner said that he had heard that rumor from a friend of his in the German War Ministry.

' 'Could I explain,' the vice-consul said, 'that in the first place I couldn't use six pounds of butter a week and in the second place I couldn't pay for them?'

The German looked uncertain.

'Anyway,' continued the vice-consul, 'I hope you don't think that I would take your Germans' butter away from you. I of course get my butter every week from Denmark, and pay for it with American dollars.'

The German subsided, and searched for another topic of conversation.

I don't know why fish was so scarce, but it was nowhere to be bought. The same system of registration and waiting lists which was used with fats, meat and fowl was in force with fish.

The mother of one of the German girls employed in our Immigration section was especially fond of fish. One day recently she saw on the sign in her butcher's window that people having numbers between 350 and 410 would be able to buy fish during that week. She had number 403, and began to look forward to a good fish dinner. Unfortunately, all the following week she was sick in bed with a cold, and her daughter came home each day too late to stand in line for the fish.

When she was well, our employee's mother went immediately to the butcher's and found that the numbers had advanced to 450-480. 'Can I buy my share of fish?' she asked the butcher. 'I was sick last week and couldn't bring my ration card around.'

The butcher was overworked and tired, as most shop-keepers in Germany are today. 'Can't you see your number has been passed?' he yelled. 'Can't you read?' The woman got no fish.

The food situation was so bad the third week of January that the ration officials had to loosen up on the only food they had available – macaroni. It became a real problem to keep the people reasonably well fed.

In the midst of all the trouble with food shortages, a ray of hope was allowed to reach the public through the government-controlled press. In a long review of the import-export situation, information for which was supplied by the Federal Farmers' Association, the following comforting sentence appeared in the Berlin *Börsen Zeitung*: 'Our requirements for jackasses can be fully satisfied in Germany itself.'

All Germans received a clothing-ration card, divided into one hundred points, which were intended to supply their needs for one year. Cloth for a man's suit was thirty points; the lining, thread and wadding required another thirty points. The man who bought a suit had only forty more points to play around with for the rest of the year. Expensive silk dresses and very expensive woolen dresses were unrationed, but they were difficult to find and later the supply was exhausted. When one German woman asked another, 'How much did that dress cost you, darling?' she was not referring to money. She meant, 'How many points did you have to give up?'[3]

Great interest was shown in articles of clothing which could be bought without giving up any points from the ration card, such as thin raincoats or cheap bedroom slippers.

When walking with Richard one day, I saw a small sign in a shoe-store window. We came closer to the window to read what it said. The sign concerned bedroom slippers (it said they were all sold out) but when we turned around we found ourselves being pressed by a crowd of people who thought we must have stopped to read about something to be bought without points. We had to push our way through twenty people before we were free.

Many cartoons and jokes appeared in the German newspapers and magazines on the subject of clothing-ration cards. One cartoon showed a pretty young lady clad in a lovely new Easter bonnet – and nothing else! 'I had only six points left,' she explains, 'and I just couldn't resist this hat.'[4]

The best introduction a foreigner could have to Berlin society was to present a pair of silk stockings to his hostess as he entered the door. In war time, if one had a show girl on his hands he didn't think of giving her pearl necklaces. Hosiery was

---

[3] Persons of the Jewish race were not given clothing-ration cards. They had to apply at special disbursing offices for permission to buy each article of clothing which they needed. The reader is free to imagine how generously these special ration cards were given to Jews. Most stores in Germany stuck signs on their doors, stating the hours when the Jewish customers might enter the stores. In Berlin, Jews were not admitted to most shops before twelve noon. This rule was enforced to assure the 'Aryans' of getting their pick each day.

[4] Clothing-Ration Card for Women: Total points for one year, one hundred. Some samples of what the points will buy.

Handkerchief	1 point	Morning dress	25 points	Lining & thread	
Pair stockings	4 points	Nightgown	18 "	for suit (if you	
Pair socks	4 "	Wool dress	40 "	have the cloth)	21 points
Pair gloves	5 "	Other dresses	30 "	3 ounces of	
Scarf	5 "	Blouse	15 "	yarn	7 "
Woolen Scarf	10 "	Jacket	20 "	Bathrobe	30 "
Sweater	25 "	Suit	45 "	Brassière	4 "
Underskirt	15	Corset	15 "		

the smart thing. Back in the prosperous days of 1938, we used to lure the girls with a pat of butter or a half-dozen eggs. Now nothing less than a pair of stockings melted a cold heart.

I know an officer in the air force who had bought a long leather coat, which reached almost to the ground. When he met a woman whom he knew slightly, he heard her exclaim disapprovingly, 'Just think! How many pairs of shoes I could have had made out of all that leather!'

Special permission was required to buy a pair of shoes. Shoes were not on the ration cards. Hanna's sister has two small girls, whose father is a soldier at the front. The sister applied every two weeks for three months straight for permission to buy shoes for the little girls.

'No,' said the official at the rationing office, 'your daughters already have shoes.'

'They only have summer sandals,' Hanna's sister argued. 'They can't go out in the snow in them.'

'They had better stay indoors, then,' the official said.

'Children can't stay indoors all winter,' the mother retorted. 'You ought to be ashamed for saying that. I care more about the health of my children than your damned rationing.'

Her arguments did not move the official. He heard them every day.

Shoes with wooden soles made their noisy appearance. The soles were carved from hard wood, and the shoes were formed by gluing a piece of brightly colored canvas to the wooden base. Many Berlin women, wearing fashionable dresses and hats, could be heard clumping along the Kurfuerstendamm in their uncomfortable, noisy wooden shoes.

If one wanted to buy a new overcoat, he had to give up sixty points from his ration card and surrender his old overcoat.

Ration card or no ration card, there wasn't a pair of rubber overshoes to be had in Berlin.

Many German business men made extra trips to Prague just to buy those articles which were unavailable in Germany. Flashlights for use in the blackouts were the most popular item, and shoes and blankets. The Germans came back from the Protectorate loaded down with supplies and foods which the Czechs themselves would soon have to do without. The same pillage occurred in Poland and was carried out even more thoroughly.

The paradox lay in the fact that German stores still displayed those articles which were not for sale. Show windows were loaded with good things, boxes of chocolates lay untouched on the counters. But they could not be sold. The displays were mainly for the benefit of the many foreigners still in Berlin. Also, they were intended to keep the Germans believing their government's claim that there were unlimited supplies in the Reich, all stored away for eventual use.

I do not think that Germany has any great amount of food stored away; I think that the rationing I have described was based on the producing power of the farms and the amount of food that could be imported. That left what supplies there were at the beginning of the war still untouched. I do not believe that these supplies are great.

Paul asked me the following question: 'If you had a thousand dollars in reichsmarks to spend in two days, what would you buy?'

I thought it over very carefully and came to the conclusion that there was nothing left in Germany on which one could spend a thousand dollars in two days, unless he bought property. One could not buy clothing, he couldn't buy food, he couldn't even spend that much money on a spree. Money had completely lost its meaning as a unit of purchase.

January 23:

Richard burst into my office shortly before noon. 'Well, I've met a pip,' he said. 'She is wonderful, and a real American.'

'Who is she?' I asked, 'and why do you have all the luck?'

'Consul Dyer's sister. Jane. She is studying music in Rome, and just came up to Berlin for a visit with her brother. I guess Dyer got her the permission to come to Germany. She is coming to lunch today at my house. Do you want to come and be the only sour note at the table?'

I did.

I pushed the dossiers aside and locked my desk. I grabbed my overcoat from the closet in the corridor and met Richard by the Information desk. The cold wind outside the Embassy quickly froze the moisture in our noses. Richard's Buick crunched heavily over the ice as we drove out of the Embassy driveway. Our cop, who double-dutied for our Embassy and Goebbels' Propaganda Ministry next door, held back traffic on the Hermann Goering Strasse, and several Germans on the sidewalk stopped to watch us go by. They were obviously envious and resentful of anybody lucky enough to have permission to drive an automobile and to have some gasoline to boot.

We drove through the Tiergarten on the new East-West Axis, past trees on either side of us which were frozen into silence. The lakes in the Tiergarten were covered with thick ice, on which children skated. I turned on the radio inside the warm car. March music blared forth at us, as always. A military band played the newest war song, *We're Going to England, to England*. It was a catchy tune, but the paradox was that Germany seemed to be going against practically everybody – except England.

Richard turned in at his driveway. Three soldiers stopped to watch us get out of the car. Germans always have time to gape at American cars, because ours are about twice as big as theirs and much more beautiful.

Jane was already in the living room; she had come by taxi. I saw at once what Richard had become so excited about. Jane was small, with brown hair and a tiny nose. Her cheek bones were high, but they did not make her face look cold. She greeted us in that frank direct manner which only American girls seem to have. In contrast with the lipstick-less German stenographers at the Embassy, Jane's lips were painted a cherry red.

'Come in out of the cold,' she said, smiling at Richard.

Richard introduced us.

'The maid and I have fixed up something good to eat,' Jane said. 'I can't understand a word she says, nor she me – but we get along.'

A large fire was blazing in the fireplace, and Richard, Jane and I backed up to it.

The maid came in, bearing a tray of cocktails.

'I showed her how to make a "Jane Dyer Special,"' Jane said. 'I hope you will like it.'

'I would like bacon grease and gin, if you mixed it,' Richard said, looking at Jane from under his eyebrows.

After lunch, we had our coffees in the living room. Jane picked out some records from Richard's really good collection and stacked them in the phonograph. I asked her to dance, and she did, beautifully. She had a husky voice, heavily Southern-accented.

'Alabama,' she explained. 'I never expected to be so far away from home in my life.'

Later, she asked, 'Is Germany really at war? I mean, I haven't seen anything to remind me of war. Everything is the same as it always was.'

'You don't feel anything yet,' Richard said slowly. 'Just like those children playing out there in the street. They don't feel the war either – yet. But the time will come when war will come home to all of us – to Americans, Russians, Africans, children and unborn babies. I think so, anyway.'

We sat quiet a few minutes thinking about that.

Later, Richard asked Jane to go skating with him on our ice rink in the Embassy back yard that afternoon. She accepted, and we drove back to the Embassy together. Jane went upstairs to see her brother, and Richard and I gently nudged our way through the crowds of immigrants to our respective offices.

About the middle of the afternoon I got to wondering about something. Consul Richard Stratton couldn't skate a lick. What did he mean, inviting Jane to skate with him? I decided to go out into the back yard and look on.

I found them there, and several others from the Embassy. Jane was laughing at Richard for the clumsy way he stood on the ice.

'Well, it's slippery,' he complained, holding on to the wire fence around the rink.

'Just let yourself go,' Jane coaxed.

'I'll let a lot of things go,' Richard said grimly, 'but not this fence.'

The clerks were looking at their boss in amusement. They were all good skaters, and executed graceful figures effortlessly.

'Look at them,' Jane said. 'You see how easy it is.' Richard looked at the spectators on the benches. Several faces peered out of the Embassy windows. 'Don't want to make a fool of myself,' Richard said.

Jane finally persuaded Richard to skate around the rink once with her. They started off together, all four hands fastened tightly together. Jane held Richard up. They were a handsome couple and everybody watched them.

'I want to try it alone,' I heard Richard say. 'Give me a push.'

Jane released him, skated around behind him and gave a strong push. The other skaters jumped out of his way in mock alarm. His feet were going like two gasoline-engine pistons. Richard wasn't almost perfect at skating.

He wasn't perfect at all.

He tried to make the curve at the end of the rink, and everybody who watched him hoped that he would make it. However, nature had other things in store for him and he crashed loudly into the plank at the end.

'Are you all right?' Jane called.

'Certainly,' Richard said. 'Just watch.'

Everybody watched him try to get loose from the plank. His skates were stuck firmly in the wood. Finally, he jerked them loose, went sailing backward a few feet, then fell flat – a perfect one-point landing.

We teased Richard about his skating for a long time afterward.

Well, there was some fun in those gloomy days, at that. Without fun, I think we would have gone slowly crazy.

The government continued to keep up the fiction of the Winter Relief collections. That is, the fiction lay in the word 'Relief'. Nobody really got relieved but the average German citizen, and he got relieved of plenty.

The collections were originally begun several years ago, under the slogan, 'A Folk Helps Itself.' Perhaps the original idea was to collect money for the unemployed, the aged and the sick, but the amount brought in by the scheme would have lined the pockets of needy people with a thick layer of gold had it been given to them.

No, it all went to buy guns, tanks and planes. No account of the way the money was spent ever appeared in any of the newspapers. Every German knew that his contribution was not being used for relief work, but such is the strange character of the German that he prefers to believe in sweet fiction rather than be doused with the chilling waters of truth.

Every week end, beginning Thursday night and ending Monday morning, Germany's streets, street cars, subways, theaters and all public places were filled with hordes of people carrying a small red bucket in one hand and a tray full of souvenir plaques in the other. The police were the collectors one week end, young Hitler girls another week end; next week the Storm Troopers, then the S.A., the soldiers, the navy – in fact, every Reich organization sooner or later had an opportunity of shaking the little red buckets in the faces of people. Since it was next to impossible to pass a week end without being forced to buy one of these plaques, enormous sums of money were collected for the government through these drives. The plaques might be toy policemen, miniature books, accordions, glass figures, traffic signals, buttons of all kinds – anything that could be hung in the lapel or hooked to an outside button. It was important that the plaques be plainly visible to all, because the government collectors descended like locusts on any pedestrian caught without a plaque. The plaques cost about eight cents, and the buying of them was 'voluntary', like everything else in Germany which one has to do.

In addition to the street collections, a member of the Party came around to every house and apartment each Sunday morning to ask for an additional 'voluntary contribution'. The names of the occupants of one's apartment house and the exact amounts of the contributions each had made were written on a piece of paper. One was free to look over this sheet while he decided how much to give to the Party worker. If one did not give as much as the Party worker thought he should, the work-er would not hesitate to ask for more.

A third bit of graft for the Winter Relief was called 'One-Pot Sunday'. Two Sundays a month, the noonday meal was sup-posed to consist of left-overs, cooked together in one pot and served in bowls.

The money which the family saved by thus depriving itself was collected that Sunday afternoon by a Party worker. The same plan applied to restaurants. A helping of the 'One Pot' was reasonably priced, and one voluntarily gave the waiter a sub-stantial contribution for the Winter Relief.

A writer who works in the Propaganda Ministry, and whom I know well, spent four days skiing in a small village in south Germany, in Bavaria. At the railroad station, he bought his tick-et back to Berlin. Before giving him his change, the ticket seller tried to sell the writer a Winter Relief plaque for twenty pfen-nigs. 'No, thanks,' the writer said, 'I have one already.'

The ticket agent asked him to show the plaque. The writer, impatient to be off, refused to do so. He stated that his word ought to be enough and that the plaque was in his pocket – as it was. The ticket agent again insisted, but the writer would buy no plaque. The writer picked up his change from a fifty-reichsmark bill and saw that the ticket agent had short-changed him by twenty pfennigs. He demanded the rest of his change, but the agent was adamant, say-ing that he considered it his duty as a good German to see that all other good Germans contributed to the Winter Relief.

Thoroughly angry, the writer found a policeman and went with him to the station master. After he had explained things, the policeman, the station master and the writer went to the ticket's agent's window and demanded a return of the twenty pfennigs.

The agent disgorged the two small coins, grumbling some-thing about the patriotic Germans and the Gestapo and Adolf Hitler and what have you.

Other Germans – those who do not work in the Propaganda Ministry and who are not on such firm footing with the Nazis – would not have dared to make a complaint.

The Nazis laid great stress on the fact that everything the nation did at their command was 'voluntary'. Even the compulsory two-year period of service in the army is 'voluntary'. Every boy is required by law to serve, so the Nazis call it volunteering. I have no doubt but that even those unfortunates who were slaughtered in the 1934 purge died 'voluntarily'.

PROPAGANDA. PROPAGANDA. PROPAGANDA.

Dr. Goebbels aimed his most powerful guns at us from every side. He filled the newsstands and the book shops with fresh material and stale material. His writers worked overtime to produce something, anything which would serve in the place of news.

Of course the food shortages and the coal shortages and the breakdown of the train schedules were not written up in the newspapers. What educated Nazi German would want to waste his valuable time reading about a mere dearth of foodstuffs? No, the soul was more important, and the political *Weltanschauung* (translation of which is, according to my dictionary: 'A view of the purpose of the world as a whole, or the course of its events, forming a cosmology or philosophical apprehension: literally, world view') of the German people was treated to a daily bath in the journals.

Not only the newspapers were subject to the strict censorship exercised by the Propaganda Ministry, but also all forms of literature and everything which went under the heading of literature.

Displayed on every subway newsstand in Berlin were such examples of Reich literature as *Was Christ a Jew?* and *Are the Roosevelts Jews?* The first pamphlet answered the question asked by the title with a resounding 'No.' The second book said 'Yes – Rosenfeld.'

From a German catalogue issued for booksellers only, I copied the following titles of books which had newly been published or were shortly to appear.[5]

---

[5] *Börsen Blatt fuer den Deutschen Buchhandel*, published at Leipzig.

There was a sprinkling of novels in the lists, but the most important and best advertised books were these:

Secret Service, England's Darkest Power.
   ('The gentle and the dark aspects; business secrets of the London murder center; bombs from the arsenal of the London Secret Service.')
Bankruptcy of English Commercial Policies.
   Dr. Walther Croll.
Great Britain's Social Arrears.
   Prof. Dr. Rauecker.
England Against America.
   ('Special light is thrown on the time of the American Civil War, when England reckoned on the final overthrow of the Union.')
   Prof. Dr. Shonemann.
England as Miracle Banker.
   Dr. Max Biehl.
England the Sea-Robber Land Reinhold Gadow.
British is Best: the System of British Self-righteousness.
   Wilhelm von Kries.
Blow On Blow: the German Air Force in Poland.
   Dr. H. Eichelbaum.
Sworn to Heaven: Five Years in the German Air Force.
   Dr. Orlovius.
Our Flyers over Poland.
   ('Birds of hell, Poland called the German pilots! Fantastically and like ghosts they appeared suddenly and with monstrous certainty seized and destroyed the Poles.')
   General Kesselring, Commander of German Air Force I.
England Fights to the Last Frenchman.
   Dr. Dranz Grosse.

England's power as it is today is founded only on a monopoly practiced by her in regard to other nations. Only through this attitude can she maintain herself. Other nations raise a row only about France; they see only her army – as if England

*were not around and everywhere a far more threatening men-
ace. Tarifa, Gibraltar, Malta – are not these English strong-
holds menacing the traffic of all other countries?*

*France is fighting for the most sacred rights of a nation,
whilst England is only defending her assumed privileges.*

*If I am fighting now and demanding so many sacrifices
from France, it is actually for the highest good of Europe. I
have only one aim: peace with England, and that means general peace. Without it, any other peace is only an armistice.*

Who said that?

Adolf Hitler?

No. The above quotation was taken from a book just published,[6] and the words were spoken by Napoleon.

The future which lies before the German boy of today is not
a glorious one. At the age of four, he enlists in a youngsters' edition of the Hitler Youth. Until sixteen he is a member of the
Hitler Youth and plays and marches in short brown pants and
black boots; then he enters the compulsory German Labor
Service for six months.

Within a year, he 'voluntarily' enlists in the compulsory army
for two years; in order to get anywhere in Germany he has to join
the Storm Troopers (the S.S.), which means wearing black boots
and suppressing all individual thoughts for the rest of his life.

When the German boy has reached his twenty-first year, he
will have spent seventeen years in boots and strict organizations.
He will have learned only what the bosses want him to know. He
is not likely to become a great writer or artist or musician.
Perhaps he may come to achieve greatness in Germany, where
nobody else will know anything anyway. He will grow up and
write a great book called 'America, the Gangster Land'. His
country will think it is a wonderful book.

January 20:

I looked at my watch. It was only five-thirty and everybody

---

[6] *Napoleon Against England,* by Dr. Friedrich Matthaesius.

had already left the Consular section. On the other side of the building, the Embassy staff still worked. Their hours depended solely on events from day to day.

These were curious times of just standing by, waiting for something to break. The Embassy continued to send its reports by pouch and cable to the President. We handled the affairs of England and France in Germany, and that was quite a bit of work in itself.

There was little or no connection between our Embassy and official German diplomatic life. We gave no parties for German diplomats; they gave none for us. The United States Embassy in Berlin occupied somewhat the same position which the Russian Embassy had during those long years of official unfriendliness between Hitler and Stalin. As far as diplomatic pleasantries were concerned, we might as well not have an Embassy in the German capital.

Before I went to the Harz Mountains, a representative of the Columbia Broadcasting System in Berlin asked me if I would go to Bayreuth to announce a Christmas Eve broadcast, part of a Columbia world round-up of Christmas carols. I read the script over and found it a harmless introduction to a group of children carolers. Before accepting the offer to go, I asked the Embassy what it thought. It thought, 'No.' I was forbidden to make the announcement, 'on principle'.

The coolness between official Germany and our Embassy was apparent in many ways. Somehow, we Americans always had extra trouble getting our ration cards through the Foreign Office. Sometimes they were lost for two or three weeks and sometimes they were just delayed for two or three weeks more and then somehow they would be lost again.

No, things were not cordial at all. We sometimes wondered how long we would be in Berlin, anyway.

From the crowds we find in our waiting room every day, one would never suspect that there are only 250,000 Jews left in Germany. The lucky ones have left for countries all over the globe from which the majority expect to emigrate to the United States.

Shanghai, Palestine, Belgium, Havana, France, Mexico, England and Italy are all full of German refugees waiting for their turns to be reached on the American immigration waiting lists. From the number of cases which we transferred to our Embassy in London, we estimated that the British admitted not less than 70,000 refugees to the British Isles in the months immediately preceding the outbreak of war.

The English were willing to take these refugees in – provided they had been registered and had affidavits which would enable them to continue on their way to the United States. If the affidavits from the United States looked sufficient to the various British consuls, the refugee was given a landing permit for England. I never could get too enthusiastic about that kind of generosity.

The first rude thud from across the Channel came early in 1939 when our consul general in London refused a visa to a German refugee. The British Immigration Office immediately called on the Consulate to explain itself, and protested about as follows: 'If we had known that this applicant, and others like him, would not be able to get a visa for the United States, we never would have admitted him.' Our consul general stuck to his guns and soon the British Passport Office in Berlin began asking us for letters stating not only the refugee's approximate waiting time on our list but also giving our opinion regarding the sufficiency of the refugee's affidavit.

War had not stopped the immigrants from flowing into America on every ship. If anything, war speeded immigration up because people now had even more urgent reasons than ever to seek the safety of the Stars and Stripes.

January 29:

The express S-Bahn train (Berlin's crack elevated system) which usually takes seventeen minutes to speed into the center of Berlin from Zehlendorf, took an hour and ten minutes today. One of our stenographers, a German-American, who lives in Zehlendorf arrived very late at the Embassy, and told the following story of what happened aboard the train:

For almost an hour the long electric train stood waiting between signal posts, held up by frozen switches. The passengers shivered in the bitter cold; the heat in the cars had been shut off to save electricity. Since the train was in the middle of a long stretch, they could not get out and walk. As good German citizens have learned to do, they sat subdued and frosty in their seats, especially since two brownshirted Nazis sat in the car with them. All were quiet; that is all except a noncom who stamped his heavy boots on the floor and muttered. Finally, the soldier said something about the 'damned state of things,' out loud.

Ears pricked up.

The Brown Shirts looked sternly at the soldier. 'Do you dare to criticize the German railways?' one of them asked in a loud voice.

With foolish courage, the noncom answered him back:

'You didn't hear me right, bud. I didn't just criticize the railways. I said the whole damned system is haywire. I get six days' vacation from the front and I have to spend three of them sitting around in icy trains.'

A little gasp ran through the car. Because of fear people did not look each other in the face.

'As a soldier, you have no right to criticize,' shouted one of the youthful Brown Shirts.

'I'm just the one who does have the right,' the soldier snapped back. 'Who else?' He looked sharply at the two well-fed Nazis. 'Anyway, why aren't you two at the front?' he asked suspiciously.

'We've been fighting,' asserted one Brown Shirt.

'Where?' the noncom asked unbelievingly.

After a slight pause, our employee heard the S.A. man give this classic answer:

'Ten long years' fighting the Brown Shirts organization!'

Several persons in the train tittered.

The soldier said quietly, 'Kiss my ass!'

The snow fell in silent white sheets on the railroad tracks outside.

Ice gathered thickly on the windows.

My prize story for the winter concerned Hanna, the New Year's goose and the temporary supremacy of the Occidentals over the Orientals in Berlin.

Three weeks before New Year's Eve, I ordered a goose from Herr Ritter, my butcher. I had first secured with great difficulty a ration card from the German Foreign Office.

Two days before the first of January, Hanna dressed up warmly and sallied out to capture the goose from the butcher shop. When she got to the store, she found the interior filled with a crowd of impatient, hungry housewives who were asking for – and not getting – a bit of goose for the holiday.

When her turn in line was reached, Hanna, full of respect for the listening ears behind her, said quietly to the salesgirl, 'I want to get "that" for Herr Russell.'

The girl was tired, rushed, busy and forgetful. '"That" what?' she boomed impatiently.

'Er–, "that,"' Hanna repeated desperately.

'Come on,' the clerk said, 'I haven't got all day. I've forgotten what Herr Russell ordered.'

Every German housewife in the butcher shop was listening intently. 'Well,' Hanna said reluctantly, 'I mean the goose.'

'Oh, now I remember,' answered the girl turning toward the back of the shop. 'Say, Poppa,' she yelled, 'which goose does the American get, the big one or the little one?'

The deep voice of old Herr Ritter came back nonchalantly from the rear room. 'The big goose is for the American,' he called. 'We're keeping the little one for that Japanese.'

With a red face Hanna took the wrapped goose over the counter from the salesgirl, painfully aware of the dirty looks she was getting from the German women.

It was a long time before I could persuade Hanna to buy any more meat in that shop. I had to come home from the Embassy a few minutes early and do it myself.

January 30:

Yesterday was quite a day. It ended all right, but I had a bad experience with Berlin's tied-up transportation system.

I had an errand to do before going home, and when I had finished I found myself in the neighborhood of Friedrichstrasse Station. Instead of going home on the safe and comfortable – though rather slow – subway, I decided to take a S-Bahn train at the Friedrichstrasse. At other times, the Berlin S-Bahn is a wonderful form of transportation; the trains are fast; the cars are clean, well heated, and above all punctual. The S-Bahn is an elevated which circles Berlin, crisscrosses it and runs out to the suburbs. Most of the track system is built on solid mounds, high enough for streets to run under. There is little waiting necessary for the S-Bahn trains because they enter and leave the stations one right after the other. Every arriving train is announced by an automatic electric sign. The S-Bahn generally runs smoothly, with no irritation to its passengers.

But this was not the case when for eight weeks there was not one night in Berlin with less than twenty degrees below zero temperature; it didn't run smoothly when the switches were frozen fast and buried under deep snow; nor when the sensitive electric motors were clogged with ice and snow; nor when so many of the railroad workers had been called to the munitions industries and into the army. In this case a smoothly functioning machine became a kind of chaos into which it was my bad luck to be thrown.

The Friedrichstrasse Station was high and black, it shook and bumped and boomed with the coming and going of ghostly trains. The dim illumination allowed in that central part of Berlin left the station as dark as though no lights had been burning. On one side of the platform the trains were headed east; on the other side, west. Sometimes there were three trains directly following each other; sometimes for half an hour not a single train came along. The passengers stood in crowded lines on the blacked-out platform, packed tightly against each other. Since no one could tell for what part of the city the incoming trains were destined, the conductor who rode in the front car with the engineer had to open the first door of the train, stick his head out into the icy station and shout the name of the station to which the elevated was going and the route. One could hardly hear him. Then the loud speaker started a staccato booming of instructions: 'Train leaving for Spandau West.' 'Careful, watch the trains!' 'Stand back, stand back, stand back.' And in between, another deep voice shouted unceasingly (for the benefit of those who were in the trains and could not see outside the ice-locked windows), 'Friedrichstrasse Station.'

'Friedrichstrasse Station... .'

A variation of these monotonous statements was an official order, 'Hurry up!' 'Hurry up!' It was something easy to say but hard to do, for the train doors which are usually opened by hand and automatically closed by air pressure became stuck fast in the intense cold. The S-Bahn trains can run with the doors open, since no continuous electrical contact is necessary to close the switches for the motors. Some doors could not be opened at all, some could be opened a narrow crack; some could not be closed at all, some could be half-closed. In spite of the trouble with the doors, the crowd of waiting, freezing, stamping, but never grumbling (one does not do that) people rushed to the trains. I saw one fat man whose circumference was almost greater than his height running in despair along the length of two entire cars, not being able to force himself through the narrow openings which the doors made. In the last moment before the train started, he found a door one foot ajar, but the whole crowd of people inside the car screamed in a discordant chorus: 'There is no room for a fatty like you! You would only get stuck in the door and hold up the train!' The pathetically fat man stood still in front of the door and sorrowfully watched his train disappear; he probably would have to wait another half hour in the biting cold.

All this time I was expecting my train any minute. It did not come. Many trains came, but not one which I could take.

Fatty might have been a funny sight, but things ceased to be humorous to the people inside the arriving trains when there was no possibility of opening the doors; when the glaciated windows obstructed their view of the signs which might have told them which station they were in (were it not for the blackout); and when passengers arriving at their station would like to get out of the cars but could not. Queer things happened then: windows were pried open and women pushed in and out of the trains through the windows like so many sacks of potatoes. They were in danger, since the train might start at the very moment when one of them was hanging between the window and the platform.

It was too much for me. I had been waiting over an hour for a train which ordinarily came every ten minutes. Worn and bitter, I left the blacked-out station and descended to the subway below the street level. A train came in, and I opened the door and got in. Passengers entering the darkened subway must watch carefully when they sit down The Berlin subways, strangely enough, often go over the roofs of houses and are, therefore, blacked-out like the S-Bahn. Sometimes one comes into a dark car and sits on something soft, and it is not upholstery but the quivering lap of an irate *Hausfrau.*

When my subway train climbed out of its underground shaft into the night, I saw that it was deep black outside. However, the electrical contacts which rub against the third rail were coated with ice and produced a continuous dazzling flash of white light which made the passengers look like ghosts and which could be seen all over Berlin. My train sped silently through the glittering sparks. Outside, a snow storm whirled thick snowflakes against the train windows. The scene was an accomplishment of the gods of darkness and winter and electricity which would have made the best movie directors in Hollywood turn pale with envy.

In any city, the most carefully blacked-out portion is the region of the railroad yard and the station. As my subway crossed over the railroad tracks at Potsdamer Station, I looked out the windows in amazement. The only place in Berlin where lights were to be seen were the railway yards which stretched out before me; the cold steel tracks shone coldly under the rays of powerful searchlights.

When I got home, and very glad to be there, I was surprised to find Niles and Jane and Richard in my living room.

'We didn't have any heat at our houses,' said Niles, 'so we came around to see you.'

'You're certainly welcome,' I said. 'But I'm not sure that it is very warm here, either.'

'It isn't boiling,' said Jane. 'But compared to Richard Stratton's ice box and my frigid hotel, it's a steam-heated heaven. I hope you don't mind.' She looked at me with her clear, laughing gray eyes.

'I couldn't be happier if I had had a raise in salary,' I answered. 'But let me rustle you up something to eat and drink.'

I fetched my large candleholder which held five long white candles. I lighted these, and placed the great thing on the living-room floor. Candles will give off some heat. Hanna brought the electric heater and set it up in the middle of the room.

In the kitchen, I found a can of pork and beans. Hanna and I cut some strips of bacon, cut slices of bread and opened a can of pineapple. There wasn't anything else there to eat. I was suddenly struck by the curious thought: I was living in Germany but everything we were fixing to eat had come from some foreign country. Even the bread was baked by Hanna from American flour.

'Oh, Herr Russell,' Hanna said, 'I'm so embarrassed for my country because we don't have enough coal to heat your apartment.'

I looked at her.

'Well, Hanna,' I said finally. 'Well. Well.'

Sometimes it is a simple thing that people say which makes your eyes moist.

When I went back into the living room, the undignified three had thrown themselves on the rug in front of the glowing electric heater. They saw the beans and were pleased.

'That's better than the Waldorf,' said Richard.

'Better than a *Smørbrod*,' said Niles, seating himself cross-legged.

'Better than an Alabama barbecue,' said Jane and that was the nicest compliment of all. We sat around on the rug in front of the heater and ate beans.

'Even eating beans makes you think of home,' said Jane. Niles quickly saw the look of homesickness pass her face, and quickly laughed.

'On a trip through France once,' he said, rubbing his long nose with a reflective forefinger, 'I found myself eating lunch in a small arbor in the sunshine. Around the edge of my plate a typical French proverb had been lettered: "When working," I read, "one does what he can. When eating, he exerts himself." '

Hanna had found a bottle or so of red wine, one of which she opened and placed on the floor by my side. We finished the pineapple, then filled our glasses with Italian wine.

'Here's to peace,' said Jane, lifting her glass in that wistful toast which we heard so often. 'May peace come soon.'

We emptied our glasses on that. Behind the long blue curtains the wind could be heard rattling the windows.

'Listen to the wind,' Niles said, shivering and drawing closer to the heater. 'Think of four or five million soldiers facing each other on the front, their feet half-frozen in their boots, their fingers so numb that they couldn't pull a trigger if it were necessary.' He drank from his wine glass. 'Winters like this one are not kind to anybody. I read in a newspaper[7] a story about a fire in Rudow, near Berlin. A mother left her three small children alone at home while she went out into the cold to search for something to eat, and I mean "search". While she was gone on her hunt for food, the kitchen stove set the house on fire, and the three small children burned to death. Their father is a soldier at the front.'

The wind whistled outside. I put a pillow under my elbow and looked into the red electric coils. The wine warmed us, and soon the bottle was empty. Hanna had thoughtfully provided for us: I found two more bottles behind the tiny electric stove.

Because of the blackout, we had to turn the lights off before we opened the draperies and the windows to let the cigarette smoke out of the room. We talked in the flicker of white candles and the red glow of the heater.

Niles was in a talkative mood. He was also restless, I could see, but I knew of no particular reason. 'Jane,' he asked, 'you have been in Germany a week or so. What is your impression of the morale of the people?'

Jane considered a moment before she spoke. 'Niles, from

[7] B.Z. am Mittag, Berlin

what I have seen and understood – and I don't speak any German – people seem to be divided against themselves. Maybe that doesn't make sense, but I mean by that that I have heard lots of people grumbling about the shortages and the food and even the war, but at the same time I hear practically everybody greet each other with "Heil Hitler." '

'"Heil Hitler" doesn't mean too much,' Niles said.

'What do young people have to look forward to in Germany?' Jane asked thoughtfully.

'Not much,' answered Richard. 'The main principle of Nazi-ism is that the individual shall be no more than what the State wants him to be. The average German boy cannot pass the Nazi Party by. If he is not a member, he will get nowhere in his profession or calling. If he joins the Party, his every step is guided; in other words, dictated. His military education and the one-sided propaganda to which he is constantly subjected keep him from knowing that any system other than Nazi-ism exists in the world. This is Nazi-ism's greatest threat to the world – the impression of its hateful ideas on the pliable minds of youth.'

I filled the glasses once more from the fat wine bottle.

We talked until late. I had to go downstairs to unlock the door and let them out.

Later, when I was ready for bed, I turned out the lights and opened the draperies and the window. Berlin was a no-city city out there in the black. I could see occasional flashes of light from the S-Bahn and the subways. There were noises of unseen automobiles passing along the street by the Tiergarten. I even heard funny little scraps of guttural conversation drifting up to me, and saw the lighted ends of cigarettes bobbing along the black sidewalk. Over there, where the beacon used to flash from the top of the radio tower, there was blackness. I heard the icy branches of the trees in the park creak as they stirred gently. There were no lights from apartment windows; Berlin was as though some giant had placed a thick blanket over it, to hide the light.

One gets a rather lonesome and sad feeling looking out his

window at a blacked-out city. It seems impossible that there can ever be light again.

One more month gone, I thought grimly.

I lit a cigarette and went to bed.

CHAPTER SEVEN

IT WAS A MIDNIGHT in February, 1940, and the darkened Berlin city bus in which I rode was filled with well-dressed people, the theater crowd on its way home. Only a small blue lamp burned in the ceiling of the bus, shedding an eerie, ghostly light over us passengers.

We swayed along the dark streets, sitting in dead silence. Suddenly, from about halfway down the row of seats, I heard a drunk muttering. 'Damn these shortages,' the voice said in a strong Berlin slang, 'can't get food, can't get coal, can't get nothing.'

I looked forward in the direction of the speaker. He was a poorly dressed Berlin laborer, his head flopped down on his chest, completely drunk from too much beer (as is often the case with Berliners). He sat there among his elite neighbors, rocking back and forth, muttering about his hard lot under the Nazi régime. I was apprehensive for the safety of the old worker.

There was a stir at the back end of the rocking bus. A Storm Trooper, clad in a long, sinister black overcoat came down the aisle. He roughly grabbed the drunk worker by the shoulder.

'What did I just hear you say?' he yelled in a good imitation of Adolf Hitler's oratory. The other passengers, the well-dressed ones, simply looked on passively and stirred themselves with distaste at the sight of the S.S. man.

The drunk old laborer was possessed of enough sense to know that he was in danger. He pretended to be even drunker than he was, which in my opinion did not need much pretending.

'What did he say?' the drunk repeated three or four times, slobbering with every sentence. 'Now, I ask you, who said what?'

The Storm Trooper, seeing that he was only making a fool out of himself before all the passengers, turned to the man sitting next to the laborer.

'I need you as a witness,' the S.S. man said in ringing tones. 'What did this traitor just say?'

The drunk's well-dressed neighbor shrugged the Storm Trooper's hand from his shoulder. 'I, my good man?' he said icily. 'Do you think I am sitting here to listen to the babble of sots? Do you think I have nothing better to do?'

Every ear in the bus was trained on the Storm Trooper; every person feared for the worker and, through that unconscious guilty feeling which everybody in Germany finally gets, feared that something might happen to them, too. In spite of their anxiety, however, their sympathies were obviously against the S.S. man. He turned in despair to a man sitting just in front of the drunk.

'Will you please repeat what this man just said against the government?' the S.S. man asked.

'Why, what man?' the passenger inquired innocently. 'I haven't heard a single thing. I have been sound asleep, and if you will just let me alone, I will go back to sleep.'

The passengers were so antagonistic to the youthful Storm Trooper that even he could feel it. There were of course several people sitting there in the gloom who would have liked to tell the S.S. man what the worker had said, but they did not dare to brave the general animosity.

Yes, it is a curious thing how intangible feelings can sometimes grow quite passively to become a force, unseen, unspoken, unrecognizable – but very real. The Storm Trooper left the bus at the next stop, and the passengers relaxed once more as we crawled through the dark streets.

As we rode, I remembered a story which an elderly army officer told me recently. He is an officer of the old Prussian school, neither Nazi nor non-Nazi, and very correct in every respect. He was riding on the S-Bahn from Potsdam to Berlin with one of his younger and more ardent officers. The two officers were on their way to Berlin for leave of a week end. Inside and outside, the train was blacked-out.

Suddenly, from somewhere in the darkness of the car, a grating, feminine voice complained loudly, 'You stop pushing me!'

From the same unseen spot came a quiet masculine voice in answer, 'But, madam, I haven't pushed you.'

Every German in the car listened to the argument. Anything, anything to break the monotony.

'Oh, yes you did!' the unpleasant voice yelled. 'Don't you try to lie yourself out of it!'

Again the old officer heard the dignified answer, 'I'm very sorry, madam, but you are obviously mistaken. I have not touched you.'

The old officer sighed, and dismissed the quarrel as the usual bickering in which Berliners love to engage. But to his intense embarrassment, the young officer with whom he was riding sprang up in the darkened car and shouted, 'This will have to be settled!'

Several Germans, seated in the security of dark corners, tittered.

The young officer might have blushed, but it could not be seen in the darkness. 'Did you push this lady or not, sir?' he asked in ringing tones. In the meantime, the long S-Bahn train was grinding to a stop, at Grunewald Station.

'I said I didn't touch this lady,' the masculine voice answered firmly. 'There is nothing else to the matter.'

'He did so, he did so,' the unpleasant voice shrilled.

The train had stopped. The young officer, making an issue over the stupid quarrel, flung open the door, jumped out onto the blacked-out platform and shouted into the darkness at the guard: 'This train stays here!'

The train guard, who had probably been working for twelve hours straight and who just couldn't be bothered with any extra trouble, flashed his green lantern at the engineer. The doors of the long train came shut with a crash, leaving the impetuous young officer standing alone on the dark platform. As the train pulled out of the Grunewald Station, the old officer felt his face grow red and inwardly thanked his stars that there was no illumination. The passengers in the coach enjoyed a good laugh.

Niles sent me word one day that he had gone to fight with the

Finns against the U.S.S.R. I held the short note in my hand and stared out the window. Traffic sped by as usual over the hard-packed snow. Pedestrians strolled along, glancing up curiously at our Embassy windows. Niles gone, swallowed up into a crazy conflict in a futile effort to retain his pride as a human being. His action made me ashamed because I had not taken up a gun and gone out to fight for the things I believed in and loved.

Richard came in, a bundle of letters under his arm. 'Hello, Bill,' he greeted me, and then paused. 'What's wrong?'

I handed him the note. He read it and whistled.

Joe stuck his head casually in the door. 'Good morning, Consul Stratton,' he said. 'Got an applicant to see you, Bill.'

'What does he want?' I asked.

Richard laid the note down on my desk. 'I'll see you later,' he said. 'That's astonishing news, though.' He left.

'He wants preference,' Joe said.

'What kind of preference?'

'Well, he says that his fiancée got her visa at Stuttgart last summer. Right after she got her visa, they got married. Now his wife is over in the United States, and she has had a baby already.'

'And?'

'Now, her husband wants preference.'

'As what? Husbands of aliens don't get any preference under the law.'

'Oh, no. This is entirely different. This applicant says that he wants first preference as the father of an American citizen.'

'Citizen?'

'Sure. His baby.'

I stared at Joe. We sometimes thought that we had heard all the fancy stories and exploded all the tricks, but almost every day brought something new. 'Explain to the applicant,' I instructed Joe slowly, 'that he has no preference. Nobody is an American citizen until he is twenty-one years old.'

The administration of Nazi Germany is shot through with paradoxes.

I am not a politician, so I have not written a political book.

I have put down the small things that happened to small people in the hope that they would give the best picture of Germany as it is today.

Still, I must at least mention one or two of the men who rule Germany. In the next chapter I shall deal with Adolf Hitler, and here I will set down a few sentences about the lesser lights, the satellites.

There is Heinrich Himmler, a little chinless man with a nil personality whose job is to keep the Nazis in power and the person of one Adolf Hitler reasonably intact.

The Frenchman Vidoc, prefect of police under Napoleon, was the author of a remark which would indicate that the Gestapo chief for Germany was well chosen: 'If you want to be a good policeman,' said Vidoc, 'you must first be an extra fine thief.'

The little man Himmler is feared by every cowardly person in Germany and hated by the others. Unmarried and completely unsociable, he finds himself more at home in a guarded underground office than attending a social function where he must look in the eye those persons whose private lives he has under surveillance.

Then there is rolypoly Field Marshal Goering, second in command of the Germans and Hitler's successor. Goering is well liked by most Germans, and is the only one of the leading Nazis who was born of an aristocratic family. When Goering appears on a Berlin movie screen, strutting and wielding his massive mace, audiences generally snicker. Jokes concerning Goering are generally harmless, and on the order of the following one: He had the telephone company install a massive telephone for him, so he could dial with his mace instead of a pencil. Hermann Goering is more of a Prussian and a German than a Nazi. There is a difference.

Another leader, and Hitler's one-time choice to succeed himself and Goering should they both die, is Rudolf Hess. He is a rather colorless individual about whom not much is known except that he is a Nazi. It would have been hard to picture Hess as head of the German State. When Hitler has an especially unpleasant bit of news to give the German nation, he lets Rudolf Hess tell it.[1]

The Reich Minister for Religion, Hans Kerrl, is a gay old rascal who is frequently seen in Berlin dives until the wee hours of the morning. Richard once saw this leader of all German churches sitting in the Kunstler Eck at four o'clock in the morning, heavily drunk, playfully chucking a pretty waitress under the chin.

The *Gauleiter* of the Nuremberg district and the owner of one of the world's more stinking publications, *Der Sturmer*, is Julius Streicher. I think it is a fact that Streicher has committed so many crimes and stolen so much money from the Party that even the Nazis couldn't cover up his crimes any longer, as was the recent rumor. Streicher was put on trial, secretly of course, by the Nazis and found guilty of every charge. At the time this was written, his fate was in the hands of his dearest and best friend, one Adolf Hitler. He probably was able to wriggle his way out of the mess.

These are some of Germany's leaders. These men who were formerly nothing have risen to unprecedented power over their fellow men, not through their own abilities or worth, but only because they were lucky enough to get on the Adolf Hitler bandwagon while it was still uncrowded.

There has been one slight cloud to mar the undisputed sway of the Nazis. Since the beginning of the present war, many of the Nazis' powers have been usurped by the army. It would not be exaggeration to say that there has been a mild revolution in the German government, a change over from absolute Party control to a combined Party-Army control. This is not pleasing to the power-mad Nazis, but there is not much they can do about it. As one example of this change in power, final censorship of what goes into German newspapers and magazines and what is broadcast over the official radio stations rests with men selected

[1] Undoubtedly, Rudolf Hess was one of the Fuehrer's closest friends before he flew to England. It is difficult to believe that the flight was not arranged with Hitler's express knowledge and permission.

by the War Ministry. The Propaganda Ministry still censors, but it can be superseded at any time by the War Ministry, and frequently is.

The most hated man in Germany is the little cripple, Dr. Paul Joseph Goebbels.

In the three years spent in Germany, I have never heard one kind word spoken on his behalf. The most that Germans would say for Goebbels was that he is a speaker. In fact, Goebbels literally talked himself into the position he occupies today. He is no Nazi or Communist or Socialist, or anything else but an opportunist of the brassiest sort. This is the man to whom is entrusted the political, moral and literary education of eighty million people.

In the next chapter 1 shall record several stories concerning Goebbels in his relationship to Adolf Hitler during the old *Mein Kampf* days. Here, I want to write a few sentences about Goebbels in his role as director of the Ministry for Propaganda and Peoples' Enlightenment.

The entire German film industry is under Goebbels' control. His rules for scenario-writing and picture-making are strict, binding and sometimes stupid. These rules are effective only in stifling creative work.

The brilliant German film actor and director, Gustav Gruendgens, who occasionally is in trouble with the authorities at the Propaganda Ministry, told a friend of mine his recipe for getting films past the censors:

'I try to direct nine bad films for every good one,' he said. 'Then nobody will notice.'

One day I was part of a crowd outside the Adlon Hotel. The public was waiting for a glimpse of Prince Regent Paul, of Jugoslavia. Dr. Goebbels appeared unexpectedly, strode across the sidewalk and climbed into a waiting car. Approximately half the Germans in the crowd deliberately turned around and looked in the opposite direction. The others gave no cheer, no Nazi salute.

Actresses who are nice to the little club-footed Doctor find that their professional paths are smoothed. Those who spurn his favors find every door closed to them.[2]

One must admit that Goebbels is adept at propaganda. The only significant failure he has had in the propaganda field is a curious one. He has forced the newspapers to run the best and most flattering pictures of himself. He had has his crews of writers dish up the most flattering news stories of his doings. He has visited the poorer quarters of Berlin and had stories published about how much he has done for unfortunates. But in spite of all this favorable press, Goebbels has not fooled a single German about his real character. They still hate his guts.

The only people who see good movies in Germany these days are the censors.

A few American films are bought each year, the number constantly declining. It is the policy of the Propaganda Ministry to buy only the worst American films, for two good reasons: poor films are cheaper than good ones, and the German film industry does not want its own poor films compared with fine American films by the German public.

Criticism about the few American films which are allowed is limited to a few scant lines in the newspapers.[3]

The reviews are generally lukewarm; the reviewers are under orders to be strictly objective and to refrain from praise.

---

[2] The Siegessäule (Victory Column) in Berlin, a tall column atop which perches a hideous gold angel, was moved by the Nazis from its former location in front of the Reichstag building to a new circle in the center of the East-West Axis. Its height was increased by the construction of a new base. Berlin quip: 'Why did they have to put the angel up higher?'

Answer: 'So Goebbels couldn't get to her.'

[3] An example of the curious lengths to which Goebbels will go to gain his ends was the German film, Lied der Wüste, ('Song of the Desert'), which starred Sarah Leander, the Swedish film star. Miss Leander, seeing what a poor job the film cutters were doing with the film, tried to take a lot of the film with her to Sweden and have it finished there. This made Goebbels angry. He was made even angrier, however, when Miss Leander refused to have her photograph taken with a German soldier as part of a propaganda stunt. Dr. Goebbels thereupon forbade reviews to be written about Lied der Wüste. So, although the film was playing at Berlin's largest theater, not a line appeared about it in any newspaper.

The long-suffering German movie public, on the other hand, ardently likes American films.

The German film writer, about to sit down to his typewriter to dash out a scenario, must remember the following hard and fast rules set by Dr. Goebbels.[4]

No movies may depict marital trouble. Marriage must always be pictured as a happy affair. A married person may not fall in love with somebody else. He or she may not cease to love his or her mate. No divorce material may appear in the movies.

No films on political subjects. The director can never be certain that Hitler will not change his political policy toward the foreign country concerned in the middle of the filming.

No large-scale musical films. They are likely to give the population lush ideas.

No spy films. This prohibition does not include the official government propaganda films instructing the people where to look for spies ('everywhere') and what to do about them.

No gangster films. No films may depict crime.

No films based on the old operettas whose scenes were laid in Russia.

No films which glorify or more than mention the Church.

Anti-Semitic films are encouraged, but no director will make them. Reasons: The directors don't want to dirty their hands with such filthy material, and the German movie public can't be induced to pay money to see such films.

No movies about America. As bad as they paint American life, it is still attractive enough to make the average German want to go to America.

Censors in the Propaganda Ministry have full power to cross out scenes and dialogue, and no writer dares even to question their decisions.

To illustrate how thoroughly the tenets of Nazi-ism are carried out in propaganda, I heard of a case where the innocent word 'church' was ordered deleted from a film dialogue.

Another scenario contained the following proposed scene:

---

[4] Told to me by a leading director in the German film industry.

A soldier, fleeing from the German army (the script implied that this occurred on the Polish border) was shot down by the Germans. He fell wounded into the dust, and crawled painfully and slowly across the road. He weakly clasped his arms about a road-side crucifix which stood there, and in the shadow of the cross he died. The Propaganda Ministry approved the script, but made one significant change. The crucifix under which the soldier died was changed to a road sign.

Dr. Goebbels is the butt of so many sharply pointed jokes that one almost regrets having to record another. The Berliners, whom he tries so hard to make like him, dismiss their Propaganda Minister with the dry remark: 'When Goebbels dies, they're going to have to kill his mouth extra.'

Hanna, who usually abstains from speaking about her rulers, or mentioning political subjects in any way, surprised me one day by telling me a joke about Paul Joseph Goebbels.

Dr. Goebbels was on the point of drowning in a lake when a young boy jumped in and saved him. Goebbels was not ungrateful. 'How can I repay you, my young fellow?' he asked the boy. 'Just tell me anything you want and it shall be yours.'

'Well, I think I would like to have a State Funeral,' the young boy answered.

Goebbels was surprised. 'At your age? Why, you're not going to die that soon.'

'Oh, no?' said the boy. 'Just you wait till I get home and tell my father whom I saved from drowning.'

And another: At one time Adolf Hitler found himself in urgent need of a week of sunshine for the annual Nazi Party rally to be held in Nuremberg. Hitler sent pompous Hermann Goering up to Heaven to ask God for seven days of sunshine. Goering came back from his trip, and told the irritated Hitler that God had promised only one day of sunshine.

Hitler sent Dr. Goebbels up to Heaven to see if he couldn't make a better bargain. However, Goebbels returned to report that he had talked himself blue in the face but that God had promised him only three days of sunshine.

Enraged, Adolf Hitler decided to go on up himself and set matters right. On being presented to God, Hitler asked why so little courtesy had been accorded his emissaries.

God explained it to him. 'When Goering came up to Heaven to make his request for you, he stole my golden staff. And when Dr. Goebbels came, he ran away with my guardian angels. The next time you want to ask me a favor, I suggest that you come yourself.'

These are the men, the most powerful men, in Germany. With one exception, these men are in the Nazi racket for what they can get out of it – and they get plenty. The one exception is the Fuehrer, and he is sincere in his beliefs.

There is a remark which I often heard during my stay in Germany. It may interest the reader.

'There is only one real National Socialist, and his name is Adolf Hitler.'

I shivered in the early morning chill of the Anhalter Station in Berlin. It was five-thirty in the morning, but even at that hour the large, unheated station was full of people. In war time Germans have learned to arrive at railway stations one or two hours ahead of train time, in order to get a seat. I sleepily followed the porter who carried my suitcase and three diplomatic pouches. We found my train, the windows of which were crowded with faces peering out.

'Ich glaube, der ist ganz voll,' observed the porter discouragingly.

I looked through the windows at the crowded compartments and overflowing corridors. I agreed with the porter that to look for a seat was useless. I cursed under my steamy breath. Ordinarily, members of our Embassy who were sent on courier trips had first-class tickets. But since the beginning of this war, first-class has been abolished in German trains operating in the interior of the Reich. Even the purchase of a second-class ticket was no guarantee that one would have a seat; a second-class ticket assured one that at least he would have the privilege of looking for standing room in a second-class car. I glumly followed the porter down the whole length of the train. Up near the front, he stopped before an open car door and put the precious bags down. The train was so full of people that the porter could not even carry the bags inside for me. I paid him off, and climbed the steps into the car vestibule. It was so packed with people that I could not move any farther. I ignored the dirty looks I got from the crowd for making it move aside to make room for me, and set the diplomatic pouches down on the floor. I turned my suitcase up on end, and sat down on it. Right at my back was the toilet door. The toilet on a European train is a primitive affair set at each end of the coach and is for the use of all sexes.

I took out a cigarette and lit it. Almost immediately a fat *Hausfrau* standing right at my elbow said angrily, '*Dieser Wagon ist Nicht Raucher, Mein Herr!*'

I glanced up at the sign which stated that one could not smoke at this end of the car. I realized sickeningly that for the next twelve hours I would be confined to this small space, unable to move about, unable to smoke. I tossed my cigarette reluctantly onto the platform. 'Damn!' I said to myself, and that was mildly put.

The Embassy sent a courier around Germany every two weeks to take confidential mail to and from our eleven consulates, including the one at Prague. These courier sacks, of which I had three on this trip, often contained secret codes and other matter so confidential that they had to be watched constantly while one was traveling. There are a lot of people who would like to get their hands on a diplomatic pouch, and they will go to almost any ends to do so.

There are several countries in Europe where one would sooner publish his secret codes in a newspaper than trust them to the mercies of the official post office of that country. Germany is certainly one such country. Yet, our Embassy has been frequently too lax about allowing secret dispatches and codes to go through the German post office rather than pay the cost of a courier.

One month, shortly before the outbreak of war, I was trans-

ferred from the Immigration section at my own request, and
assigned to the Mail Room to take the place of the regular clerk
who was on vacation. We regularly received shipments of diplomatic mail from Washington, usually on American ships to cut
down the danger of tampering. One day I was given a packet of
envelopes containing new secret codes. These envelopes had
been carefully handled and sealed in Washington, sent in a
diplomatic pouch entrusted to the personal care of the captain
of the ship on which they traveled, brought from Holland to
Berlin by couriers carefully selected for their integrity. I put the
envelopes in a safe, according to instructions, to keep them until
a courier should be sent around to the consulates inside
Germany and in Prague and Danzig. They were there a week
before the consul in charge of the consular section of the
Embassy came to the Mail Room and asked to see them. I of
course took the valuable envelopes out of the safe, and handed
them to the consul. To my surprise he told me to send them out
that afternoon, by registered mail. I said that I had been
instructed to send them out by American courier, only.
'Nonsense,' the consul said. 'We can save a lot of money this
way.' I had the German assistant in the Mail Room take them to
the German post office and register them.

An envelope from the Embassy, registered, plastered all over
with red wax seals and addressed to American Consulates inside
Germany just screams to the Gestapo, 'Here I am! Open me up
and see what's inside!'

Some time later, another consul asked me what had become
of the codes. I told him.

'My God!' he said.

I sat there in the crowded vestibule and remembered a story
I had heard of pouch-tampering during the World War. The
Dutch sent their diplomatic pouches to their legation in London
via the regular ferry between Holland and England. During the
four hours' trip, the contents of the official Dutch pouches were
removed and photostated down to the last sheet. The Dutch
never knew what was going on, since the pouches arrived in
London and in Rotterdam with their locks and seals untouched.

The English merely used the old trick of pulling the threads out of the bottoms of the pouches, removing the contents, photographing them, replacing the envelopes and sewing the sacks up again with the same thread which they had removed.

I don't want to leave the impression that the British are more unscrupulous about pilfering their neighbor's diplomatic post than other nations. The British themselves attach diplomatic pouches to their couriers' arms with small chains which cannot be removed in transit. We Americans are a bit too naïve about our diplomatic pouches; we even sent them on German boats before the outbreak of war when there was no convenient American ship available and we never sent a man along with the pouches.

The heavy wax seals which we trustingly put on the envelopes may easily be removed by sliding a hot razor under them. After the contents of the envelope have been examined, the seal may be stuck back in its original place.

Practically every foreign country has a supply of wax seals, wax, paper, and envelopes which are identical with those used by other countries. The U.S.S.R. is perhaps the most adroit in the use of these falsifications.

From one of our Paris-Berlin-Warsaw couriers I heard a story about a Russian courier. He was disliked by his foreign colleagues with whom he sometimes traveled. For both personal and official reasons these colleagues wished to get at the contents of the Russian's pouches. During one long and tiring trip across the plains of Poland, the Russian courier stuffed his pouches up over the train's steam pipes and dozed off. Soon enough the heat from the pipes had melted the wax seals and a foreign courier seized the golden opportunity to examine the contents of the Russian's diplomatic post.

In spite of all the discomfort of traveling in wartime Germany, I was glad that I had been chosen to make a courier trip. It gave one a chance to get out of Berlin for a week or two; one visited other consulates and got the views of men stationed all over Germany and one saw for himself what was actually going on.

There was one serious drawback to making a courier trip. This drawback was another official, against whom I have a deep and abiding prejudice. Each of us has such a person in our memory. Unfortunately my such person happened to be our Embassy Disbursing Officer – the man who made out the checks.

After one had made a courier trip – which involved putting out a large sum of money – our Berlin Disbursing Officer would take several months to come across with a check to reimburse the person who made the trip. In my case, after the two courier trips which I made for the Embassy, I had to live for several months on borrowed money before I got mine back from the Disburser's Office.

We had a little clerk in the Embassy who is every inch a lady, but somewhat shy. This clerk is not an American, but she speaks excellent English – and several other languages. One day she was in the Disburser's Office, and attempted to explain to this august personage a new ruling which had come from Washington and about which she knew more than he did.

The Disbursing Officer looked coolly at the shy lady, and said, 'I can't read English.' The clerk did not understand that the officer was being heavily sarcastic, and tried again to explain the new ruling. 'I can't understand English, either,' the Disbursing Officer said, leaning back in his swivel chair. The lady clerk was so embarrassed and angry that she made a vow – as many others of us did – never to return to that man's office.

This same man, this official of the United States government, authored a memorandum to a friend of mine which I shall always keep in my possession.

Early in September, 1939, as I have written, the Embassy chartered two special train coaches to take American women and children out of Berlin. The female employees of our Embassy were strongly advised to go to Copenhagen on the train, to await further orders. Some decided to go, and some decided to remain.

On orders from Washington, the Embassy paid the railroad fares of the girls to Copenhagen.

After they had arrived at the Danish capital, tired, broke and discouraged, to their dismay they received telegrams from the Embassy stating that they had been fired effective as of the day of their departure from Berlin. This whole business was engineered by our Disbursing Officer. One clerk, who had a mother to support, had to arrange for passage back to America as best she could. Another one of our clerks who could book passage on no boat before the middle of October found life so expensive in Denmark that she had to return to Berlin and live with friends until her sailing date. The Disbursing Officer raged at her for returning and, after thinking things over, sent her the following classic: 'It would be appreciated if you would refund 31.90 marks which the government paid for your railway ticket Berlin-Copenhagen as you have invalidated your evacuation by returning to Berlin.'

The former employee, who was not rich at all and who had had to pay for her return to Germany, was forced to dig up the price of her ticket and pay it to the Disbursing Officer.

The train pulled slowly out of the station, half an hour late in starting. There was no hustle and bustle about the departure; no loud 'all aboards,' no shouting of 'good-byes' from friends to friends. There was merely a 'Close the doors,' echoed hollowly from the loud-speaker system, and the train silently rolled away. I glumly surveyed my traveling companions. On their part, the Germans in the vestibule looked curiously at the diplomatic pouches which I had propped against my upturned suitcase. I knew that I had a long vigil ahead of me. I glanced at the Germans to see if one of them could possibly be a government agent. I decided that none was, because they had all been in the vestibule ahead of me and they could not have known that I would pick that particular car to sit in. Still, to guard against the possibility that somebody might try to snatch one of the bags I had to keep my eye on them constantly, or let my foot rest casually against them.

The *Hausfrau*, the one who had objected to my smoking, folded her arms and resigned herself to a long journey. She was still feeling a glow of moral satisfaction for having made me observe the rules. Nothing could affect her now, not heat nor cold nor weariness nor anything but non-observance of authority. Her nerves were steeled against the long hours ahead.

The train gathered speed slowly as it rolled through Berlin's snow-covered suburbs. I noticed that the air was becoming chillier. Quickly suspicious, I reached over and touched the heating apparatus; it was dead cold. The engineer had shut the steam off the moment the train had left Anhalter Bahnhof, to save coal.

Day was beginning to break. The snow-covered fields were streaked with gray light, giving the appearance of half-cleaned landscape painting. I looked at the Germans, one by one, trying to guess what they were like and whether they were Nazis or not. In addition to the *Hausfrau*, there were five persons sitting or standing in the vestibule. There were many more people packed into the long corridor which extended around the corner of the toilet, but I could not see them. Sitting next to me on his suitcase was a browned man, probably a small-town storekeeper who owned a farm on the side. His suit was of the usual conservative German gray-black (does not soil quickly), and in his lapel he wore a Nazi Party swastika. Two young girls stood near the door, about twenty-two years of age. Their hair was clumsily tied up over their heads, their dresses were neat, clean prints, and they wore dark gray coats. In the region of their hips there were excess bulges which unfortunately seem to afflict most German women. Their faces looked old, and although we American men are wont to complain about the amount of paint, powder and lipstick which goes on our American girls' faces, I assure you that the unfinished product is even less attractive. The faces of German girls resemble a painter's canvas, on which nothing had yet been painted. From their bulging coat sleeves, I guessed that the girls had muscles which were well developed from years of intensive sport. Their practical knapsacks lay on the floor. They also looked as though they could stand there for hours without complaining.

Two young soldiers were also in the vestibule, clad in the gray-green of the German infantry. They had laid their knapsacks on the floor and had exchanged their stiff military hats for tiny khaki caps, cocked jauntily over their ears. Their faces were healthy and they looked strong. The inevitable heavy black boots were on their feet and legs, and around their waists they wore wide leather belts to which were fastened ammunition pockets and pistols. They talked together in loud, laughing tones, glancing at the young girls constantly.

I extracted a small book from my overcoat pocket. It was a Penguin edition of a novel which I had bought in the Anhalter Station. I read the first paragraph three times in boredom, then went on to the second paragraph without even having compre- hended the meaning of the first. A shadow fell over my book, and I looked up. I saw a young mother, her hair straggling down her neck, a kicking baby in her arms. She obviously wanted to get past me, though I couldn't at first imagine why. Then I remembered the toilet door against which I sat, and I sprang up in embarrassment. None of the Germans in the vestibule was even slightly fazed by the incident. In fact, when the mother and baby squeezed back out of the door again, the Nazi storekeeper- farmer said sympathetically, 'They never want to go until they get on a train, do they?'

The mother laughed and nodded. She continued to shove her way between the crowded passengers back to the special compartment which is reserved for mothers on every train with- out extra cost.

I opened my book again, but it was too cold to read. The train rocked from side to side and actually seemed to be speeding. Because of the biting cold air, the two soldiers stamped their boots heavily against the floor to keep blood circulating in their feet. One of them accidentally kicked my diplomatic pouches and he looked down curiously to see what his foot had struck. Reading words in a strange language written on the outside of the sack, he stared at the sack fixedly, then he stared at me. He called his com- rade's attention to the courier pouches and they both stared for a while. Then they started looking at the two girls again.

I glanced at my watch. Only three hours had gone by. My hands were numb from the cold, and I was hungry. I thought of a dining car, and almost laughed out loud because the idea seemed so absurd. When I pulled a bar of American chocolate out of my pocket and unwrapped the silver wrapping, an electric shock ran through the vestibule. The other passengers eyed my chocolate openly and hungrily. I felt suddenly embarrassed. There wasn't enough to pass around, so I slid the rest of the bar back into my over-coat pocket.

The train rolled on, past snowy hills, whistling mournfully over intersections, rumbling over bridges and the ice became thicker on the windows, inside and outside. The two soldiers had struck up an inevitable friendship with the two girls. They began to tell jokes to each other, to exchange experiences and laugh over them. The girls told the soldiers that they were on their way home for a three days' vacation from the munitions factory where they worked.

'Just look at my fingers,' I heard one of them say as she held up her hands for inspection. I glanced casually at her hands and saw that the fingers were completely yellow. 'We girls in the munitions factory all have these yellow fingers. It is caused by the gunpowder we handle.'

'Do you have to work very hard?' asked one of the soldiers.

'Oh, it's not so bad,' said the other girl. 'We do have to work long hours, but our foreman has explained to us that long hours are necessary if Germany is to have all the bullets she needs.'

'And can you quit the factory when you want to?' the other soldier asked curiously. I looked at the red and yellow sign which hangs in every railway car: 'Watch out what you say; the enemy is listening.' I squirmed, and adjusted my necktie. But the girls were obviously not concerned with the remote possibility of an enemy overhearing them in that cold train vestibule.

'No, we can't quit until the war is over,' the girl told the soldiers. 'Our foreman explained that to us, too. He said that when a soldier at the front gets tired or homesick he can't leave his post and go home. We are just like soldiers, the foreman told us. We have to keep on working until they let us go.'

The four young people continued to talk together, flirting and making dates which each of them must have known could never be kept.

I looked at my little book again. I had read only twenty pages in all these hours of riding. To one who is acting out a great play, taking a major or even a minor part in an event which affects the lives of hundreds of millions of people, small black words on the pages of a book seem trivial. I was too restless to read.

A shadow passed across the book again and interrupted my thoughts, if not my reading. It was the mother with her child again, and I stood up dutifully to let them go in.

The door clicked after a time, and I rose again to let the mother and the baby make their exit.

Time passed. The soldiers and the girls had exchanged addresses with each other – a custom so common in Germany that by now I think every German should have every other German's address.

At Nuremberg a few passengers got out, the two healthy, muscle-bulging girls among them. After a long wait in the snow-filled station, the train pulled out again and I found myself missing the gay chatter among the girls and the soldiers which had helped to pass the time.

Darkness began to settle in the vestibule. It was the middle of the afternoon, but the daylight was already fading. I shivered.

The two soldiers looked at each other lonesomely. They were obviously thinking of the two friendly girls who had just got out of the car, of the war, of all the boredom and misery and danger which they themselves had to face.

There was a long silence. Finally, one soldier slid his heavy leather gun belt around his waist and said to his comrade, 'Oh, well – '

His companion looked drearily out of the ice-covered window and repeated meaninglessly, 'Yeah. Yeah – '

More time passed. I stirred myself. The train had stopped at a small station, and I got up to look out the window. I struggled with the window until it came loose from the ice which held it, and lowered the glass. I looked out at the snow and the ice which covered everything. The few employees who worked on the station platform seemed more frozen than alive. Their beards were iced. A vender of bottled drinks pushed his wagon to the train windows, but he could not sell anything because the contents of his bottles were frozen solid. Another vender sawed meat which was piled on a wagon; it was too frozen to be cut with a knife. I looked back to see what was holding up our train.

I could see soldiers disembarking from the back car, their equipment already piled on the snow. They were probably destined for an air field hidden in one of the near-by forests.

I heard a grumbling in the vestibule, and looked around behind me. The *Hausfrau*, who I had sincerely thought was made of iron, was weakening. She sat dejectedly on the end of her suitcase. She raised her head long enough to say sternly, 'Close the window! Can't you see that it is cold enough already?' I obligingly closed the window and sat down again.

With a jerk the train started again. It traveled slowly, but any kind of motion was better than that eternal sitting in stations. I decided to see if by any chance a seat had become vacant. I took the three heavy diplomatic pouches and pushed and shoved my way into the corridor. I saw that a large number of passengers had left the train at Nuremberg. I looked into compartment after compartment, until I finally saw one small vacant seat.

'Is this place free?' I asked.

Nobody in the compartment answered me at first. They sat there, cold and resigned, not wanting to be crowded any further by another passenger. Then a gray-haired woman answered me reluctantly.

'Yes, I think so.'

With a joy which I cannot describe, I squeezed past the Germans in the corridor who had not imagined that a vacant seat could exist. I got my suitcase, and what with trying to get past people with the four bags (I could not leave my pouches alone for a second, of course) I encountered a lot of Germanic grumbling which I cheerfully ignored. Back in the compartment, I stuffed the bags overhead. The seven other passengers in the dark compartment looked at me tiredly. They were worn out with traveling; they were cold and discouraged. It was a typical winter train crowd.

It grew darker outside. The conductor came through the car,

pulling the flimsy curtains together over the windows. He switched on a tiny, painted-over ceiling light, whose somber glow was even more depressing than total darkness. The train was already five hours late.

One woman stirred herself. 'It's awful,' she said bitterly.

The other passengers looked at her.

'It's just awful,' she repeated, slapping her hands together to warm them.

'Watch out what you say,' spoke a gruff voice. 'A woman's place is in the home already or in the war factories. She should not be making trips on the trains for pleasure.' The speaker sat next to me; he was obviously a Party member. The implied threat in his voice was enough to silence the woman who had complained. The other occupants of our compartment were silent, looking at the woman and the Nazi with no expressions on their faces.

I worried about the safety of my pouches. It was so dim in the compartment that I could hardly see them. I glanced upward constantly to see their shadows above me. It was impossible to sleep, I could not read in the dark, it was even out of the question to relax. It would have been the most sensible thing for the Embassy to send its couriers around Germany in private cars because the courier could have kept a close watch on his pouches, he could have made twice as much speed as the trains and he would not have frozen to death. But the German's wouldn't give us enough gas to make the trips. I often wonder if the German diplomats in the United States had enough gas for their cars, or if they were rationed to a few pints each week. Of course I knew the answer, but it was still something to contemplate.

I must have nodded, for my head jerked suddenly. I opened my eyes and saw shaded lights bobbing outside the frozen windows. The passengers in the compartment were rising to take their suitcases down from the racks. I could not believe it, but we had arrived in Munich.

I miraculously found a porter in the dimly lighted Munich Station. We walked down the platform into the brightly lighted dining room. It was warm there, and I could smell food and see large foaming mugs of beer sitting on cleanly scrubbed wooden tables. Going out into the darkness again, I looked for a taxi. On the opposite side of the street I saw one, out of which some people were climbing. The porter and I rushed madly across the black street, and I saw that there were already several Germans pleading with the taxi driver to take them where they wanted to go.

I stuck my head in the window, too.

'Are you free?' I asked anxiously.

The driver looked me over. 'I can't take you unless you are an official, or unless you have a lot of baggage or unless you are an old woman or unless you are going to have a baby,' he repeated in a parrot-like voice. 'I just told all these people here that I can't let them ride because I would be fined if they caught me.'

I produced my identification card. 'I can't qualify for some of your classifications,' I said, 'but I don't think you will be fined if you let me ride.'

When he saw the identification card from the Berlin President of the Police, he became more cordial. He helped the porter put the pouches into the taxi.

'To the best hotel you've got in Munich,' I said, recklessly.

The hotel to which he took me was full of Munich citizens who had rented rooms because they had no coal or hot water at their homes. I engaged a room, and was taken upstairs in a typical rickety European elevator.

I ran hot water into the large tub, and leaped in joyfully. Of course I had to climb back out again to fetch my soap from my suitcase since even the most expensive European hotels provided no free bars of soap.

After I had eaten and given up my ration cards for what I had eaten and crawled into bed, I could still feel the vibration of the train. My brain could not forget the depressing picture of the vestibule in which I had ridden for so many hours, the snow-blown stations through which we had passed, the frozen bottles of soda pop, the bleak despair written on the passengers' faces.

Those diplomatic pouches spent the night under the blankets with me.

The next morning, I dressed early, ate some breakfast and carried the pouches around to the Consulate. For two hours I talked about conditions in Bavaria with our consul general who was stationed in Munich. There were some things which he preferred telling me rather than to run the risk of setting them down on paper. It seems that our consuls scattered around Germany had more respect for the Germans' ability to search our diplomatic pouches than the Embassy itself had.

The consul general told me that the food situation in Bavaria was far better than in Berlin; vegetables were plentiful and even eggs were to be had. However, all fats, mainly oils and butter, were extremely scarce.

He told me a theory of his – new to me then, but now commonly known in Germany – that the Nazis were systematically using the war as a means of eliminating those groups of people who were not too strong in their adherence to Nazi-ism. For instance, regiments from Munich and Vienna (cities whose populations are less ardent in their belief in Nazi-ism than the military-loving Prussians) had been ordered to the very front line of the fighting in Poland, while the Prussians and the Storm Trooper regiments had been purposely held back. What an opportunity war presents for the calculated elimination of possible opposition! Hundreds of thousands of the people of whom the government was not sure could be shoved up front and killed. The consul general told me that losses in the Bavarian and Tyrolean regiments had been enormous. He told me, but I already knew it, that North German regiments had suffered few casualties.

The Storm Troopers' regiments came through the Polish campaign practically unscathed, German newspaper propaganda to the contrary notwithstanding. Feeling ran high in Bavaria against the S.S., especially among the families who had given up a son or a husband.

The consul told me that one afternoon in Munich, a long trainload of Bavarian youths was waiting in the station before starting off to the front. On the station's platforms stood numerous S.S. men, who had been sent down from Prussia to act as policemen in the Bavarian provinces and capital. As the train pulled out of the station, the soldiers cursed the Storm Troopers, asking why the Black Ones were allowed to stay behind while the Bavarians had to go off to the very front.

I myself later saw several military trains in the Munich Station which had large signs painted in chalk on their sides: 'FAST TRAIN – WARSAW, PARIS, LONDON,' one sign read. 'GOING IN THE DIRECTION OF OUR PROTECTORATE FRANCE,' another stated.

After the consul had dismissed me I parked my pouches in the Consulate safe and walked out into the soft Munich sunshine.

The thousands of tourists who have visited Munich know of its peculiar charm for the stranger. I know of no other city which so completely welcomes the newcomer. The moment one enters Munich, one has a desire to walk and swing one arms, to gaze for hours at the huge old buildings and fountains and palaces from another day, to drink beer and make friends with people.

Munich is a student's city, and the atmosphere of youth penetrates every heart – no matter how old.

Even the Nazis have not ruined Munich. Now you know how nice the city is.

That night, I went to a small cabaret to drink beer, smoke and watch the floor show. The chief attraction was an enormously fat Bavarian comedian named Weissverdl, who kept the crowd of singing, beer-drinking, smiling Germans roaring with his jokes.

I was surprised to hear 'Fatty' tell this joke:

A German and a Dutchman, he told, were standing down on the Netherlands border with Germany (in the days when there was a border), talking over the bad food situation in the Reich. The Dutchman, who had plenty of food in his belly, was sympathetic with the plight of his hungry neighbor.

'I hear that it's so bad in Germany,' he said to the German, 'that you're even eating rats.'

'Gosh, and were those rats good!' the German exclaimed

reminiscently. Then his face fell. 'But now they're all gone, and the government is feeding us *ersatz* rats.'

I left Munich, and visited our consulates in Vienna, Prague, Frankfort, Stuttgart, Cologne, Bremen and Hamburg. Vienna was the saddest place I visited. The city was dead, a shell of the once gay city which was the envy of postwar Europe. There is nothing so melancholy as a dead city which is still inhabited by people.

There are bitter things enough for us to read about today. I will not add to the supply by writing my impressions of Vienna. I will merely express my hope that the city may live again, I should have said 'my belief.'

I rolled into Berlin one afternoon at dusk, into the Stettiner Station. An icy wind was blowing along the platform; there were no porters; outside the station not a single taxi waited. I telephoned the Embassy, and somebody was sent to pick me up.

I was almost glad to see our familiar Embassy building again. I shook the snow off my shoulders as I went into the warm hallway, and remembered that I had a lot of work to do.

CHAPTER EIGHT

IN THE LONG PERIOD which I lived in Berlin, I was invited out innumerable times. I was invited to parties at which diplomats, merchants, artists, pretty young girls, old hags, worthy men, poor hangers-on, rich rascals, proper and improper people, Aryan and non-Aryan people were present.

I attended those parties where the food was good and where the food was bad; parties where much and where little was drunk.

Whatever kind of party it was, there was constantly present one guest – a guest who would not be excluded, even as he could not be persuaded to come in. A guest who really existed, but who at the same time was a ghost. A guest who provided us with puzzles, the solutions of which were impossible in the eyes of decent men.

When the guests knew each other well, their conversation slid immediately to this man. If they did not know each other intimately they first experimented carefully, behaving like two people who are dancing together for the first time.

This guest always became the center of the party. Sometimes early, sometimes late, this time exclusively, that time sharing the spotlight with others. No matter what the circumstances, he was always with us.

His name was Adolf Hitler.

I don't think that I could explain Adolf Hitler. He is a phenomenon; as such, the better one tries to understand him the more Sphinx-like he becomes.

Of the abundance of things which are part of Adolf Hitler, I write only the facts, certified stories, and psychological tendencies which I have learned from authoritative sources.

What I put down here are truths, and not my personal opinions. I must ask the reader to form his own conclusion of this Fuehrer of eighty million people. What the interior of this man is like may be seen from these stories, all told of him by the men and the women he calls his friends.

This man, who once lived in Vienna roofless, who never learned any profession correctly, has only one attitude toward himself: Uncompromising worship of one Adolf Hitler.

He is possessed by the god of language; physically he is also a curiosity.

This man, to whom every possibility for recreation and exercise stands open, appears in public leaning on a balcony railing, or sitting or standing next to his chauffeur in his long car. He has covered thousands of miles sitting silent beside his chauffeur, without once taking the steering wheel in his own hands.

Adolf Hitler could possess the finest horses, and ride on the most beautiful courses. Several years ago, he actually did take one riding lesson in a sternly closed circle of friends. The lesson was a miserable failure, and today Hitler could hardly be associated with any kind of horsemanship.

He has a princely estate in the beautiful Bavarian mountains. Nobody has ever seen him on skis. He does not play tennis, he does not swim, he does not fish, he plays no golf.

Hitler has flown thousands of miles in his airplanes. Although his colleague Benito Mussolini years ago passed examinations in bomber piloting, Adolf Hitler is content to sit in a heated cabin and let himself be flown. During hours of flying, he just sits in his comfortable seat, looking out the window at the landscape below, ignoring the officers and Party members who fly with him.

There is not a bicycle on Hitler's entire private mountain.

The things which give pleasure to other people do not interest Hitler. He is a colossus of inactivity and bodily laziness. There is only one part of his body that is constantly active: his mouth.

As proof of that statement, I have a speaking witness.

Benito Mussolini invited Adolf Hitler to visit Italy for the first time, as his guest. Later, the Italian Duce expressed himself on the subject of his visit to the ambassador of a certain Western power:

'I showed that man Venice,' Mussolini told the ambassador, 'where one finds the most beautiful architecture in the world. I ordered served to him the finest of foods in the most magnificent of rooms.

'Around him sat the most beautiful women of a country blessed with beautiful women. The most expensive wines waited to be drunk. And he?

'What did he do?

'He did nothing. He talked.

'He talked on the Grand Canal, he talked in the hotel corridors, he talked during our automobile trips around the countryside. Nothing, nothing but talk!'

That was in the year 1935, when Benito Mussolini was already a 'big shot' and Hitler still had to become one as far as foreign politics was concerned. Later, things changed.

When Mussolini finally repaid Hitler's Italian visit by coming to Germany in 1937, he again had to listen to the Fuehrer talk.

Hitler himself related to a small circle of friends later that Mussolini's visit had caused him extraordinary worries merely over the matter of the Duce's personal safety while he was in the German Reich. After Mussolini had left Berlin, his jaw jutting out an unusual distance for the benefit of German gapers, Hitler ordered that hourly messages be sent to him from the railway stations through which the Duce's train passed on its way to Italy. Hitler lowered his voice, and told his friends confidentially: 'And what a breath I took when he was finally in Kufstein,[1] I can't tell you at all!'

On the same occasion Hitler related to his awe-struck friends: 'Naturally, I had my elite Storm Troopers with me, who can shoot the whites out of an assassin's eyes at twenty yards, but –' and he paused meditatively, '– once they might shoot too late.

'And then the "Yugoslav"[2],' he continued, 'rode with me through a dark tunnel. Then I really thought again of the dan-

---

[1] A small railway station on the former Austrian-German border.

[2] Hitler used this impolite term to refer to Prince Regent Paul, former ruler of Yugoslavia.

ger of assassination. I can tell you, my heart was so small – I don't know; I guess as small as a pinhead.'

One more note on royal visits to Germany.

When former King Carol of Rumania visited him at Obersalzburg, Adolf Hitler drank a cultivated tea with his guest, and spoke comparatively little – for the simple reason that King Carol answered all of Hitler's high-flown statements with surprising cleverness.

When King Carol had left, as the royal automobile drove down the long winding road of Obersalzburg, Hitler looked after the departing guest, rubbed his hands together in pleasure and astonishment, and said to his attendants:

'There goes a very clever rascal.'

King Carol did him the favor of letting him down with a thud, for a few days later Carol ordered the Fuehrer of the Iron Guard, Codreanu, who was being supported by Nazi money, 'shot in flight' according to approved Balkan custom.

Does Hitler have any friends? One must admit it – yes.

At first there was Roehm, who was shot during the purge of June 30, 1934, because of insubordination to his Fuehrer. Another fast friend was forced to take leave of Hitler.

This time, the cause was brain disintegration The name of Hitler's friend was Schreck,[3] and he was Hitler's personal chauffeur for many years. In the main, Schreck was a genial character who had taken over the court clownship which had formerly been held by fat Putzi Hanfstaengl with his beautiful piano playing. Schreck was a man of the common people, a real Bavarian whose strongest points were his accordion and his hill-billy songs.

Today, the Fuehrer's friends like to describe a picture of a halt by the side of the road during the old *Mein Kampf* days. All the campaign party leaned against Hitler's car, laughing and happily listening to the singing Schreck. From other sources, I learned the text of Adolf Hitler's favorite hill-billy song, one

---

[3] Translation Into English: 'Horror.'

which he ordered Schreck to sing to him hundreds of times. If I remember correctly, the refrain went as follows:

I don't care about my virginity,
I don't care about all of life.
For that girl who took it away from me,
Can't give it back to me again.

When Schreck died, it took the most powerful arguments and persuasion to restrain Adolf Hitler from honoring his faithful chauffeur with a State Funeral.

One of the men who knew best how to dissuade Hitler from carrying out this grotesque State Funeral for a chauffeur was the Fuehrer's last remaining 'du' friend, and certainly one of the most remarkable figures in the leadership of the Third Reich: Heinrich Hoffmann, Germany's only official photographer.

Heinrich Hoffmann is a small, somewhat misgrown, heavy-drinking man. He had the luck to have supported Hitler from the very beginning, although Hoffmann himself was not at all prosperous at the time.

Hoffmann formerly belonged to the lowest caste of photographers – he was a school photographer in Munich. In that city, he went from class to class, persuading the school children to pose prettily, then squatting behind a black cloth to squeeze the camera bulb. In a lackadaisical manner Hoffmann got through life, often more wrongly than rightly.

But this simple school photographer had the good luck to believe in Adolf Hitler at the right time. He bought the Fuehrer a hat once, and as a mark of Hitler's great love for him, even today, wears the Fuehrer's cast-off gloves.

Today, Heinrich Hoffmann addresses Adolf Hitler, his oldest and best friend, as 'Herr Hitler.' Hitler himself still addresses the photographer as 'Heini' and 'du.'[4]

---

[4] In German, as in French, the formal and familiar forms of address are still in use. The familiar, the 'du' in German, corresponds to our outmoded 'thee' and 'thou.'

In the meantime, the school-photography days have long since been forgotten. Heinrich Hoffmann possesses a monopoly which has made him one of the richest men in Germany. One of the greatest reasons for his prosperity is the fact that in every German '*Beamten*' (official's) office (and God alone knows how many there are of these!) a picture of Hitler is hung on the wall. This picture can be bought only from the firm of Heinrich Hoffmann, Inc.

But Hoffmann has not stopped with mere riches. He has also become the Reich's leading art expert, art dealer and Maecenas – right next to Hitler. Hitler himself once commented: 'I can be mistaken about politics; about art, never!' In the same fashion, Heinrich Hoffmann is really convinced that he is an art expert, and he conducts himself accordingly.

From priceless private collections in Germany, he was suddenly able to out-bargain the owners and procure for his own house the most beautiful Gobelin tapestries at laughable prices – he was the friend of the Fuehrer.

One time, Hoffmann let himself be hung with a false Makart and when the difference between what he had bought and the real original was noticed, he was able to get rid of the falsification at a price double what he had paid for it – he was the friend of the Fuehrer.

At a time when there was no foreign currency available in Germany, not even for five-cent International Postal Coupons, it was possible for Hoffmann to buy a Gobelin after Donatello for 180,000 Italian lire – he was the friend of the Fuehrer.

But the little school photographer is also thankful. He likes to tell anecdotes about Hitler in a style reminiscent of typical brave and pretty school primers. These anecdotes which Hoffmann tells generally concern Hitler and himself, and they always show Hitler to be a great, great man far above petty considerations of the workaday world.

Here is an example – an anecdote which Hoffmann has related hundreds of times, when he was in his cups and when he wasn't:

During *Mein Kampf* days, Hitler stayed one night at a castle which an already Nazi-converted aristocrat had placed at his disposal. Before retiring, Heinrich Hoffmann strode boldly through the palatial rooms and happened to discover a Nymphenburger porcelain figure. He was mad with joy, and rushed to Hitler: 'Only look, *Mein Fuehrer*,' he exclaimed, 'here is the fourth figure of our quartet. You know, we have only three of them and this one might well be the fourth. That is wonderful. Now I at least know where to find it.'

Hitler agreed with Hoffmann, applauding his cleverness in finding and recognizing the fourth figure. Weeks later a package reached the future leader of the Germans. When the wrapping was torn away, it was seen that the aristocrat, not too surprisingly, had forwarded the Nymphenburger figure as a present for Hitler.

'And what do you think?' Hoffmann is fond of relating to his friends. 'Of course I was very happy to see the fourth figure. But what do you think our Fuehrer said? "Heinrich," he said to me, "there is only one correct thing to be done. You must pack up the other three figures and send them all to our friend, in order that he may have the complete set."'

When telling this story, Hoffmann leans back enjoyably, drinks a fresh gulp of whisky and says, 'That's the way a Fuehrer behaves.'

Art. And again Art.

That is Hitler's true passion He has a few other interests, but his greatest liking is for art. And as he likes art, so he likes the artists. However, this liking is seldom reciprocated. One gets a peculiar feeling from listening to the very artists whom he spoils talk about their Number One patron. Those artists who have remained faithful to his wishes owe him very much, but they repay Hitler with pure ingratitude – sculptor, actor, cabaret artist, tightrope walker and dancer alike.

I never heard one of his beloved artists speak well of Hitler. It often seemed to me that he might be compared to a lover who is very rich but very fat and very old and who supports a very pretty, very young and very attractive girl. The girl will never say anything good about her big, fat old man; I never heard any word of appreciation about Hitler's personality from those he pampered.

Of course – on the other hand – every one of Hitler's wishes is automatically an order for the artist; this is especially true of the German film industry. The men in responsible positions, the directors, the producers and so on, do not want to make good films, they do not want to make bad films, no hits, no artistic films and above all no experiments. They only want to produce films which Adolf Hitler will like. The trouble is that in many things the Fuehrer has a peculiar taste. A director may suddenly receive a telephone call from Obersalzburg and be overwhelmed with compliments from Hitler because he has made an average film. Others, however, who think they have found the 'pattern' and who try to imitate the average film which so pleased Hitler, will be criticized and condemned for their productions.

For Hitler, favorite actors do not exist. Today he likes this actor or actress, tomorrow he likes another one. There are two exceptions; it is well known that Hitler speaks of Greta Garbo as 'the woman.' He continues to have all her new films shown to him in spite of the fact that these films are not allowed to play before the German people because they have Jewish managers or producers. His other favorite actress: Marlene Dietrich. In 1938, she was about to sign an excellent and promising contract with a German film company. But a healthy and wise instinct caused her to refuse. Even though Adolf Hitler is no prince of godly munificence, he has completely assumed the caprices and infidelity to his favorites which only a prince would dare to exhibit.

Hitler and the artists.

There was once a fascinating young girl from an artist's family, who was born and reared in a circus tent. This girl starred as a dancer in the Winter Garden in Berlin.[5] Hitler saw her dance

[5] In normal times, Hitler sees every program presented in this somewhat provincial and gaudy music hall.

there, he liked her and she presently received an invitation to tea.

The girl appeared at the Chancellery, was greeted enthusiastically, excellently entertained and was allowed to listen to a Hitler monologue on the difficulties of tightrope dancing. The Hitler monologue lasted over an hour. Over the second cup of tea, Hitler asked his charming guest:

'Now, my dear little girl, what can I do for you; let me know your wishes. Tell my your troubles.'

The 'little girl', a fine artist in her profession, began without hesitation:

'The end of the month is coming soon,' she said, 'and our worries over the expensive railway tickets start again. We artists have to travel constantly from one city to another. Could you make it possible for us artists to receive reduced fares for these professional trips?'

Laughing generously like a real patron of the arts, Hitler called one of his uniformed adjutants to him and gave an order: 'Give this young girl a first-class pass for all German railways.' Grinning with satisfaction, he turned to the pretty young artist to find an astonished face.

'But *mein Fuehrer*,' she objected, 'I didn't mean it that way. I didn't ask anything for myself. I thought I would be able to request something for all of us artists.'

Hitler was irritated. He rose brusquely and left the tea table and disappeared through a door into the inner rooms of the Chancellery. The young and confused artist was bid farewell only by Hitler's frozen-faced elite Troopers.

Another incident:

During a reception, a well-known German composer and musician was asked by Hitler: 'Tell me what you think about this. In Munich, my conductor of the State Orchestra wants to use only four basses in a Strauss operetta. What do you think of that?'

The composer really did not know what to say.

'Well,' Hitler continued, 'to play Strauss, one needs at least eight basses, don't you think?'

'Yes, *mein Fuehrer,*' the composer answered obediently.

'Excellent! We are of the same opinion,' said Hitler. He then pulled the composer into the next corner, sat down with him and talked 'at' him for over forty minutes. The other guests were astonished at this special mark of attention. They became envious, and after the reception was over the composer and his colleagues rushed to an artists' bar in Munich to recuperate. The other musicians assailed the composer with questions:

'What did Hitler say?' 'What did he say?'

To these questions, the composer made a dazed, though sincere, answer: 'It was wonderful! Hitler is a genius. What all he knows about music, how much he understands of music!'

The friends assailed him further, begging the composer to be more specific. 'What did Hitler *really* say to you?'

The composer who had received the signal honor of having Hitler talk to him for forty minutes was silent for a couple of minutes. Suddenly, the scales dropped from his eyes and he said quite honestly and very reflectively and in a very low voice: 'In reality, Hitler said nothing.'

Later on, the composer told me: 'He simply talked me drunk.'

There are numerous stories about Hitler's relations with women. But these stories all have the appearance of being improbable. It does not seem worth while to waste any time on them. There are such nonsensical stories as these going about:

That wherever Hitler travels, a blonde girl with long hair sits among his adjutants. According to the story, after Hitler's victorious entrance into the ancient castle overlooking Prague, high above the thousands of lights of that unhappy city, this girl was supposed to have sung to him on the castle balcony to the strains of her guitar: beautifully, softly and, in addition, nakedly. But that is all nonsensical, very probably nonsense.

Renate Mueller told a friend of mine (and indeed, I think all the world) the story of her first *tête-à-tête* with the absolute ruler of eighty million people.

It happened at a big reception in the Reich Chancellery. Dr. Goebbels, the Mephisto of the Nazi Party, sidled up to the lovely Mueller, drew her aside into a corner in his inimitable manner and whispered: 'Today you can make your fortune, the fortune of Germany and the fortune of its people. I know that the Fuehrer likes you very much. He has expressed the wish to speak to you alone. I will arrange a meeting during the course of the evening. Be wise, Renate, make the most of your opportunity and prove yourself worthy of my recommendation.'

Renate Mueller was at that time, and for many years following, the sweetheart of a very rich Jewish industrialist and consequently felt no fluttering of her heart at the prospect of the *tête-à-tête*. She waited calmly during the reception, and everything was arranged as Goebbels had told her it would be. On the pretext of showing her the other rooms of the spacious Chancellery, Hitler asked her to leave the crowded drawing rooms with him. The two came to his private living room, and Hitler sat down next to Renate Mueller. She did not feel her heart fluttering at his presence.

She did nothing. She just listened to him as he talked and talked. Hitler talked without end of quite ordinary things concerning which neither she nor he could possibly have any interest. But isn't that exactly the method of a bashful lover? Renate sat next to him, and he talked on and on.

Suddenly, he ran out of something to say. There was an awkward pause. He eased himself over a little closer to her. She could feel his nearness. She did not feel her heart flutter. He, perhaps?

At any rate, he suddenly got up – no, he jumped up from the couch, raised his right arm in the stiff Nazi salute, the salute he invented, and said:

'What do you think, how long can I hold my arm up like this?'

Renate shook her head. She did not know what to answer the Fuehrer. That was no matter because Hitler told her the answer:

'I can hold my arm like this for hours without getting tired.

It is not true that I have an apparatus built in my arm sleeve to support my arm. That's all nonsense, my dear, all twaddle. I can stand this way for hours. And when I think about fat old Goering, I always must remember that he gets tired after a couple of minutes.'

Miss Mueller looked at Hitler standing before her with his arm stretched out in stiff salute. 'That is really wonderful, *Mein Fuehrer,*' she said.

Hitler smiled like a man who has received too much applause. He lowered his arm, approached her once more, looked deeply into her eyes and said: 'Come, my dear. Let us go back to the guests again.'

And that was the *tête-à-tête.*

Another actress told me:

'I was this man's guest for eight days. It was fascinating, he was fascinating. Other men look at my mouth, but Hitler only looked into my eyes. And when I told him that I was a divorcée, the man nearly jumped to the ceiling with joy.' This is true, no matter how untrue it may sound.

Hitler and art.

He has suffered much from his disappointments in art, but he has suffered even more from the artists. Once, a nice young fellow who spent his early youth on one continual spree after he inherited a large fortune told me an authentic story about Schwabing, which happened in 1920.

It was during the inflation in Germany, and the night life of the Munich Bohemian quarter was extravagant and insane. Night after night, a mixed society of artists, writers, dancers and students sat hilariously in the Green Ship, a bar and taproom in Munich. At the piano sat an old man who had been an insurance official in his better days. He had a small wart on his forehead. He had composed a hit song, which he always sang when the crowd was at the height of its gaiety. Hitler heard this song often when he came to the Green Ship. The song was a bit of gay foolishness, and the words might be translated about as follows:

Rosalie, since yesterday morning you have had a red
  spot on your knee.
Rosalie, the spot won't disappear any more.
Yesterday you were in love with me; today you have
  deserted me.
Rosalie, the spot will never disappear.

Hitler went many, many nights to the Green Ship. His appearance in the doorway was enough to freeze the good humor of all the guests to below zero. Hitler was a well-known 'horror guest' in the Schwabing artists' bars; when he appeared, all the others disappeared. They did everything possible to protect themselves from him, but not because they feared him. On the contrary, Hitler was lean, shabbily dressed and practically penniless, but he had one passion which never left him – he talked. He talked without interruption, mainly about art. No wonder that the flight from his table would begin when he came, and whispers of horror could be heard above the clink of the beer mugs: 'Jesus, here comes Hitler!'

He has never forgotten this bad treatment. Psychoanalysts who are students of Sigmund Freud frequently explain Hitler's unbridled insanity for building new buildings, his mania for pulling down everything in order to build it back again in his curious barrack-Greek style,[6] as a typical symptom of the secret wish to supersede everything and everybody. Hitler's invasion of well-behaved, though antagonistic, neighbors may be due to his own personal ego. He cannot stand the thought that other nations are free to ridicule him in their press and on their radio and still go unpunished; the easiest way to stop this criticism (unjustified, of course!) is to march in and take possession of the offending neighbor. Hitler still tries to revenge himself with all the power he now possesses for the injuries which he had to endure in the old days at the hands of the Schwabing artists.

[6] Whole blocks of Berlin's wealthiest business center disappeared under our very eyes. On returning from a month's vacation in France, I rode down the Potsdamer Strasse in a taxi in growing astonishment; near my apartment, five whole blocks of buildings had vanished in my absence.

Since he was of course not noticed by the real society of Munich, he also wants to revenge himself on the Wittels-bachers, the royal family who made the Bavarian capital such a charming one. This is perhaps the reason why Hitler did not make Munich the capital city of the Third Reich, as he had originally intended to do.

He likes the artists, although he is not liked by them. But he indescribably hates intellectuals – who have much in common with artists – for reasons which once more arise in the dim realm of the psychological. Before a large group of guests, he once declared bitterly that of all the people in Germany he hated only one class – the intellectuals.

'These impudent rascals,' Hitler snarled, 'who always know everything better than anybody else, these rascals who grin scornfully at every one of the Party's failures and say, "We already knew that was going to happen!" These rascals, who only possess their intellect in order to play with it. These rascals – I would like to exterminate them like rats, even if it meant killing ten, twenty or thirty thousand of them. I would like to kick them out tomorrow!' Hitler unclenched his fists, and said in a quieter voice, 'But, unfortunately, we need them.'

He hates intellectuals because he cannot stand the thought that there is anybody in Germany who does not see in him God. That is also the reason why he hates – and not at all lastly – the press. It is true that the German press is tamed, toothless and so hellishly watched over that it is necessary for Hitler to concentrate his hatred against newspapers on the foreign press. But from time to time he also has his troubles with the docile German press.

There was a widely traveled, cultured gentleman who was ordered into uniform at the beginning of the invasion of Poland to become a soldier-correspondent. His duties had nothing to do with journalism, in the old sense of the word. He was compelled to serve as blindly as every other soldier who wears the field-gray uniform does. It did not make any difference if his news stories were appreciative or derogatory, sensational or bad. The censor struck out the 'sweets', anyway. One day, this gentleman wrote a feature article concerning a visit to the headquarters of a German general on duty in Poland, and the story was very well liked by all concerned. It was, of course, censored three times, changed, made worse, perhaps improved again – but at any rate, this article finally found its way into the German press.

Adolf Hitler, who otherwise reads very little, sometimes with the cleverness of the devil can find articles in the really harmless German press which do not meet with his approval. It happened that way in this case.

There was a terrible thunderstorm over the publication of the article, although it had been well liked and approved of by the proper officers and Propaganda Ministry officials. For several long minutes, Hitler expressed his rage in the presence of his adjutants in unintelligible screams. When he managed to get himself somewhat calmer, he shouted at his unfortunate companions:

'This miserable writer! What is this skunk thinking of when he attempts to glorify the generals? Why does he see fit even to mention their names?

'Who won the campaign in Poland?' he shouted.

'I did!

'Who gave the orders?

'I did!

'Who had all the strategic ideas which made victory possible?

'I did!

'Who ordered the attack?

'*Ich! Ich! Ich! Ich!*

'And this liar comes along and tries to assert that the generals had something to say about the campaign! He is instinctless, and stupid!'

The poor writer, who of course immediately heard about Hitler's rage over his article, did not dare to write a line for the next few weeks through fear that the sight of his name would throw Adolf Hitler into another rage.

No man who must work in Hitler's presence wants to experience one of these rages. Hitler likes others to be in trouble but only he is allowed to cause the excitement.

An eye witness of the event told me the following story:

The German battleship *Deutschland* was one of the ships belonging to the international non-intervention patrol off the coast of Spain during the Spanish Civil War. A Communist-Spanish airplane bombed the *Deutschland*, killing thirty-four German sailors. As a reprisal, the *Deutschland* then promptly shelled the innocent Spanish coastal town of Almería.

A large public funeral was planned for the thirty-four dead sailors, to take place at Kiel, Germany. The Party was determined to make great propaganda out of the funeral, and it was arranged that Adolf Hitler should speak and then review the members of the crew of the attacked battleship.

In a three-sided square stood sailors and infantry, the sailors from the *Deutschland* standing just behind a line of relatives of the deceased. On the open side of the square there was a platform. At the beginning of the ceremony, a German admiral spoke. Hitler followed him, and spoke to the assemblage (and over the German radio) long and passionately.

It had been arranged by the Propaganda Ministry that following his speech Hitler would walk down the line of survivors and then review the infantry and naval units drawn up to stiff attention. Everything had been set up: the newsreel cameramen waited at prearranged points all around the square; thousands of spectators looked on from a distance.

Perhaps he spoke too well. Perhaps the visible pain and suffering of the surviving relatives lined up before him was too much. In any case, the first widow with whom Hitler spoke a few words cried violently. Her child, who was ten years old and who stood next to his bereaved mother, began to cry heartrendingly. Hitler patted him on the head and turned uncertainly to the next in line. Before he could speak a word, he was suddenly overcome. He spun completely around, left the whole carefully planned program flat. Followed by his utterly surprised companions he walked as fast as he could to his car and had himself driven away from the parade grounds.

Hitler's days are pretty well filled with duties of state. What does he do at night?

Concerning his nocturnal activities, there is rather exact information available to insiders. Hitler has a weakness for light entertainment. It is well known that he saw the *Merry Widow* performed seven times in one winter season – an old dusty operetta which had its *première* thirty years ago. As I have already noted, he sees every change of program at the Berlin Winter Garden.

In dancing, Hitler has decided likes and dislikes. For expressionist dances like those of Mary Wigman or Palucca he has a deadly hatred. He likes light tap dances which are performed with the upper part of the dancer's body remaining immovable. Hitler likes dances done only with the legs, a style in which American tap dancers excel. If you consider his taste, you will not wonder that Hitler saw a young American dancer perform in this fashion four times;[7] you will not wonder that he ordered her competitor, Marion Daniels, to come to Munich from Marseille by special train. You will not wonder that of all the comedians who broadcast in Germany, he best likes the bold Manfred Lommel who, although he was formerly an army officer, relates the most stupid nonsense imaginable. Yes, Hitler responds most favorably to the light muses in his private entertainments.

This man has never seen one of Shakespeare's plays. He probably never read a line of Goethe. His most exalted artistic activity is listening to Wagner. Hitler goes to the operas because he loves them. A short time ago I read an excellent article about Wagner. The article stated that he was the Barnum of the opera world. Barnum – that means swindle, ballyhoo, obtrusiveness, noise, rudeness, roaring, and a little itching for sex.

Is it astonishing that Hitler orders 'Wagner-Barnum' to be

---

[7] This young girl, who was known to many Americans in Berlin for her simplicity, her sweetness and her charm, was immediately the object of adverse publicity in American papers and magazines, described as 'the girl who danced before Hitler.' On returning to the States, she found her contracts canceled because Hitler had liked her dancing – which was certainly no fault of hers. The girl was a dancer, not a politician.

played on every occasion? Not only on the official radio, but also at every other opportunity is Wagner performed in Germany. Hitler likes the *Meistersinger* Overture. Probably he even dreams about it.

He spends his other evenings seeing movies. In his Berlin Chancellery there is, besides a completely equipped dental laboratory for his teeth, a very elegant movie theater where he sees all the newest films, occasionally seeing the same movie three times straight. More than once he has procured Charlie Chaplin films through representatives in foreign countries and has amused himself highly over them.

Hitler decides whether Hitler may see non-Aryan movies or not.

It is known that Hitler once saw *Pancho Villa*, an excellent American movie starring Wallace Beery, twice in a row. The film was rough and coarse, but filled with manly vitality. Afterward, Hitler said to his attendants: 'I found this film excellent, but far too good for the German masses.'

His mentor and advisor in all these amusements is the little intellectual, Dr. Paul Joseph Goebbels. I would like to relate here a characteristic story from the thousands told about Goebbels.

Goebbels plays a role in the Third Reich which is incredibly great. Though he has periods of decline and sometimes falls from favor, he still has one great consolation: Goebbels is the only man in Germany for whom Adolf Hitler ever proposed a toast.

An acquaintance of mine once had the pleasure of going on an excursion with Dr. Goebbels and a large party of government officials. During the ride into the country, my friend sat next to Goebbels. He later told me the exact content of their whole conversation, even to the smallest details.

It happened in the summer of 1939, six years after Hitler had come to power. It was astonishing what subjects Goebbels could introduce in the middle of a wonderful landscape, a peaceful place far removed from strife. He suddenly revealed in himself an abyss of deepest hatred against the former German

Chancellor Bruening. His hatred was founded on good reasons as far as Goebbels was concerned since Bruening was a man who was clean, correct, honest, who handled government funds conscientiously, who did not live in luxury, who did not even like luxury, who thought clearly and sanely. In other words, Bruening was the exact opposite of Hitler, Goebbels and the other rascals who were to take over later.

After venting his spleen on Bruening, Dr. Goebbels started to talk about our 'Kampf'. Filled with simulated admiration, my acquaintance asked Dr. Goebbels how he had ever managed to conquer Communistic Berlin for the Nazi Party. Then Goebbels related the following story:

'You see,' he said, 'that was not so difficult at all. It was only necessary for me to use my brain. The German Nationalist Party attacked me week after week in their newspapers and demanded that I give my answers to their questions in public. Of course, they wanted to silence me publicly with their arguments.

'I waited for quite a while, and then got a brilliant idea for a plan – which worked out exactly as I had wanted it to. Through the columns of my daily newspaper, Der Angriff, I challenged the chief brawler of the Nationalists to arrange a public debate within the next fourteen days in one of Berlin's largest auditoriums. To my joy, he accepted. The auditorium I had in mind seated four thousand people.

'After waiting for five days,' Goebbels continued, 'several of us went to see the printer who had the contract to print the admission tickets for this auditorium. He had already printed the four thousand tickets and had delivered them to the Nationalist Party committee. This dishonest printer was quite willing to talk turkey with us, and we therefore bribed him to deliver to us another set of tickets which were identical with the first set. We distributed three thousand of these tickets to our own most ardent Party members, who were all to be relied upon. Five hundred of the tickets I ordered given to our mortal enemies – Communists. They were our avowed enemies but they also wanted to destroy the existing system of government, and that put them in our good graces for the time being.

'My boys then got an order to be at the auditorium, not at eight o'clock, the time set for the meeting, but at six o'clock. Everything went beautifully, I can tell you. At an early hour the auditorium was completely full. Five hundred of our opponents had been able to enter but the others, who had good tickets, had to turn around and go back home.

'I sat at my opponent's side, near the speaker's table. I had given our boys exact instructions as to how they should behave during my speech. If I put my hand on my chin, they were to cheer; if I touched my forehead with my right hand, they were to roar with laughter; if I folded my hands on the speaker's table as though in prayer, I wanted a screaming demonstration from them. The debate and the demonstrations were broadcast by radio to the entire German nation and therefore the crowd's reaction was very important to our cause.

'Things went smoothly. I rose and spoke for twenty minutes on the advantages of Communism. Of course after a short time I had every one of the five hundred Communists present on my side. Then I spoke against the German Nationalists. From this moment on I had no more need for my signals to our boys. The crowd screamed denunciation of the Nationalist Party; it roared approval of the National Socialists. I had all my Party friends yelling into the microphones and when the 'show' was over, I can assure you that we had again won several thousand more votes.

'You see, my friend, that's how we did it. It was not so difficult after all.'

But these things were the pleasures of peace times. Now that war is in progress, Goebbels as well as Hitler has other troubles and both have other things to occupy them in the evenings.

Hitler does not trouble himself too seriously over the situation which exists today. This illustrates another one of the important differences between Adolf Hitler and Joseph Stalin.

Stalin, the Asiatic who was once a bank robber in his youth, knows well the weaknesses of the U.S.S.R. He knows that his transportation system is worthless; he knows that the Russian army is poorly equipped; he knows that official corruption in

Russia is enormous; he knows that Russian indolence and laziness have not been diminished one whit by Bolshevism; he knows that he is surrounded by hundreds of intriguers, of whom he orders several killed off from time to time to maintain peace a little longer. Stalin knows about all these Russian weaknesses and worries about them.

Not so with Adolf Hitler. He is indescribably blind; he sees many things, but he does not want to know about them. And nobody dares to tell him anything exact about conditions in the Reich, about the people's reaction to unpleasant new government decrees, for instance. His habit is to postpone disagreeable things as long as possible. It is a fact that Germany's Minister of Finance had to wait four months for an audience with Hitler and when he was able to see the Fuehrer, only one person spoke – and it wasn't the Minister of Finance.

It is, therefore, not true that Hitler works long and hard at the business of being a dictator. He does everything illogically, according to his emotions. He spends his evenings accordingly.

Since Hitler really has an exceptional memory, he spends hours learning by heart the tonnages of the various ships in the British navy; he knows exactly what kind of armament, the kind of armor plates, the weight, the speed and the number of the crew of every warship in the British navy. He knows the number of rotations of airplane motors in every model and type existent. He knows the number of shots a machine gun fires a minute, whether it is a light, medium or heavy one, whether it was made in the United States, Czechoslovakia or France.

In other words Hitler greatly resembles William II, who was also a 'specialist in everything'. Both ignored the important fact that it is not sufficient to know mere figures and facts to be a specialist in any given field – numbers and facts may also be learned by a parrot.

Hitler neither knows the deep significance of government nor does he have any vital insight into its operation. He helps himself out of this lack of perception by a diligence in the study of details. No wonder that he fools his visitors and subordinates with a bluff-knowledge which seems to be astounding.

Even in war time, his chief activity is the study of details and figures. He sits alone in his fabulous office for long, long hours often the whole night through. An expensive magnifying glass lies on his desk; a complicated built-in electric lighting system spreads an even glow over the desk (Hitler has failing eyesight, and must wear glasses in order to read); on the surface of his desk are laid enormously enlarged aerial photographs which German air force pilots have brought back from their reconnaissance flights over enemy territory. Hitler studies their every detail over and over. He knows from what height the pictures have been made. He knows exactly the difference between the camouflaged trenches and the easily recognizable military establishments. He knows exactly how the harbor and the port of Scapa Flow look. He knows the entrance by heart.

He knows exactly where in these enemy ports the docks of neutral countries lie. Only now and then he summons a specialist, who gives him even more details on any subject. Even when he has been studying maps and photographs in this way for hours, he never gets tired.

Hitler can stand only light meals and is indescribably frugal regarding his food. A raw apple, a pear, a banana, a glass of milk or, as an exception from time to time, a piece of cake are all he will eat. Such a diet makes him fresh again. After eating something at night, he will have people who may happen to come to his mind telephoned, even if it is one o'clock in the morning. Or he will order another movie shown to him.

He goes to bed as late as possible because he suffers from insomnia. There are many visions which might keep a man of this sort from sleeping.

In Nuremberg, during the Nazi Party rally of 1937, I myself saw Hitler going to his room at six o'clock in the morning. Before retiring, he had been sitting and talking with an intimate group of friends in a restaurant. It was Hitler who had done all the talking, and his listeners got more and more tired as the hours wore away. Their eyes became heavy and they could hardly pay any attention anymore but their Fuehrer did not notice that.

At last he got up and went to his hotel shortly before six o'clock in the morning.

Three hours later, he was seen reviewing a parade of one of the Nazi Party organizations. Probably Hitler was glad that the still and lonely night had passed so quickly.

This is a picture of the man whose name is known in every corner of the world.

This is the man whose slightest moods may become harsh law to over a hundred million people in middle Europe.

This is the man who has in his hands a power greater than that ever held by any ruler in history – a power multiplied by the airplane, the radio, the fast printing presses.

He is uncontrolled, he does not have to give account to anybody, he crassly and ruthlessly conceals his every failure, he puffs himself up with every success.

Today he follows an impulse. Tomorrow he condemns it as wrong – without admitting that he has been wrong.

To promise something and never to do it; to forget things which were never meant seriously; to break every promise but to faithfully keep every threat. That is the psychological picture of *Der Fuehrer*.

Will history in years to come deal with Adolf Hitler as an enduring hero – or as a mere rascal who came to power?

I glanced at the map hanging on the wall. What would happen next? How many changes in boundaries had been made since I came to Europe! Three capitals had come under the jurisdiction of our Berlin Embassy. Three of our legations had been dissolved – Vienna, Prague, Warsaw. Would we soon see Copenhagen under our jurisdiction? I wondered. Or Berne, Switzerland? The Nazis were systematically and ruthlessly destroying the good life of Europe for their own selfish ends. Why should they stop with only part of the continent under their rule?

I guess I like Germans as individuals. I like their personal honesty, their energy, their cleanliness. I like the way they bring up their children to know how to behave. I like the pleasure Germans get from simple things – which is more a European trait than a German one. I like the unity of family life as it was in Germany before the coming of the Nazis. I like their books, their music, their stage, their operas. This is something harder to explain, but I like the absence of fierce competition, the absence of the rush rush rush which is too typical of America. I like to feel that I can sit down for five minutes without having somebody push his way into my job. I like the way German families walk on Sundays; walk slowly and enjoy their walking – while in America every member of the family must have his own car if the Sabbath air is not to be rent with family squabbles.

I hate the Nazi government. I lived under it for three years, and I know it well. I know how the Nazis have lied and cheated and persecuted the people unlucky enough to live under their power. No Nazi threats, promises, arguments or pleading could influence my opinion of their way of governing.

In 1933 when Hitler came to power, many people in Germany shrugged their shoulders and said, 'Oh, let him come. He's tried long enough. It's only another form of wild socialism and it will cool off in six months.'

Intelligent Germans found themselves in a trap. Their rights were squelched, their privacy invaded, their every action watched by the Secret Police. They found themselves dominated by a man whose main passion it is that every individual shall live for the State alone – which means, Himself.

Their children were snatched away from them and taught the strange new philosophy of uniforms and heavy boots. The former country of thinkers became known as a land infested with political, moral and intellectual degenerates.

For those who liked the land of Germany, who admired its physical beauty, its orderliness and its genuine culture, this change was saddening.

I have talked with simple German citizens who spent months in concentration camps merely because they had made an indiscreet remark which had been reported by some rat to the Gestapo.

I have seen fine Germans who were excellent people in every respect forced to give up their homes, their possessions and their friends merely because they were – Jewish.

I know of a baker in a small town in the Harz Mountains who is now in an insane asylum.

This baker fought in the recent war with Poland and he was wounded in action. He returned to his small village an invalid and tried to take up his life again where it had been broken off, His experiences, however, left him no mental peace.

Perhaps I should explain that the baker was not a Nazi. Neither was he a Nazi-hater. He was a simple baker, wanting to live his quiet life at peace with his neighbors.

On New Year's Eve, the simple baker baked his neighbors some doughnuts – the traditional New Year's Day food in Germany, forbidden this year because of the shortage of flour and lard. Somebody reported the baker to the police (his competitor across the street, most likely) and he was fined 1,000 marks and sentenced to a month in jail.

He felt that he had been disgraced in the eyes of his townspeople. He tried to hang himself three times.

They have had to lock him up in an asylum.

I think that is the most typical story I know to illustrate what is happening to the people of Germany under the Nazis.

My door flew open. Paul Coates struck his fat head in. I pulled myself out of my reverie.

'Say,' he said, looking important with his news, 'I just heard that the Russians have offered peace terms to the Finns. The terms are hard, but the Finns will sign. I knew all the time they couldn't hold out.'

'Yes,' I said tiredly.

'It's big news,' Paul said, leaving hurriedly. 'I'm going to tell Richard.' He was gone.

I heard the immigrants chattering in the waiting room, typewriters banging from the adjacent rooms, automobiles speeding past my window. Niles, of course, had offered himself in vain, as had thousands of other men. Where is Niles now? I wondered, looking at the map on the wall.

What a waste of good, solid people war is, I thought. What a tragic waste! My fingers were nervous from the accumulated tension of seven months of war.

Outside my window a column of soldiers marched. Left, right, left, right, left, right. Their heavy boots made a muffled thump on the pavement as they all struck together. Their hair was hidden under steel helmets, their feet were clad in the identical black boots, their brains were filled with similar dull thoughts. There was no joy in their faces. They had begun to sing, under orders, 'We're going to England, to England, to England.'

Every soldier must believe in the thing for which he is about to give his life. Every soldier, when he crawls through the barbed wire fence with his officer just behind or before him, when he watches enemy shells curve over into the mud of the trenches, when he sees his comrades spit out blood and die before his eyes, must know that his country is in the right. Otherwise he could not force himself to fight.

That is something to remember.

I looked at my watch.

With one hand I crushed out the cigarette.

And with the other I drew a fresh dossier toward me.

CHAPTER NINE

ONE MORNING a German girl whom I knew well, an intelligent and spirited girl, sat with me in a parked car in our Embassy back yard. We had not gone there to spoon, but to listen to the automobile radio.

It was April, the tenth of April, 1940, and the first slow signs of spring were visible in the German capital. The snow had melted from the sandbags piled against our Embassy basement windows. Our former ice-skating rink was a big, wet tennis court. The sun was shining. It was warm enough for us to go out into the courtyard without our coats.

That morning the sickening news had finally come. German soldiers were at that moment occupying Denmark and Norway. This step was a bitter blow to those Germans who had still hoped that Hitler might at last acquire some sense of honor and decency. The occupation of Denmark and Norway by German troops meant that Adolf Hitler was not satisfied with the conquest of Poland – he had embarked on a course from which there would be no turning back.

Every Berlin newspaper that morning screamed the news at us in bold black headlines. This German girl, who had come by to see me for a few moments, sat in the car and listened tensely to the official broadcasts. Over and over we heard a recording of a statement by Dr. Paul Joseph Goebbels explaining the step to the German people. The message was also repeated in Danish and in Norwegian. Dr. Goebbels also read the German government's memorandum (ultimatum) to Denmark and Norway. The girl and I listened to his harsh voice enumerating the terms which these two countries would have to accept. We heard his shout that 'neither of these two countries will be used as a base for operations against the enemy.'

'Germany,' he lied further, 'has no territorial ambitions or demands against either Denmark or Norway. So please accept our invasion as a necessary step for your own protection; do not attempt to withstand the German army. We do not want any of your land. We will leave when the war is finished.'

I started to make a sarcastic answer to Goebbels' latest pack of official lies but when I looked at my companion in the automobile, my German girl friend, I stopped.

She had tears in her eyes. 'That hateful damn liar!' she said bitterly.

'That hateful damn liar!'

Several months before, I had tendered my resignation to the Embassy. I was, of course, pleased that the officers did not want to let me go and that they offered to try to squeeze a raise in pay and a rise in position out of the Department of State. But the cold reality of our Foreign Service is that if a clerk gets his job in a foreign country he will always be shoved behind clerks who have gotten their jobs through Washington. For that matter, if a young man intends to make a career for himself in our Foreign Service he must take the examinations in Washington for a vice-consulship.

In other words, there were no more worlds for me to conquer in Berlin. I wanted to come home to finish this book and try a novel or so. Therefore, on April 13, 1940, I said good-by to a flock of people – Americans, Germans, Nazis, anti-Nazis, rich, poor, intellectuals, bums – whom I had more or less collected over a period of three years. In a newly acquired miniature car I *putt-putted* down the Reich *Autobahn* in the direction of the Brenner Pass – in the direction of Genoa and freedom.

A few days later I arrived in the beautiful Austrian city of Innsbruck, capital of Tyrol. It was late at night and I drove to the first garage I came to. The sleepy and taciturn Austrian garage attendant, noting that my car carried a Berlin license plate, motioned me to a parking space. He did not bother to have me fill out a registration slip for my car – an omission which caused me some uncomfortable moments the next day.

I spent the night in a small hotel. The next morning I walked over to the garage to get something out of my luggage compartment. I found four large German policemen standing stiffly around my car, waiting for me. One of the policemen told me that my car had been reported to the police from all up and down the *Autobahn* because it was being driven without the small red 'v' on the license plate which shows that the car may be driven in war time.

I pulled out my wallet and leafed through my library of identification papers. I showed the police my permission from the President of the Berlin Police to drive the car from 'Berlin to the Brenner Pass, using the shortest possible route.'

The four policemen were satisfied with this certificate. They walked out of the garage and I began to search in my luggage. The manager of the garage came over to me. 'You're not a German?' he asked.

'*Nein, Amerikaner.*'

He looked around over his shoulder. 'They searched through your car last night,' he whispered.

'Who did?'

'The Gestapo. They went through everything you have there.'

I checked on that. I had left most of my baggage in several suitcases stacked in the luggage compartment. I saw immediately that my effects had been disarranged. In sudden alarm I searched for the notes and the partially completed manuscript of this book. They were strewn around a little, but they were all there. I thanked the garage manager for his information. I left my car there and walked through Innsbruck's narrow streets, looking with uneasy interest at the beautiful old churches and walls and university buildings. I took an incline trolley, then a suspension cable car, then another suspension car and found myself at the top of the Hafelekar, a glorious snow-covered mountain to the south of Innsbruck. From the top of the Hafelekar I looked over to the peaks of the Italian Alps. The slopes of the mountain were dotted with skiers. I ate lunch there in a pleasant restaurant.

Afterward I descended to Innsbruck and went around to the garage to get my car. I found a solitary motorcycle policeman standing guard over that innocent piece of tin. 'I will have to take you to Gestapo headquarters,' he said apologetically. 'They want to ask you a few questions.'

He got on his motorcycle and led the way. The garage manager gave me a compassionate look as I drove away.

It is a trivial thing to record, and of no significance whatsoever, but the fact is that the motorcycle policeman got completely lost in Innsbruck while leading me to the Gestapo's headquarters. He had to ask questions of several pedestrians before we finally reached the grim building. I got out of my car and was led through a forbidding iron gate. The gate was closed after me with an unpleasant clank. I walked down a long corridor to a small office. I found myself before a serious Gestapo official whose hair had all been shaved off with the exception of a small tuft over the middle of his forehead.

At last, I thought. After three years' stay in Germany I too have had my invitation to a Gestapo tea party. I guessed that I could kiss my trip to Genoa and the S.S. *Washington* and freedom good-by for a while.

The Gestapo official asked me questions, probing questions, all of which I was able to answer to his satisfaction. He looked at my American passport and seemed impressed by the gold letters stamped on the red cover – 'SPECIAL PASSPORT'. Finally he relaxed and said that I was free to go.

He did not mention the manuscript.

I did not mention the manuscript.

I left.

As I was about to get into my small car, glad to feel the warm sunshine shining on me once more, I heard an agitated voice behind me call, 'Russell!'

I turned around quickly and saw an American friend of mine, a young newspaper man from the Associated Press bureau in Berlin. 'Why – hello, there,' I greeted. 'What the hell are you doing down here?'

The young reporter looked tired and worried. 'They've taken my passport away from me and won't let me leave Innsbruck.'

'Why?'

'I've been here three days already. I have to report to the Gestapo every hour. I'm not arrested, you understand, just have to come here every hour.'

'Well, why? What did you do?'

'Nothing. I didn't realize it but I was in a border zone without special permission. I'm on a few days' vacation.'

'Can I help you?' I asked. 'Call up the Embassy or something?'

'No,' the worried youngster said. 'I just called Mr. Lochner in Berlin. He will probably be able to make them turn me loose. There is nothing you can do.'

'I'll try, anyway.'

'No, but listen. Wait here ten minutes. If I am not back out in ten minutes, go on and leave.'

I protested but he overruled me. He went into the grim doorway, sweat visible on the back of his neck. I sat down in my car. The street there was paved with large cobble-stones; opposite the Gestapo headquarters there was a high stone wall. The sun shone brightly, birds sang in the trees, the silent, white-capped mountains formed a majestic background to the old city of Innsbruck.

Ten minutes passed, twenty minutes, half an hour. Then I saw that a full hour had gone by. The newspaperman had not returned. I asked the Gestapo guard at the iron gate about my friend, but, of course, he would give me no information. Then I decided that his boss in Berlin would effect his release if anybody could. I got in my car and cranked-up. I looked behind the seat once more to be sure that my manuscript was intact. My car left an impertinent blue cloud of exhaust as I *putted* away from the Gestapo headquarters, bound for the Brenner Pass.[1]

Late in the afternoon, I reached the (former) German-Italian

---

[1] Recently I received a letter from the newspaperman. He did not mention the incident, but the obvious conclusion is that he was freed and allowed to resume work in Berlin.

border. I met with politeness there, none of my baggage was examined, none of my papers unfolded. The border patrol had obviously been informed that I was on my way.

The customs official was a fat, pleasant old fellow who stamped my passport with a flourish.

'Now, why do you want to leave Germany, young man?' he asked me. 'You had a good time here, didn't you. You liked our country, didn't you?'

I was looking across the strip of land which separated Germany from Italy at the gaily dressed Italian soldiers who marched up and down their side of the border. 'Yes, yes,' I said absently.

'You come back when we have peace, eh?' the fat old guard asked me. 'You come back and see us then.'

'I hope to,' I said, and he lifted the striped pole and let me drive through.

'Heil Hitler' the official called after me. '*Auf Weidersehen.*'

As I drove over the strip of road between the German barrier and the Italian barrier I had a curious feeling that hundreds of eyes were staring down at me from the mountain heights. I looked up at the steep, wooded slopes. Not a gun to be seen, not a building, not a soldier. Yet I knew those woods were teeming with soldiers, bristling with guns. The hills were quiet; I heard the distant calls of birds. Overhead billowed the rain clouds which are always to be found at the Brenner.

When the Italian officials had finished searching me, stamping me and loading me down with travel literature, I looked back at the white mountains of Germany beyond which lay Munich and Berlin and three years of my life. On the whole, they were an agreeable and certainly an exciting three.

I stared at the snow-covered mountains a few minutes before I turned around in the seat and pressed my foot to the starter.